SOCIOLOGY OF EDUCATION SERIES
Aaron M. Pallas, Series Editor

Advisory Board: Sanford Dornbusch, Adam Gamoran, Annette Lareau,
Mary Metz, Gary Natriello

Where Charter School Policy Fails

The Problems of Accountability and Equity

Edited by
AMY STUART WELLS

Teachers College, Columbia University
New York and London

Published by Teachers College Press, 1234 Amsterdam Avenue, New York, NY
10027

Copyright © 2002 by Teachers College, Columbia University
Chapter 7 Copyright © 2000 by Corwin Press, Inc.

Library of Congress Cataloging-in-Publication Data

Where charter school policy fails : the problems of accountability and equity /
edited by Amy Stuart Wells.
    p. cm. — (Sociology of education series)
   Includes bibliographical references and index.
   ISBN 0-8077-4249-X (paper) — ISBN 0-8077-4250-3 (cloth)
   1. Charter schools—Government policy—United States. 2. Educational
equalization—United States. 3. Educational accountability—United States.
I. Wells, Amy Stuart, 1961– . II. Sociology of education series (New York,
N.Y.)
LB2806.36 .W54 2002
371.01—dc21   2002067315

ISBN 0-8077-4249-X (paper)
ISBN 0-8077-4250-3 (cloth)

Printed on acid-free paper
Manufactured in the United States of America

09 08 07 06 05 04 03 02   8 7 6 5 4 3 2 1

To all the women and men who struggle
under the current charter school laws
to better serve poor students and students of color
and who envision a more progressive future for this reform.

Contents

Acknowledgments

During the two and a half years we spent on the UCLA Charter School Study and the subsequent months of further analysis and research on charter schools, so many wonderful people have helped to shape our work. From researchers who asked us hard questions at conferences in which we presented our findings, to the funders who allowed us to do this work in the first place, to the charter school educators and parents who answered our questions and forced us to rethink simple assumptions, to our most patient editor, we have benefited greatly from input, support, and feedback. Thus, while there are too many people to thank everyone individually for his or her contribution, we would like to single out a few people upon whom we lavish extra praise and gratitude.

First of all, the UCLA Charter School Study and the editor's follow up work reviewing charter school research from other states would not have been at all possible without the most generous support of several important institutions. First of all, the Spencer Foundation funded the editor during the summer of 1995 when she attended a Summer Institute on Educational Policy at the Center for the Advanced Study in the Behavioral Sciences. It was during this summer institute that she reviewed the literature on decentralization and, with the help of Cynthia Grutzik, wrote the proposal for the UCLA Charter School Study. This study proposal was funded by both the Ford and the Annie E. Casey Foundations. In addition, Janice Petrovich at the Ford Foundation played a central role in helping us publicize our initial set of findings from this study. She was also instrumental in helping us frame these findings for a broad audience that included advocacy groups and parents.

In addition, the Spencer Foundation continued to support this work when it awarded the editor a post-doctoral fellowship. This allowed her to be more involved in the study in a hands-on way. We would also like to thank the Spencer Foundation for providing fellowship support to four additional members of our research team during the course of this study. And finally, the Russell Sage Foundation also supported the editor's work on this project through its fellowship program. This allowed her to systematically review the growing body of literature on charter school reform from various states.

We also remain hugely indebted to our thoughtful and supportive advisory board members: Richard Elmore, Michelle Foster, Pedro A. Noguero,

Annette Lareau, and Kenneth Wong. Throughout our data collection and analysis processes, their insights and constructive criticism were most helpful. In addition to our formal advisory board, we benefited from the input of several more informal advisors who periodically read our work and gave us very helpful feedback. These colleagues and friends include Carol Ascher, Michael Apple, Edward B. Fiske, Bruce Fuller, Jeannie Oakes, Eric Rofes, and Geoff Whitty.

Then there was the invaluable support of several UCLA students and tape transcribers that enabled us to collect, organize, and analyze our huge body of data. These include Ligia Artilles, Ricky Lee Allen, Allen Choi, Kiyoko Clemons, Khue Duong, Lisbeth Espinoza, Audrey Gallego, Raquel S. Hunter, and Quiana Whitfield.

We also want to thank Susan Liddicoat at Teachers College Press—our editor who stuck with us through the complicated process of editing a book by authors who are now scattered around California and the country.

And last, but certainly not least, we want to express our appreciation to all of the extremely generous and thoughtful charter school educators and parents, state policy makers, and school district officials who gave us their time and input. We cannot thank them enough for teaching us some very valuable lessons.

Where Charter School Policy Fails

The Problems of Accountability and Equity

CHAPTER 1

Why Public Policy Fails to Live Up to the Potential of Charter School Reform

An Introduction

Amy Stuart Wells

There are early warning signs that charter school reform is entering a recession. That is not to say that the movement has quit growing, only that its rate of growth is beginning to slow. While charter school counts vary depending on who is counting, the estimated number of charter schools across the country grew from about 1,500 in 1999 to 2,000 the following year. The number jumped to only 2,372 for the fall of 2001 (Center for Education Reform, 2001; see RPP International, 2000). This slower growth rate occurred even as the number of states with charter school legislation expanded from 32 to 38.

There are, no doubt, several reasons for this lull in a reform movement that only a few years ago had so much political momentum that then-President Bill Clinton called for 3,000 charter schools by the year 2000. Yet, after spending the past 8 years studying charter school reform, I am convinced that sheer exhaustion on the part of charter school founders and educators is a major factor in the slowdown. In other words, the energy and enthusiasm that once sustained this effort to free schools from public bureaucracies, while giving them public funds to educate students, have waned as more and more educators, parents, and would-be educational entrepreneurs have learned that running autonomous schools without adequate support is extremely difficult. It seems there are a limited number of people with the knowledge and experience to educate children, the business acumen to keep an autonomous institution running, the political connections to raise the private funds needed to keep schools afloat, and the ability to forsake virtually all of their personal life in order to work 6 or 7 days a week for 12 to 14 hours a day. As one charter school principal stated in an article on charter school leader burnout, "It's sometimes painful to think about how long and intense this process will be" (Bowman, 2000, p. 1).

Educational management organizations, or EMOs, now running an estimated 10 to 20% of all charter schools across the country, help alleviate much of this burden. But they also come with their own philosophies and agendas—often including making a profit for their shareholders—that are not always in line with community-based groups who want to start charter schools (Bowman, 2000; Horn & Miron, 2000; Scott, 2002; Willard & Oplinger, 2000).

Thus, I speculate that charter school reform is a late-20th-century, laissez-faire reform that will die of its own weight some time early in the 21st century. This is not to say that all of the existing charter schools will fold; many of them could continue for years, as have some public alternative schools from the 1960s and 1970s. But it is fairly clear to anyone who spends a great deal of time in charter schools that this is not a public policy that will transform the public educational system into a more effective, efficient, or academically accountable system. Yet, at the same time, charter school reform's downturn should not be used as a rationale for vouchers—that is, an argument that if you can't transform the public schools via charter school reform, you should put them out of business. That would be the wrong interpretation of the story. Despite the rhetoric of many right-wing charter school supporters, I argue that this movement has begun to lose its momentum not because charter schools are stifled by the public education bureaucracy, but rather because of the lack of support these schools have received from the public policies that created them.

Furthermore, this book is not about the failure of individual charter schools. Indeed, charter schools are so diverse and so disparate in terms of their quality and viability that it would be misleading to try to generalize about the success or failure of these "schools" as if they were one entity. As the following pages demonstrate, my co-authors and I have been to many solid charter schools that are run by caring and committed educators. We also have been to far less stellar charter schools that were mostly in the business of making money for a small group of operators by enrolling students who had few other options and providing them with minimal educational services. We know quite well that the spectrum of charter school programs, goals, constituents, and quality is extremely broad.

For instance, we have studied charter schools that are rural, home-schooling collaboratives serving mostly Christian fundamentalist families, as well as urban "ethnocentric" charter schools serving families of specific racial/ethnic groups and focusing on the history and culture of those groups. We have seen back-to-basics charter schools—some serving mostly low-income students of color, others more middle-class White students from conservative communities. In addition, we have examined more progressive charter schools that offer open classrooms and integrated curricula—some in urban areas serving more racially and socioeconomically diverse students, others in more middle-class and White communities. We are also familiar with charter schools that serve suburban White students whose parents think they are too smart for regular public schools, and independent study and in-house charter schools that are last resorts for failing students. There are charter schools run by for-profit EMOs and those run by non-profit grassroots community groups. Furthermore, we know of schools where these categories collide—for example, a back-to-basics, Afro-centric school operated by a for-profit company.

Indeed, the only consistency across this diverse and diffuse reform "movement" is that charter schools all operate under the guidelines of state policies that promise greater autonomy in exchange for greater academic accountability, but generally fail to support the efforts of committed educators, especially those serving the most disadvantaged students in grassroots and non-profit charter schools. In other words, educators and parents in poor communities that are generally the most frustrated with the unequal public educational system often lack the support they need to create viable charter schools under the current policy framework. What's more, charter school laws fail to provide a viable infrastructure for holding schools accountable in any meaningful way.

This book, therefore, helps readers understand the connections between the problems that many charter schools face or perpetuate and the state policies under which they must work. In other words, the chapters in this book help readers understand that it is the ambiguity, the lack of support, and the complete absence of equity provisions within the charter school laws in most states that have led to the beginning of the end of yet another school reform movement. Our central theme, then, is to be true to the "multiple meanings" of charter school reform that exist at the school and community level, while at the same time pointing fingers at the poor public policies under which they exist. As an introduction to this argument, I examine the political and philosophical roots of charter school reform and the context in which these laws were passed. Here, it is easy to see how and why things got to be the way they are.

THE POLITICAL ORIGINS OF CHARTER SCHOOL REFORM

Charter school reform was definitely *not* a child of the 1960s. Although there were progressive voices advocating for more autonomous schools, this movement was born in the late 1980s and early 1990s between the end of Reagan's second term and the Contract with America. The political rhetoric of the day was not to ask what your government could do to solve the problem of educational inequality, but rather how could you pay fewer taxes and get big government out of your life (Edsall, 1991; Frank, 2000; Yergin & Stanislaw, 1998).

Clinton offered a kinder, gentler version of this rhetoric. After all, Clinton was a "New Democrat," which meant he emphasized restraint by government in contrast to the more traditional liberalism that critics had taken to calling "tax-and-spend." In his 1995 State of the Union address, Clinton declared, "The era of big government is over." In 1996 he signed the Welfare Reform Act, which both limited the duration of support for needy families and required recipients to enroll in job searches and take whatever jobs they could find (Yergin & Stanislaw, 1998).

In education, the equivalent backlash against big government was targeted at the large and bureaucratic public educational system in general. More specifically, frustration was aimed toward many of the equity-based policies of the 1960s and 1970s, particularly programs such as special education, desegregation, compensatory education, and bilingual education, whose enforcement had required lengthy rules and regulation (see Petrovich, forthcoming). The focus had shifted in the 1980s and 1990s away from equity toward so-called "excellence" in education—as if the two were mutually exclusive (see Fuller, 2000; Reyes & Rorrer, 2001).

Gone was the political emphasis on redistributing resources and opportunities toward students who had the least. In this brave new world of educational reform, equity would occur "de facto." In other words, rather than focus directly on the needs of students who were most disadvantaged in the educational system, policy makers would try to improve the quality of the overall educational system via an emphasis on higher educational standards—that is, "excellence"—as well as an infusion of choice and competition (see Petrovich, forthcoming). The argument was that a rising tide would lift all boats and that both standards-based accountability systems via systemic reform and a strong dose of competition via deregulation and choice would force all schools to respond to the needs of all students. Charter school reform was in sync with both of these efforts and thus is grounded in the ideology of each.

Systemic Reform and the Standards Movement

What later became known as "systemic reform" began with former President George Bush and the National Governors Association—then headed by Bill Clinton—at a 1989 educational summit. That summit helped to launch what is now a massive movement in public education to create more standards and assessments and hold schools and students more accountable for "outcomes," even as schools were freed of some of the more onerous regulations of the public educational system (Clune, 1993; O'Day & Smith, 1993).

The theme of systemic reform—a trade-off of greater autonomy for accountability—became a centerpiece of the Clinton administration's educational policy agenda. Thus, the landmark Goals 2000 legislation, which was supported by Clinton and a bipartisan group of legislators, became law in 1994 and had a major impact on the way in which many subsequent pieces of legislation—federal and state—were written. For instance, Goals 2000 provided more than $500 million annually for states to develop academic standards and matching assessments. Shortly thereafter, Congress passed the Improving America's Schools Act, which withheld major federal funding from states that did not develop standards.

Thus, the primary focus of systemic reform was on setting standards and assessments (O'Day & Smith, 1993). Yet at the same time individual schools were, in theory, given newfound freedom from rules and red tape in exchange for greater scrutiny of their student outcomes. In this way, systemic reform represented a shift from an input-based accountability system, where school resources are regulated by districts and states, to an outcome- or performance-based accountability system, where schools have greater autonomy from regulations but must demonstrate their success in terms of student achievement (see Chapter 2).

Following Congress' lead and funding, policy makers in state capitals across the country have bought into this seemingly logical and straightforward trade-off of greater school autonomy in exchange for greater accountability regarding student learning. As of spring 2002, 49 of 50 states have established state standards, and 46 states have mandated assessments aligned with their standards in at least one subject area (Quality Counts, 2002). All of this occurred prior to the federal 2001 "No Child Left Behind Act" that now mandates states test students every year in reading and math in grades three through eight (Olson, 2002). Meanwhile, most of the states with the new accountability systems also have designed policies—such as charter school laws—that grant schools freedom and flexibility in how they use these resources.

Charter school reform, then, fits into this autonomy-for-accountability framework because it provides the "autonomy" side of the equation within a broader "accountability" context. According to the authors of the federal charter school study:

> The school's charter gives the school autonomy over its operation and frees the school from regulations that other public schools must follow. In exchange for the flexibility afforded by the charter, the schools are held accountable for achieving the goals set out in the charter including improving student performance. (RPP International, 2000, p. 1)

One of the fastest-growing systemic reform policies during the late 1990s, charter school reform grants individual schools freedom from state and local regulations in exchange for a written charter proposal stating goals for student outcomes.

Market Metaphor for School Reform

A second major political theme that has driven charter school reform, at least at the policy level, is the market metaphor or what political scientists would refer to as "neo-liberal" ideology.[1] Proponents of this view argue that the best way to improve public education is to force schools to compete for "customers" by providing parents greater choices of where their children attend school. From this perspective, the educational system can only be improved via greater deregulation and privatization of large bureaucratic systems and the simultaneous infusion of competition, high-stakes incentive systems, and supposed unfettered consumer choice. Proponents of this view trace the problem with education to government's intrusion into the daily operation of schools, thus shielding them from beneficial market forces, especially competition (Chubb & Moe, 1990).

The argument is that, acting through self-interest, individual consumers—as opposed to paternalistic public policies—will drive improvement of the educational system (see Chubb & Moe, 1990; Cookson, 1994; Friedman, 1962). In general, neo-liberalism advocates an increased reliance on market forces, volunteerism, and individual demands to achieve social ends. Deregulation, or cutting back on governments' regulatory systems that were put in place to help protect the public, particularly the most disadvantaged, is the goal. Yergin and Stanislaw (1998) argue that the neo-liberal objective of the 1990s was to move away from government control and toward greater reliance on competition in the marketplace as a more efficient way to provide public services.

Thus, the fall of communism in Eastern Europe only strengthened the argument that highly deregulated, free-market capitalism is the only logical economic system—for individual countries and for the world economy at large. As Lester Thurow noted in 1996, "The market, and the market alone, rules. No one doubts it" (p. 1).

Indeed, too much government regulation or direct delivery of social services via the welfare state is seen by neo-liberals as both expensive and isolationist in nature, putting countries at an extreme disadvantage in a global economy (see Callaghy, 1993; Thurow, 1996). This argument became so pervasive, so much the "common sense" of the late 20th century, that those who questioned its soundness were easily dismissed. Thus, basically, for the past decade and a half, this theme has dominated much of the political imagination of those with the ability to influence policy and structure debates about the future of education (Yergin & Stanislaw, 1998). And it is clearly one of the most prominent themes behind charter school reform.

According to an article in the *New Republic*, "Those who invented charter schools were not just out to create a few thousand good schools. Rather, they wanted to improve all 88,000 public schools in the country by creating enough competition for money and students to force school districts to innovate" (Osborne, 1999, p. 2).

Decentralization: Local/Community Control

There is yet another political theme that shaped the demand for charter school reform and that is the age-old call for decentralization and giving more control over governance and decision making to the local school community. Like the market metaphor, the call for greater decentralization is, for some anyway, an attack on government—at least federal and state government—involvement in education. This political theme also more closely links charter school reform to what have become known as "new social movements," because it represents very localized activity around issues of recognition, identity, difference, voice, and empowerment.

Still, it is important to remember that historically, decentralization has had different implications for different communities. Thus, in the United States we have used two different phrases—local control and community control—in describing this political push. At first glance, the two phrases seem quite similar in that they both express a demand to devolve decision-making powers from distant, centralized bureaucracies to more localized political contexts. Yet, historically, these terms described very different political phenomena and were used by people from different social, economic, and political standpoints to accomplish very different—and sometimes contradictory—goals.

For instance, the term *local control* is tied historically to efforts by those who already have social, economic, and political power and are thus resentful of any government infringement on their right to exercise that power. In contrast, efforts to establish community control of schools generally originated from people who had little power in the educational system—the poor and the disenfranchised—and who argued that the public schools in their neighborhoods were not serving the needs of their children. Historically, community control efforts in education, which became quite popular in the 1960s, were linked to the Black power movement and efforts by urban African American parents and activists to have more say in how their neighborhood schools were run. They sought to systematically change the culture and climate of those schools via grassroots, community-based reform (see McCoy, 1970).

Thus, while there are similarities in terms of the call for devolution of power, the goal of local control is to allow those who historically have had power within local educational systems to maintain it, and the goal of community control is to alter those very power relations. These political and social distinctions between the objectives of the advocates of these two different forms of devolution remain with us today. For instance, the theme of local control was echoed by political conservatives throughout the 1990s—in everything from the Contract with America to 2001 Congressional proposals for the reauthorization of the Elementary and Secondary Education Act. This is the neo-conservative ideology of the so-called "New Right" and hearkens back to the "states rights" and "local control" movements in the South in the 1950s and 1960s as Whites resisted federal government intervention for school desegregation and affirmative action (see Apple, 2001; Edsall, 1991; Lewis & Nakagawa, 1995).

While the Republican call for local control is grounded in various political attitudes, including the backlash against government-enforced civil rights laws, the demand for community control has come from the political left, as racial and ethnic minority groups have continued to struggle for greater freedom from oppressive state-run institutions. Historically, however, this push for greater community control is not solely an anti-state political movement. For instance, community control efforts among African Americans in the 1960s were taking place parallel to the civil rights movement, which relied heavily on the federal government and the U.S. Constitution for enforcement of basic rights. And finally, in a related but distinct effort, many educational progressives throughout the history of this country have called for policies creating greater localized control of teaching and learning—policies allowing for the creation of schools as localized sites of democracy (Maynard, 1970; McCoy, 1970).

But the most recent political push toward greater local/community control of schools, manifest in policies such as charter school reform, is different in that it tries to be all of these things at once. Thus this reform is more similar to other so-called new social movements, branching out in various political and cultural directions (see Wilgren, 2000). Fraser (1997) refers to this as the politics of recognition—of a new political "imaginary" centered on notions of identity difference and cultural domination—that mobilizes groups around race, ethnicity, gender, and sexuality. I would argue that in the case of charter school reform, groups mobilize around these and other beliefs and identities about schooling and whose knowledge is valued in schools. These beliefs tend to overlap and intertwine with identities of race/ethnicity, social class, and religion and "morality."

But whether it is the Christian right in a small rural town or a Latino community in a crowded urban center, charter school founders and operators clearly are engaging in a politics of recognition. They are trying to escape the "cultural domination" they say they have experienced in the regular public schools, and they seek to create school communities in which they can define the identity and culture of the school.

WHERE IDEOLOGY MEETS PUBLIC POLICY

Indeed, these powerful political arguments—systemic reform, free-market reform, and the renewed push for local or community control of schools—shaped much of the policy-making agenda in the mid- to late-1990s, especially when it came to charter school reform.

First of all, as I noted above, charter schools represented the ultimate accountability-for-autonomy trade-off of systemic reform. Thus, in exchange for greater freedom from the educational system, charter schools must, in theory, be held accountable for student outcomes in ways that regular public schools are not. According to most charter school laws, charter schools must administer mandated state tests, and a chartering agency theoretically can close a charter school that fails to meet specified performance objectives. In fact, a very compelling argument for charter schools is that they replace the current rule-based accountability system, in which schools are held accountable for meeting regulations on inputs, with an outcome- or performance-based accountability system. Since charter schools that do not achieve results can be shut down, the argument goes, this threat forces charter schools to be more accountable, particularly for student outcomes and success (Finn, Manno, Bierlein, & Vanourek, 1997; Hassel, 1996; Kolderie, 1992; Manno, 1998; Manno, Finn, Bierlein & Vanourek, 2000; Millot, 1996).

Yet, despite charter school reform's direct link to systemic reform, in many ways it has been the free-market or neo-liberal argument that has most directly shaped state charter school policies. Indeed, advocates of this view are the most active and organized at the political and policy-making level in terms of influencing the scope of charter school legislation. For instance, under the "strong" versus "weak" charter school law distinction advocated by the Center for Educational Reform (CER)—a conservative think tank in Washington, DC—"strong" charter school laws are those that are more deregulatory and those that spawn the largest number of charter schools. According to the center's definition, so-called "strong" laws include the following provisions:

- No cap on the number of charter schools allowed
- Multiple charter-granting agencies
- No formal evidence of local support required before start-up
- Greater legal and fiscal autonomy

- Automatic waiver from state and district laws
- Exemption from collective bargaining and work rules
- Guarantee of full *per-pupil* funding, but no more and no special support for those schools serving poor students

For instance, the CER webpage notes that the state with the strongest law is Arizona because in that state, an unlimited number of charter schools may be established, virtually any individual or organization may petition to start a charter school, three different public bodies are empowered to authorize charter schools, and full per-pupil funding follows students to the schools, which are legally and financially autonomous and exempt from state laws and regulations, district policies, and collective bargaining agreements. So-called "weak laws," on the other hand, are those that are seen by the free-market advocates as more regulatory.

These free-market reformers are mostly silent in terms of equity issues, except to say that, de facto, school choice will force schools to be more accountable to parents and competitive for students and the dollars they generate. But there is no discussion of "redistribution" of opportunities or resources—for example, targeting more resources to charter schools in low-income communities, or ensuring that the most disadvantaged students have access to popular charter school programs. In fact, federal funding for charter schools is now more than $100 million a year, and none of it is targeted specifically toward low-income communities, in part because such redistribution would be antithetical to charter school reform, at least as free-market reformers see it.

Meanwhile, the CER webpage, which offers far more up-to-date information on charter schools than the federal government, boasts of its unique role in influencing the specifics of charter school legislation in statehouses across the country. Each year CER evaluates the "strength" of the state charter school laws across the country and posts this ranking on the website, which states:

> Using well-established criteria, the Center offers the nation's only comprehensive evaluation of all charter school laws. . . . The evaluation components are based on sound, objective measures of how to evaluate progress toward the intended goal that charter laws seek: To provide the maximum capacity and flexibility within a state to yield the establishment of highly successful charter schools.

Unfortunately, this strong versus weak law distinction advocated by this incredibly conservative think tank became the "common sense" of the charter school movement, the nomenclature by which good versus bad laws were defined. For instance, an *Education Week* article describing the growth of charter school reform noted that the most recent state to pass charter school legislation was Indiana, which "has been given an 'A' for the strength of its charter school legislation by the Center for Education Reform (*Education Week* on the Web, 2002). This sentence, which lacks any qualification regarding what CER is or what its "A" rating stands for, is followed by a direct link to the CER website.

Meanwhile, those seeking more local and/or community control of schools have found it in charter school reform but at a price to those who lack the local resources to supplement the meager public funding. In other words, the devolution aspect of charter school reform works better for some than others. In particular, it works very well for those with the private wealth to shape the laissez-faire policy to their advantage. This means that it is more likely to serve those who seek local control from the standpoint of social, economic, and political privilege and not those who seek to empower the most disempowered communities via charter school reform.

EMERGING THEMES ACROSS THE RESEARCH

Evidence abounds that the accountability-minded systemic reformers and the equity-minded community controllers have lost the most ground in the process of translating ideology into charter school policy. Indeed, after conducting one of the most thorough reviews of the research literature to date on charter schools, I have concluded that of all the promises and sets of assumptions behind charter school reform, the claims of increased accountability and de facto equity have proved to be the furthest from the truth. Here, I offer a brief review of what I have learned and point to chapters and sections of this book that corroborate these findings.

Accountability and Student Achievement

Thus far, there is no strong or consistent evidence that charter schools have improved student achievement—as measured by state-mandated assessments anyway—or that they are being held more accountable for academic outcomes than regular public schools. Aside from anecdotal reports from individual schools, none of the methodologically sound state-level reports show significant increases in overall achievement of charter school students, and many show decreases. In fact, the lack of academic or outcome-based accountability in charter schools is perhaps one of the most robust findings across the states and reports.

Therefore, even though most state charter school laws require that charter schools administer state assessments, there does not yet appear to be any consequences for those charter schools that are not performing well academically. Studies from a number of states and jurisdictions, including Massachusetts, Michigan, Ohio, Pennsylvania, Texas, and Washington, DC, to name a few, draw similar conclusions (see, for example, Henig, Holyoke, Lacireno-Paquet, & Moser, 2001; Massachusetts State Auditor, 2001; Miron & Nelson, 2000; Public Sector Consultants, 2000; Texas Center for Educational Research, 2001; Willard & Oplinger, 2000). For instance, the Massachusetts State Auditor (2001) reported:

> We found that DOE [state Department of Education] did not establish specific performance objectives for charter schools or provide formal guidance on how these objectives should be established, measured, or reported to ensure that charter schools perform at an acceptable level. As a result, we found that many of the performance objectives established by the charter schools for themselves that we reviewed were unclear and unmeasurable. . . . We found erroneous performance measures being reported by charter schools to DOE that were not detected by DOE. Further, one of the seven charter schools that we visited had no supporting documentation to substantiate how it measured the achievements of its objective as reported to DOE. (p. 2)

Indeed, many of these studies demonstrate that when charter-granting agencies do attempt to hold charter schools more accountable, it is in the area of fiscal as opposed to academic accountability. One set of findings from our study of California—the focus of Chapter 2—helps explain this phenomenon. In that chapter, my co-authors and I argue that the process of holding charter schools accountable for measurable student outcomes is a highly political one and that district officials are uncertain of just how to do it. We also learned that charter school proposals tend to be extremely vague regarding "to what" they should be held accountable. And finally, we learned that the political popularity and clout of charter schools affects the degree to which their charter-granting agencies are likely to revoke a charter. In other words, there is a political context to accountability that systemic reformers greatly underestimate. It seems it is much more difficult to close down a politically popular charter school regardless of how far the school is from meeting its proposed goals (also see Bulkley, 1999).

Echoing our more nuanced explanation of why charter school accountability is so illusive, a 1997–99 study funded by the U.S. Department of Education found that across six states, the autonomy-for-accountability trade-off remains an unrealized aspiration (Hill, Lake, Celio, Campbell, Herdman, & Bulkley, 2001). Indeed, paralleling so many of the findings discussed in our UCLA Charter School Study (1998) report and Chapter 2 of this book, Hill and colleagues (2001) report that charter school authorizers, particularly conventional school district offices, are struggling to learn how to relate to schools on the basis of performance rather than compliance.

In short, there are now massive amounts of evidence that the systemic reform vision of charter schools and their autonomy-for-accountability trade-off has not materialized. We are left with a reform that, in many cases, provides a great deal of autonomy for individual schools but little public information or feedback about what takes place within them. Chapters 2, 3, and 7 of this book provide greater insight into the many ways charter school reform affects school-level autonomy or accountability. For instance, Chapters 2 and 3 illustrate that charter schools rely on the "traditional" public school system more often and in many more complex ways than would be implied by the rhetoric of the reform. At the same time, they are held far less accountable for academic outcomes than the rhetoric would imply. And finally, as Chapter 7 reveals, while charter school educators for the most part enjoy their greater autonomy from the public educational system, most admit that their classroom pedagogy is similar to what it was before they came to the charter schools. This suggests that they do not feel any more or less accountable than they did before charter school reform.

Therefore, the lesson to be learned from our research and that of our colleagues across the country is that despite the high level of support that advocates of systemic reform have given to the charter school movement, assuming all the while that charter school reform was part of systemic reform, it is now clear that this is not the case. Charter schools are many things to many people, but they are not systematically more accountable for their student outcomes than the public schools down the street.

Equity Concerns

If charter school policies as they are implemented at the school level are not exemplars of accountability and systemic reform, then what are they? Whose interests are being served by this reform? The answer is, rarely the most disadvantaged students. And this clearly echoes research findings from the United States and abroad regarding the effect of school choice policies (see, for instance, Fiske & Ladd, 2000; Gewirtz, Ball, & Bowe, 1995; Whitty, 1996). Indeed, there are several findings from our research—discussed in detail in Chapters 4, 5, and 6 of this book—and many, many other studies that suggest this reform movement is leading to even greater inequalities within the educational system. In this section, I introduce several of these findings regarding equity and charter schools.

Lack of Public Funding Leads to Reliance on Private Resources. Several studies from various states across the country demonstrate that charter schools are funded at a lower level than other public schools, especially when their costs for facilities are taken into account (see, for instance, Public Sector Consultants & Maximus, 1999; Texas Center for Educational Research, 2001). Furthermore, as Slayton demonstrates in Chapter 4, not all charter schools receive the same amount of public funding from their districts. While recent legislation in California is supposed to address these inequalities, given the insidiousness of the problem as described by Slayton, chances are that many of these inequalities remain.

Meanwhile, due to their lack of public support, charter schools are forced to constantly seek private support. With some states not even giving full per-pupil funding to charter schools and no states covering all or most of the capital expenditure needed to house a school, charter school founders and educators are generally left to their own devices to obtain private resources by any means necessary. This, of course, is less generally problematic for charter schools located in wealthy communities where private resources abound, as opposed to low-income communities. These issues and how they complicate the lives of charter school educators and students are described in detail in Chapter 5 of this book.

This finding helps to explain the popularity and rapid growth of the educational management organizations. Because EMOs usually provide start-up funds and help charter school educators and parents locate sites for their schools, they are becoming especially popular in low-income communities where it is often more difficult to raise the private capital necessary to open a charter school (see Scott, 2002).

And, as I mentioned above, the issue of EMO-run charter schools raises concerns about just how much autonomy individual charter schools have or just how much local and/or community control their founders and educators have. Depending on the management company—its size, for-profit as opposed to non-profit status, and its organizational culture—these concerns may be more salient in some instances than others (Horn & Miron, 2000; Scott, 2002; Willard & Oplinger, 2000). Furthermore, researchers, journalists, and auditors are uncovering more and more stories of ethically problematic behavior on the part of these companies. For instance, the Massachusetts State Auditor's report (2001) found "a number of deficiencies relative to management companies' operation of charter schools" (p. 3). Such inadequacies included potentially excessive profits provided to these management companies; in one instance, more than 24% of a charter school's funding went to the school's management company rather than to program services.

All of this suggests that to the extent that low-income communities are more likely to find themselves in a situation with less public funding, more reliance on private resources, and more dependence on EMOs to bring in the start-up funds needed to get off the ground, these communities are much less likely to benefit from the autonomy offered via charter school reform.

Signs of Increasing Racial/Social-Class Segregation in Charter Schools. Another major equity concern that our review of the existing literature on segregation and charter schools confirms is that charter schools are generally not very racially or socioeconomically diverse. For instance, we found ever-increasing evidence that when the demographic data are broken down and the school-level information is examined, charter schools are more racially and socioeconomically homogeneous than the already highly segregated public schools (Wells, Holme, Lopez, & Cooper, 2000). Yet, we also found important state-by-state differences in terms of the racial/ethnic makeup of charter schools. For instance, in some states—especially Connecticut, Illinois, and Michigan—charter school reform has been embraced as a mostly urban reform designed to serve predominantly low-income students of color. In other states, such as California, Arizona, and Colorado, it has appealed to a much wider range of people and communities, including many that are predominantly White and well-off.

In fact, our analysis of the U.S. Department of Education (RPP International, 2000) data from 1997–98 suggests that the more racially/ethnically and socioeconomically diverse a state's K–12 student population is, the more likely the charter schools in that state are to enroll White and non-poor students. Conversely, in states with a general public school population that is predominantly White and relatively wealthy, charter schools are more likely to enroll a higher percentage of students of color and low-income students; only four out of 18 states do not fit this analysis (Wells et al., 2000).

Related to this issue is what appears to be a correlation between the geographic size of school districts and the likelihood that they enroll White and wealthy students. In other words, it appears as though in states such as Connecticut and Michigan, which have smaller geographic school districts that are distinguished by impenetrable urban–suburban and suburban–suburban boundary lines, the demand for charter schools in the suburbs is far less. On the other hand, in more southern and western states with larger, county-wide school districts that include urban and suburban-type communities, charter schools are more likely to appeal to White and wealthier families (see Wells et al., 2000). This correlation suggests that segregation and separation along race and class lines need to be examined within the context of the districts and states in which the schools reside.

Furthermore, the closer we looked at the local communities in which these new schools are being founded, the more evidence we saw of the segregative effects—in terms of race and social class—of charter school reform. For instance, a national study by researchers at NYU demonstrated that within their local contexts, charter schools are often more racially and socioeconomically isolated than nearby public schools (Ascher, Jacobwitz, & McBride, 1999). That is, when you examine the school-level data, charter school enrollment tends to be comprised of either predominantly White students or predominantly students of color. At the same time, charter schools tend to enroll either mostly non-poor students or predominantly poor students. In fact, those researchers found that two-thirds of the 552 charter schools they looked at enrolled either predominantly White students or predominantly students of color, compared with less than 50% of the districts in which these schools are housed. In other words, the charter schools were much less diverse that their surrounding school districts. Similarly, another study out of Arizona State University found that charter schools in the metropolitan Phoenix area tended to have much higher White enrollments than surrounding public schools (Cobb & Glass, 1999).

In terms of social-class segregation, most data support the argument that, like racial segregation, at the school level, charter schools tend to be more segregated by social class than even the already segregated public schools. Moreover, there is some evidence from various studies to suggest that even in poor communities, the relatively more advantaged of the disadvantaged students are enrolling in charter schools, and the percentage of the lowest-income students served in charter schools across the country may be declining. And finally, there is some preliminary evidence to suggest that to the extent that charter school reform does serve low-income students and students of color, they frequently are enrolled in some of the most impoverished schools or those with the least challenging curricula (see Wells et al., 2000, for a review).

Although it has become more and more apparent that charter school reform has led to greater racial and social-class segregation and isolation, it is less apparent just how the specifics of charter school policies have allowed this to happen. Chapter 6 of this volume provides a more in-depth explanation of the relationship between the state law and who ends up enrolling in charter schools. Clearly, what we argue in that chapter is that state charter school laws that fail to provide students with transportation and allow charter schools to have some sort of admissions criteria, such as a required parent involvement contract, contribute to racial and social-class separation. In addition, virtually all charter schools have a very limited and narrow method of recruitment that most likely taps into the relatively well-off families even in the low-income communities.

And finally, as Chapter 6 so carefully documents, starting a charter school is very much about the process of community building around a set of shared values and beliefs. While such community building is often seen as an important asset of charter school reform, it also leads to racial/ethnic and social-class segregation via exclusion of people who are "different."

In this way, the evidence of greater segregation within charter schools, which happens to be one of the most consistent findings across the various studies, speaks to charter schools being more about the politics of recognition as more homogeneous groups of people come together to form charter schools. But it also speaks to the lack of a charter school policy framework that would support those charter school operators who want to create more diverse schools. For instance, the lack of transportation and outreach for charter schools leads to a situation in which it is difficult to create racially and socio-economically diverse charter schools. Furthermore, as we illustrate in Chapter 6, the license to create more homogeneous school communities in terms of the values and beliefs of those within these schools often leads to the creation of charter schools that are more homogeneous in terms of race, class, and culture.

Taking Stock

Other cross-state findings that have emerged from charter school research include a lack of evidence that there is much, if any, meaningful collaboration between charter schools and the regular public schools. In this way, charter schools are not serving as "models of innovation" for the public system (see, for example, Rofes, 1998; UCLA Charter School Study, 1998).

Furthermore, related to the finding from Chapter 7 that we discussed above, many of these research reports argue that charter school educators generally are not employing any new instructional practices. In other words, it appears as though this reform is more about the deregulation of funding and the ability to create school-level policies, such as parent involvement requirements, and less about changing the process of teaching and learning in any meaningful way. Study after study reports that despite all the hype around charter schools, the teaching and learning that go on within them are often the same as what is found in traditional public schools. For instance, a study looking at charter schools in Massachusetts, New Jersey, and Washington, DC found a lack of true innovation in many charter schools (see Teske, Schneider, Buckley, & Clark, 2000). Research from Michigan draws the same conclusion (Arsen, Plank, & Sykes, 1999).

Clearly, it is difficult to read the emerging body of research literature on charter schools and not come to the conclusion that the free-market reformers won the battle for the soul of a movement that promised to be so much more than merely a deregulatory reform. In other words, despite the diversity of people and political interests represented in this reform, the legislative agenda in the statehouses across the country has been dominated by those who want deregulation for the sake of competition and school-level autonomy. The interests of those who would like to see greater accountability in exchange for that autonomy, or those who would like to have gained more meaningful community control of schools in low-income communities, have not been at the forefront of the policy-making agenda. Meanwhile, more economically privileged charter school founders who seek to create their own separate schools and enjoy a strong degree of local control have faired far better under this deregulatory agenda.

The suggestion I make at the end of this book is for more progressive and equity-minded charter school supporters to come together to imagine a policy world in which charter school legislation may better support their efforts to create and sustain schools that serve the students who traditionally have been the most disadvantaged in the public educational system. Or how about a world where the criteria of academic accountability could be tailored more closely to the needs of students and educators—not just in charter schools, but in all schools—and school communities could work with their districts or charter-granting agencies to find helpful and appropriate ways to measure progress and growth? Why not a policy agenda that focuses on quality over quantity and seeks to support charter schools that are open to all students while simultaneously serving as laboratories of good pedagogy? And why can't policymakers write a charter school law that supports and provides incentives for groups that want to start racially diverse charter schools?

As I note in the Conclusion, several state legislatures are beginning to grapple with many of the shortcomings of their charter school legislation. Indeed, state policy makers from Texas to Massachusetts are beginning to question in a more careful way whose interests are being served under the current policy conditions. Efforts to curb the deregulatory aspect of the movement are on the rise. Whether a more progressive policy agenda will follow remains to be seen.

In the meantime, this brief overview of the charter school reform movement and the emerging themes in the research helps us to better understand "what" is happening in charter school reform across the country. The following chapters of this book are intended to help explain the "how" and "why" of these findings. Our findings from California, a state that has been at the forefront of charter school reform, offer a chance to see how these emerging themes from the research relate to the day-to-day experiences of charter school educators and students. Answers to "how" and "why" questions can be derived only through a methodology that is sensitive to the understandings of individual actors as well as the unique social context in which they are situated.

THE UCLA CHARTER SCHOOL STUDY

The data presented in this book are drawn from an ambitious study of charter schools in 10 California school districts. Our research team conducted in-depth case studies of each district and 17 of the charter schools within them. Additional charter schools also were examined in a less in-depth manner during the course of this study, although they eventually were dropped from the study for various reasons—for instance, one converted back to a regular public school, or we needed to focus our data collection on two or three schools within the large urban districts. Still, these additional charter schools are discussed in Chapters 3 and 4 of this book.

The main purpose of our research was to understand how a seemingly straightforward policy such as charter school reform interacts with different local communities. We knew from prior research on charter schools in California that they existed in a wide range of diverse communities across our vast state—from urban poor to wealthy suburban to middle-class rural (SRI International, 1997). Thus, we purposefully sampled districts and schools based on their diversity from each other. In other words, rather than use random sampling techniques employed by quantitative, survey researchers, we sampled based on the phenomenon we wanted to study—namely, the diversity of experiences within the charter school movement (Merriam, 1998; Schofield, 1998). This study, therefore, helps move the debate on charter school reform beyond global generalizations of whether it is "working" into a more thoughtful discussion of when it is working and for whom.

With this in mind, we selected 10 districts that differed on several key factors, including size; racial and socioeconomic diversity; position in an urban, rural, or suburban community; geographic location in southern, central, or northern California; and number, percentage, and types of charter schools in the district. Our sample consisted of five large urban districts, three that were mostly rural but also had some suburban housing, and two that were mostly suburban, although one included a rural section. All totaled, these 10 districts housed 39, or almost one-third, of all the charter schools in the state at the time we selected the sample in 1996 (SRI International, 1997).

We selected the 17 charter schools within these districts by once again sampling for diversity along various dimensions—for example, grade levels served; size and demographics of the students; type or format of the school, including home schooling and independent study charters; philosophy of the school; dependent versus independent relationships with districts; and duration of the charter. The final sample included two suburban, five rural/suburban, and ten urban charter schools. All the names of the districts and schools have been changed to protect the identity and confidentiality of the people we interviewed.

Data collection included 462 semistructured interviews with school district officials; various members of the charter schools' communities, including school founders, leaders, teachers, parents, governance council members, and community supporters; and educators at nearby public schools. We also conducted observations of district and charter school meetings and of classrooms in charter schools. And finally, we collected hundreds of district and charter school documents. In addition to the data collected in these 10 school districts, we also interviewed 50 state-level policy makers in six states in order to better understand bipartisan support for this reform (see Wells, Grutzik, Carnochan, Slayton, & Vasudeva, 1999).

This extremely large and rich data base was then carefully and systematically analyzed according to the themes that emerged during the data collection process, including accountability, funding and resources, and student access. In this way, the findings that emerged were truly grounded in the experiences of charter school founders, educators, and parents, as well as school district officials and state policy makers.

THE CALIFORNIA CHARTER SCHOOL LAW— THE POLICY CONTEXT

Our study was of charter school reform in California—the second state in the country to pass charter school legislation and the state that has consistently had the largest number of students enrolled in charter schools. As with so many other educational reforms, California has been a bellwether state when it comes to charter schools. In order to help readers better understand the connection between the policy and the practice of charter schools in California, I outline the parameters of the legislation that shaped the experiences of the districts we studied.

The original California charter school law, which was passed in 1992 and went into effect in early 1993, was amended considerably in 1998 to make the chartering process easier for schools and to reduce the power of school boards to deny or revoke charter proposals. Since 1998, additional state legislation has been passed that affects the experiences of California charter schools—either directly or indirectly—most of which does not address the central issues of accountability and equity discussed in the following chapters of this book. In this way, as I discuss in more detail in the Conclusion, most of the constraints of the original California charter school policy that affected the schools in our study remain intact. A brief description of that legislation follows.

The Stated Intent

In the prefatory statement of the intent of the California charter school law, the legislators wrote that this policy is designed to help low-achieving students and to enhance academic accountability in the public educational system. Thus, the themes of equity and accountability were present up front in the legislation even if they were not supported by the specifics of the law.

For instance, as stated in the "General Provisions" of the California charter school law, the primary intent of the legislation is to improve pupil learning and increase learning opportunities for all students, especially those identified as low achieving. Regarding the accountability issues related to this intent, the legislation stipulates that this reform is designed to "hold the [charter] schools . . . accountable for meeting measurable pupil outcomes, and provide the schools a method to change from rule-based to performance-based accountability systems" (pp. 2–3). Yet, as the wording of the legislation shifted from intent to content, the process by which charter schools were to be held accountable for serving low-income students was confusing, to say the least.

Granting, Denying, and Revoking Charters

One of the defining features of the California charter school law is that charters are granted to schools almost exclusively through local school districts. In fact, the original 1992 law specified that only local boards of education could grant charters, although petitioners could appeal to their county board of education if their local district rejected their initial request. The 1998 amendments, however, allow charter petitioners to apply directly to their county board of education and, if denied a charter by their local board or county board, to apply directly to the state board of education for a charter. In 2000, the California charter school law was amended again to allow the State Board of Education to grant charters to schools. Even with these new provisions, a defining characteristic of California charter schools is that the vast majority of the approximately 358 operating charter schools in the state as of 2001 are local entities, generally granted through and governed by their local school districts (CANEC, 2001; RPP International, 2000).

There are two routes to creating charter schools in California: The first is to convert an existing public school into a "conversion" charter school and the second is to create a new, "start-up" charter school. The original law included a statewide cap of 100 on the number of charter schools, and a limit of 10 per district. The 1998 amendments to the legislation, however, raised the cap to 250 charter schools for the 1998–99 school year and 100 more per year after that. The limit of 10 charter schools per district was removed.

California charters are valid for 5 years, at which time schools must renew their charters with the granting agencies. The law specifies conditions under which a charter may be revoked or not renewed, including a "material violation" of the standards of a school's charter, failure to "meet or pursue any of the pupil outcomes" specified in its charter, failure to meet generally accepted accounting principles, or fiscal mismanagement. The law also specifies that charter school proposals should describe the method by which public progress in meeting the schools' pupil outcomes will be measured. In this way, the law attempts to enforce the accountability aspect of charter school reform. However, as we demonstrate in Chapter 2, this provision is not enough.

Charter School Operations

In terms of the day-to-day operations of the charter schools, the law waives most of the California Education Code regulations except for those related to non-discriminatory admissions based on race, gender, and national origin; basic health and safety standards; and participation in the state assessment program. In these specific areas, charter schools are required to abide by the same rules and regulations as regular public schools. Also, the California law requires that each group of charter school petitioners state in its proposal the means by which the school "will achieve a racial and ethnic balance among its pupils that is reflective of the general population residing within the territorial jurisdiction of the school district to which the charter petition is submitted" (p. 4). Still, as Chapter 6 and our prior report (UCLA Charter School Study, 1998) clearly show, this aspect of the legislation is not being monitored, let alone enforced.

As noted in Chapter 4, public funds for charter schools are, in most cases, routed through the local districts that grant the charters. Originally, the funds that all charter schools were supposed to receive were to be equal to the "base revenue limit" per pupil for the district. In 2001, the state legislature reduced the funding for non-classroom (independent study, home-schooling) charter schools.

In addition to basic, general funds, charter schools are entitled to receive state and federal categorical funds—for example, Title 1 or special education—for students who qualify for them. The law does not state, however, that charter schools are eligible for any of the capital funds from the state or those generated by local tax revenues to pay for facilities. Subsequent state legislation and a ballot initiative, Proposition 39, have made it easier for charter schools to gain access to public funds for facilities or to the facilities themselves. Still, finding a home for a new, start-up charter school remains one of the major challenges.

Given these criteria, the California law is not too dissimilar from the vast majority of charter school laws that exist in the other 37 states and jurisdictions. In fact, the Center for Education Reform gives California a "B" in its A–F grading system because it allows for healthy growth of charter schools but also contains some provisions that may impede growth. Thus, California's law is not the most deregulatory, free-market law, but it is by no means the most restrictive either.

In this way, our in-depth findings from California are helpful in terms of not just California, but other states as well. To the extent the same phenomena are occurring elsewhere, we hope the chapters that follow help to shed some light on the reasons why charter school reform has failed to produce greater accountability and why it comes up so poorly on equity dimensions.

OVERVIEW OF THE CHAPTERS

Thus, the two themes that cut through more than one of the chapters of this book are (1) despite the rhetoric to the contrary, there is no additional academic accountability for charter schools, and (2) because the charter school legislation was, for the most part, not centrally focused on issues of equal educational opportunity, serious equity issues related to resources and access have arisen.

Meanwhile, there are several cross-cutting themes that emerge across different chapters. For instance, Chapters 2, 3, and 4 examine charter school–district relationships and the ambiguity inherent in those. For instance, as I noted above, Chapter 2 by Wells, Vasudeva, Holme, and Cooper, provides a close examination of the way in which issues of "accountability" play out in the daily relationships between charter schools and their charter-granting agencies—namely, their local school districts. This chapter demonstrates that neither academic nor fiscal accountability is a simple, straightforward, and rational process. Rather, it is a messy, ambiguous, and political process. Clearly these findings from California must relate to other states and their experiences with charter school accountability.

Chapter 3, by Carnochan, looks more closely at three charter schools in one large urban school district to examine the relationship between charter schools and their charter-granting or host school district. Her findings lead to several policy recommendations—for all schools, not just charter schools—in terms of their relationships to districts, including that districts should assist charter schools in obtaining skills related to self-governance, consider how to allow schools greater authority over hiring decisions, and attend to the lack of adequate facilities for schools in poor areas. Thus, Carnochan argues that urban districts can use charter school reform to change district practices and challenge the prevailing sentiment that such districts are but inefficient, change-resistant bureaucracies. It also suggests that charter reform, with its supposed autonomy-for-accountability trade-off, does not provide solutions to long-term problems, especially in urban settings.

Slayton's Chapter 4 shows us that despite explicit wording in the California charter school statute regarding how charter schools should be equitably funded, the actual process of funding these schools is arbitrary and capricious. Indeed, despite the technical language of the law, how much public funding a charter school receives depends on the savvy and know-how of the principal and the politics of the school district leadership. This chapter provides a segue into the chapters that follow, which focus more explicitly on equity issues as they relate to charter schools.

Chapters 5 (Scott and Holme) and 6 (Lopez, Wells, and Holme) focus explicitly on equity issues. Namely, Chapter 5 discusses the ability of low-income communities to garner the necessary private resources to participate in charter school reform, while Chapter 6 illustrates the limited student access to many charter schools. Both of these chapters also reveal disturbing trends about the ways in which charter school reform can contribute to growing inequities in the public educational system in general.

Chapter 7 (Vasudeva and Grutzik) focuses on teachers' lives in charter schools and also raises important equity concerns of another sort—namely, which teachers at which stages in their careers can participate in this reform. Yet, at the same time, this chapter shows the attraction of charter school reform for professionals who seek more autonomy and freedom to serve students. In other words, teachers who want the autonomy to teach in a more deregulated school can do so, but often at a professional and personal cost.

In the Conclusion, I ask a central question about how a reform movement that is so diverse at the grassroots or school level has become so narrow and so conservative at the policy level? I then offer some suggestions for reworking the language of "strong" versus "weak" laws to serve a more progressive agenda.

In all, the in-depth look at charter school reform in 10 California school districts presented in this book helps us understand the broader cross-state findings that are emerging in the charter school literature in general. Therefore, when policy makers and advocates of charter schools are looking for answers to questions about *how* and *why* this reform movement has not lived up to the expectations, they will have a place to turn. What this book will help them understand is that in many ways the tensions and inconsistencies between the three different political themes shaping this reform—systemic reform, free-market reform, and local/community control—are more pronounced in the experiences of those engaged in charter schools than are the platitudes about what these more autonomous schools can accomplish. Yet, it ultimately will be up to more progressive forces within and alongside the charter school movement to make it something else—a reform that serves the needs of the most disadvantaged students in schools that are held accountable for their growth and achievement. Who could ask for more?

NOTE

1. We realize that it is difficult to discuss "neoliberalism" in the U.S. context because of the traditional use of the term "liberal" here to describe supporters of more, and not less, government intervention and activism as opposed to a classical economic definition of "liberal," which describes the views of libertarians or free-market advocates. Thus, the international term "neoliberalism," which stems from

the classical meaning of "liberal" and refers to contemporary free-market reformers, often is misinterpreted in this country to be the equivalent of a "New Democrat." While many so-called New Democrats are neoliberal and subscribe to the ideology that deregulated competition between non-government service providers will cure all social ills, the term better describes more right-wing pundits who argue for extreme shifts toward total deregulation and free-market reform.

REFERENCES

Apple, M. (2001). *Educating the right way.* New York: Routledge.

Arsen, D., Plank, D. N., & Sykes, G. (1999). *School choice policies in Michigan: The rules matter.* East Lansing: Michigan State University Press.

Ascher, C., Jacobwitz, R., & McBride, Y. (1999). *Charter school access: A preliminary analysis of charter school legislation and charter school students.* New York: New York University, Institute for Education and Social Policy.

Bowman, D. H. (2000, December 6). No rest for leaders of charter schools. *Education Week, 20*(14), 1, 14–16.

Bulkley, K. (1999). Charter school authorizers: A new governance mechanism? *Educational Policy, 13*(5), 674–697.

Callaghy, T. M. (1993). Vision and politics in the transformation of the global political economy: Lessons from the second and third worlds. In R. O. Slater, B. M. Schutz, & S. R. Dorr (Eds.), *Global transformation and the third world* (pp. 161–258). Boulder, CO: Lynne Rienner.

California Education Code (1992). § 47600-16, Chapter 781 (pp. 1–7).

CANEC (California Network of Educational Charters). (2001). Legislative Summary. [www.canec.org]

Center for Education Reform. (2001). [http://edreform.com]

Chubb, J. E., & Moe, T. M. (1990). *Politics, markets & America's schools.* Washington, DC: Brookings.

Clune, W. H. (1993). Systemic educational policy: A conceptual framework. In S. H. Fuhrman (Ed.), *Designing coherent education policy: Improving the system* (pp. 125–141). San Francisco: Jossey-Bass.

Cobb, C. D., & Glass, G. V. (1999). Ethnic segregation in Arizona charter schools. *Educational Policy Analysis Archives, 7*(1). [http://epaa.asu.edu]

Cookson, P., Jr. (1994). *School choice: The struggle for the soul of American education.* New Haven, CT: Yale University Press.

Edsall, T. B. (with Edsall, M.). (1991). *Chain reaction: The impact of race, rights, and taxes on American politics.* New York: Norton.

Education Week on the web. (updated March 13, 2002). Hot Topics: Charter Schools. [www.edweek.com]

Finn, C., Manno, B., Bierlein, L., & Vanourek, G. (1997). *Charter schools in action: Final report.* Washington, DC: Hudson Institute.

Fiske, E., & Ladd, H. (2000). *When schools compete: A cautionary tale.* Washington, DC: Brookings.

Frank, T. (2000). *One market under God: Extreme capitalism, market populism, and the end of economic democracy.* New York: Doubleday.

Fraser, N. (1997). *Justice interruptus.* New York: Routledge.

Friedman, M. (1962). *Capitalism and freedom.* Chicago: University of Chicago Press.

Fuller, B. (2000). The public square, big or small? Charter schools in political context. In B. Fuller (Ed.), *Inside charter schools* (pp. 12–65). Cambridge, MA: Harvard University Press.

Gewirtz, S., Ball, S. J., & Bowe, R. (1995). *Markets, choice and equity in education.* Buckingham, UK: Open University Press.

Hassel, B. (1996). *Autonomy and constraint in charter schools.* Cambridge, MA: Taubman Center for State and Local Government.

Henig, J., Holyoke, T., Lacireno-Paquet, N., & Moser, M. (2001). *Growing pains: An evaluation of charter schools in the District of Columbia 1999–2000.* Washington, DC: George Washington University, Center for Washington Area Studies.

Hill, P. T., Lake, R., Celio, M. B., Campbell, C., Herdman, P., & Bulkley, K. (2001). *A study of charter school accountability.* Seattle: University of Washington, Center on Reinventing Public Education.

Horn, J., & Miron, G. (2000). *An evaluation of the Michigan charter school initiative: Performance, accountability and impact.* Kalamazoo: Western Michigan University, Evaluation Center.

Kolderie, T. (1992). Chartering diversity. *Equity and Choice, 9*(1), 28–31.

Lewis, D. A., & Nakagawa, K. (1995). *Race and education in the American metropolis: A study of school decentralization.* Albany: State University of New York Press.

Manno, B. V. (1998). Handout on charter school accountability. Distributed at Hechinger Institute Session on Charter Schools. Teachers College, Columbia University, New York.

Manno, B. V., Finn, C. E., Bierlein, L. A., & Vanourek, G. (2000). Charter school accountability: Problems and prospects. *Educational Policy, 14*(4), 473–531.

Massachusetts State Auditor. (2001, October 22). Independent state auditor's report on the activities of the executive office of education's and the department of education's administration of the charter school program. Boston: Author.

Maynard, R. C. (1970). Black nationalism and community schools. In H. M. Levin (Ed.), *Community control of schools* (pp. 100–111).Washington, DC: Brookings.

McCoy, R. A. (1970). The formation of a community-controlled school district. In H. M. Levin (Ed.), *Community control of schools* (pp. 169–190). Washington, DC: Brookings.

Merriam, S. B. (1998). *Qualitative research and case study applications in education.* San Francisco: Jossey-Bass.

Millot, M. (1996). *Autonomy, accountability, and the values of public education: A comparative assessment of charter school statutes leading to model legislation.* Seattle: University of Washington/RAND.

Miron, G., & Nelson, C. (2000). *Autonomy in exchange for accountability: An ini-*

tial study of Pennsylvania charter schools. Kalamazoo: Western Michigan University, Evaluation Center.

Nathan, J., & Power, J. (1996). Policy-makers' views on the charter school movement. Minneapolis: University of Minnesota, Hubert H. Humphrey Institute of Public Affairs, Center for School Change.

O'Day, J., & Smith, M. (1993). Systemic reform and educational opportunity. In S. H. Fuhrman (Ed.), *Designing coherent education policy* (pp. 250–312). San Francisco: Jossey-Bass.

Olson, L. (2002, January 9). Testing systems in most states not ESEA-ready. *Education Week, 21*(16), pp. 1, 26–27.

Osborne, D. (1999, October 4). Healthy competition: The benefits of charter schools. *The New Republic Online* [www.tnr.com]. pp. 1–8.

Petrovich, J. (forthcoming). Introduction. In J. Petrovich & A. S. Wells (Eds.), *Bringing equity back: Research for a new era in American educational policy.* New York: Teachers College Press.

Public Sector Consultants. (2000). *Issues in Michigan's public school academy initiative phase 2.* Lansing, MI: Author.

Public Sector Consultants, & Maximus, Inc. (1999). *Michigan's charter school initiative: From theory to practice.* Lansing, MI: Author.

Quality Counts. (2002). *Education Week* on the web. *www.edweek.com.*

Reyes, P., & Rorrer, A. (2001). US school reform policy, state accountability systems and the limited English proficient student. *Journal of Educational Policy, 16*(2), 163–178.

Rofes, E. (1998). *How are districts responding to charter laws and charter schools?* Berkeley: Policy Analysis for California Education (PACE).

RPP International. (2000). *The state of charter schools 2000: National study of charter schools, fourth-year report.* Washington, DC: U.S. Department of Education, Office of Educational Research and Improvement.

Schofield, J. W. (1998). Increasing the generalizability of qualitative research. In E. Eisner & A. Peshkin (Eds.), *Qualitative enquiry in education: The continuing debate* (pp. 201–232). New York: Teachers College Press.

Scott, J. (forthcoming). *Charter schools, privitization and the search for educational empowerment.* Unpublished doctoral dissertation, University of California, Los Angeles.

SRI International. (1997). *Evaluation of charter school effectiveness.* Menlo Park, CA: Author.

Teske, P., Schneider, M., Buckley, J., & Clark, S. (2000). *Does charter school competition improve traditional public schools?* (Manhattan Institute Civic Report No. 10). New York: Manhattan Institute.

Texas Center for Educational Research. (2001, September). *Texas open-enrollment charter schools fourth-year evaluation. Executive summary.* Austin, TX: Author with University of Texas, Arlington, School of Urban and Public Affairs; University of North Texas, & University of Houston, Center for the Study of Education Reform; Center for Public Policy.

Thurow, L. C. (1996). The future of capitalism: How today's economic forces shape tomorrow's world. New York: Morrow.

UCLA Charter School Study. (1998). *Beyond the rhetoric of charter school reform: A study of ten California school districts.* Los Angeles: Author. [www.gseis.ucla.edu/docs/charter.pdf]

Wells, A. S., Grutzik, C., Carnochan, S., Slayton, J., & Vasudeva, A. (1999). Underlying policy assumptions of charter school reform: The multiple meanings of a movement. *Teachers College Record, 100*(3), 513–535.

Wells, A. S., Holme, J. J., Lopez, A., & Cooper, C. W. (2000). Charter schools and racial and social class segregation: Yet another sorting machine? In R. Kahlenberg (Ed.), *A notion at risk: Preserving education as an engine for social mobility* (pp. 169–222). New York: Century Foundation Press.

Whitty, G. (1996). Creating quasi-markets in education: A review of recent research on parental choice and school autonomy in three countries. *Review of Research in Education, 22,* 3–47.

Wilgren, J. (2000, October 9). Blacks turn to school vouchers as civil rights issue. *New York Times,* p. A1.

Willard, D. J., & Oplinger, D. (2000, September 13). Whose choice? An introduction. *Teachers College Record* On-line [http://www.tcrecord.org]

Yergin, D., & Stanislaw, J. (1998). *The commanding heights.* New York: Simon & Schuster.

CHAPTER 2

The Politics of Accountability
California School Districts and Charter School Reform

AMY STUART WELLS, ASH VASUDEVA,
JENNIFER JELLISON HOLME, and CAMILLE WILSON COOPER

The political framework discussed in Chapter 1 helps to explain why "account-ability" became one of the most popular educational reform slogans of the past decade. Indeed, under the "systemic reform" banner, individual schools are, in theory, given newfound freedom from rules and red tape in exchange for greater scrutiny of their students' academic outcomes (see Ladd, 1996; O'Day & Smith, 1993). As Wells noted in Chapter 1, this reform marks a paradigm shift in education from an emphasis on input-based accountability, where school resources are regulated by districts and states, to outcome- or performance-based accountability, where schools are less regulated up front but must demonstrate their success in terms of student achievement or "out-comes" (see Elmore, Abelmann, & Fuhrman, 1996; Ladd, 1996).

Policy makers in Washington, DC and state capitals across the country have bought into this seemingly logical and straightforward trade-off of greater school autonomy in exchange for greater accountability regarding student learning. As a result, there has been a proliferation of federal and state policies designed to establish new standards and assessments (performance-account-ability measures) as well as decentralization policies that grant schools free-dom and flexibility in how they use resources (Elmore et al., 1996).

Left out of the equation of more centralized performance measures and more autonomous schools, are the local school districts. Caught between the state's demands in terms of outcomes and schools' demands for more free-

An earlier version of this chapter was published in the *Stanford Law & Policy Review, 11*(2), pp. 325–342.

dom, school district officials are no longer sure of their roles. In fact, some observers question whether school districts will continue to exist in this new era of state-imposed standards and school-level autonomy (Elmore, 1996). Others argue that local school districts simply will evolve into agencies that focus mainly on managerial and financial accountability (Radnor, Ball, & Vincent, 1998).

Nowhere is this conundrum over the future role of school districts more visible than in the case of charter schools—the quintessential autonomy-for-accountability reform. One of the fastest-growing deregulatory policies, charter school reform grants individual schools freedom from state and local regulations in exchange for a written proposal stating goals for student outcomes, among other things (Sugarman & Kuboyama, 2001). But the role that local school district officials should play in charter reform is not clear, despite the fact that in the vast majority of states with charter school laws, local school boards are either the only or one of a few charter-granting agencies.

In fact, according to the report, *The State of Charter Schools* (RPP International, 2000), based on data from 36 states and the District of Columbia, in 14 of these states, including California, charters are granted almost exclusively through local school districts. In another 16 states, school districts are one of two or more charter-granting agencies. In fact, only seven of the 37 charter school laws mandate that charters be granted to schools only through a state entity—either state boards of education or state commissioners or both—bypassing the local school districts completely (RPP International, 2000).

In states where districts grant charters, district officials theoretically find themselves in the awkward position of freeing individual schools from their own bureaucracy, while continuing to argue that that very bureaucracy is legitimate and necessary. It occurred to us that this situation could create an odd political dynamic, especially in instances where charter school founders and supporters espouse an anti-public education ideology grounded in a critique of the bureaucratic and unresponsive public system (see Wells, Grutzik, Carnochan, Slayton, & Vasudeva, 1999).

Using documents and interview data with district officials, including administrators and school board members, as well as the principals or directors of charter schools included in the UCLA Charter School Study, we explore issues of accountability. Because all the charter schools in our study—indeed, all the charter schools in California at the time of the study—were granted through local or county school districts, we were able to examine "accountability" as a dynamic between the charter-granting school districts and the charter schools.

While other research on accountability in education examines to whom and for what school-level educators believe they are accountable (Abelmann & Elmore, 1998), we wanted to explore accountability in charter school reform primarily through the eyes of the officials who are supposed to hold these autonomous schools accountable. We wanted to know whether school district officials saw their role as straightforward and clearly defined under the state law or whether they struggled to understand to whom and for what charter schools are accountable in this age of deregulatory reform. Thus, the point of this chapter is not to arrive at one single and universal "truth" about accountability in charter school reform, but rather to understand how those who are supposed to impose the accountability requirements make meaning of their roles and their authority.

We learned that holding charter schools accountable was as much a political process as it was an administrative matter. Thus, despite any technical or rational policy talk about accountability, the day-to-day experiences of people struggling to define charter school accountability were complicated, contradictory, and deeply enmeshed in their political contexts. *In many instances, the amount of autonomy and the degree of accountability charter schools experienced were no more or less than those of the non-charter public schools.* Virtually all other researchers studying this issue in charter school reform corroborate this finding, making it consistent across states and districts (see especially Massachusetts State Auditor, 2001; Miron & Nelson, 2000; and Willard & Oplinger, 2000). Yet, as we demonstrate in this chapter, the specifics of how and why greater accountability for charter schools is not enacted differ to some degree depending on the local political context. Such research evidence should inform future debates and discussions about the autonomy-for-accountability trade-off in education.

THE POLITICS OF CHARTER SCHOOL ACCOUNTABILITY

In thinking about the political issues related to charter school accountability, we were drawn to the work of political sociologists, many of whom write about the political aspects of policy implementation. For instance, we considered Raab's (1994) argument that policy is powerfully shaped by practice and is thereby deflected from its legislated intentions. Raab notes that in studying how practice recreates a policy, "human agency" must be taken seriously, but so, too, must "the context of action," which provides the constraints and opportunities for action.

In other words, both the agency of the actors involved, as well as the local, state, and national context of charter school policy, profoundly shape what accountability looks like. Indeed, our findings demonstrate that the policy talk about accountability in exchange for greater autonomy is what Simola (1998) would call "wishful rationalism"—or the rather naive way in which educational reform discourse frames the goals and levers of the policy apparatus without consideration of the cultural and historical contexts of reform. He writes, "It is only through underestimating the institutional, historical, and cultural frames of schooling that the goal-rationalism could be seen as the omnipotent basis for educational reform" (p. 741).

In our study, we learned that as charter school reform interacted with different school districts and their local constituencies, different understandings of what was possible in terms of holding charter schools accountable emerged. Both Hargreaves (1985) and Mehan (1992) argue that educational policy has to be negotiated and implemented through interaction. These interactions and the resulting interpretations are related to Simola's "institutional, historical, and cultural frames of schooling"—that is, how these different actors make meaning of what it is that charter schools and districts are supposed to do. In fact, many times, what ultimately happened in each school district we studied in terms of charter school accountability was highly sensitive to the local political context. In this way, a school board's ability to hold a charter school accountable for anything was circumscribed in part by the political popularity of the charter school and the political vulnerability of the district.

For instance, in several of the 10 districts we studied, charter school founders and operators, as well as their larger network of supporters, brought to their interactions with the school districts a strong anti-public school ideology. In fact, many of these charter school advocates were engaged in this reform specifically because of their disdain for what they saw as an overly regulated and bureaucratic public educational system. This critique and antagonism, which were particularly strong in the large urban school districts, often shaped the interactions between charter schools and their districts. Yet in other districts—generally, the more suburban and rural districts—the relationships between the charter schools and district officials were much more amicable (see Wells & Slayton, 1997; Wells, Slayton, & Scott, forthcoming).

Despite these context-specific issues, we also found some common themes across the 10 districts. For instance, in all the districts, officials talked about the ambiguity of the legislation and the tension it created as they reconsidered their roles in light of charter school reform. In particular, issues of liability plagued these officials as they worried about something happening at the charter school that could bankrupt or financially jeopardize the entire district. Thus, while some of these officials attempted to define a new role for their districts and new relationships between the districts and the charter schools, most of the officials we spoke to were trying simply to keep the charter schools under district control, particularly when it came to issues of fiscal accountability. The goal of academic or student-outcome accountability—one of the central purposes of the autonomy-for-accountability trade-off—did not, therefore, materialize.

At the same time, district officials said they felt trapped between charter school founders who demanded more autonomy from district bureaucracy, and state and federal regulations that dictate the way in which districts and their non-charter schools must function. This chapter provides a window into understanding the interactions, meanings, and contexts that shape charter school reform and create a much messier and more uneven form of accountability than the "wishful rationalism" of policy talk would lead us to believe.

THE POLITICS OF ACCOUNTABILITY IN CONTEXT

The basic guidelines outlined in the California charter school legislation and discussed in Chapter 1 of this book make one thing clear: Many of the specifics of the relationships between charter schools and their charter-granting districts are not addressed in the statute. While the California charter school legislation has created a state-level policy framework for school-level reform, it is ultimately up to the charter-granting agencies—school districts in most cases—to make this reform happen.

In the context of these decentralized struggles to implement charter school reform, one of the most striking themes to emerge from our data is how complicated and unpredictable "accountability" is when the rational and technical policy talk meets the real-life experiences of people working in schools and districts. These experiences are mediated by a local political context in which power, control, and authority are differently ascribed to various actors—such as school board members, superintendents, or charter school leaders—depending on the historical relationships between the public educational system and its constituents, especially the most powerful constituents within the local community.

This section focuses on ways in which this local context matters regarding who has political leverage to hold whom accountable in charter school reform. We learned, for instance, that as charter school reform interacted with different school districts and their local constituents, different understandings of what was possible in terms of holding charter schools accountable emerged. Oftentimes, charter school founders and operators were steeped in a powerful critique of the public educational system and their animosity toward that "system" framed much of the negotiation between the charter schools and the districts over issues such as funding, facilities, student-outcome measures, and so forth.

As one official in the urban Mission Unified School District noted, "There's this real sense that they [charter schools] don't belong to a district, and quite frankly, I've been told they're encouraged along these lines, by outside folks that are either community people or they've got their own network that they meet with, and they're encouraged to push the envelope."

Depending on the extent to which the anti-public school ideology resonated with large segments of the school districts' constituencies, district officials would be more or less threatened by that ideology. Generally, it was the large urban school districts that faced the harshest criticisms from their constituencies for being too bureaucratic and too ineffectual (see Wells & Slayton, 1997). Thus, it was within these more politically vulnerable districts that the anti-public school ideology struck the loudest chord and made the political act of holding charter schools accountable very difficult and delicate.

For instance, the very large and urban Madrona Unified School District had been politically under siege for decades and was, at the time of our interviews, facing loud opposition from several different communities within the district boundaries. A former school board member described the rhetoric associated with charter school reform: "So, 'School districts get out of the way, let them be free, let them go, don't meddle, you don't get it, you're not hip to this reform, let them do whatever the heck they want.'"

In this same district, several of the charter school leaders, in opposition to the district, had garnered a great deal of political support for their schools. One school in particular had received a lot of favorable news coverage, and one district official noted that the principal used her connections to the media to get what she wanted from the district. Another Madrona district official said that how the district handled this particular school was "very political."

Relating the popularity of a school to issues of accountability, some noted that it would be more detrimental politically for a district to revoke the charter of a popular school than it would be for the board of education to allow a charter school to continue despite the lack of strong evidence that student achievement—as measured by standardized tests—was improving. For instance, a Madrona administrator who acted as a liaison between the charter schools and the board of education questioned whether or not the board would ever have the "political wherewithal" to revoke a charter if after 5 years one of the charter schools was not "moving in the right direction" in terms of student achievement. Meanwhile, several charters were renewed in Madrona for a second 5-year period even though the schools had not shown consistent test score improvements.

Similarly, another urban school district, Edgewood, was under fire from various constituents in its racially diverse, but highly segregated and divided, community. An Edgewood official noted that it would be very difficult for the school board to deny a charter even to a group proposing to create a school based on an unsound educational philosophy. He said that given the current state of public education in this poor city, the school board did not have much leverage.

> If the people who elect them don't get what they want, they can make corrections. [If] the staff member don't go along with what parents want, they may complain to governing board members. It's a tough

one there. . . . Perhaps the resistance to some experimental effort is properly not fairly strong because what we fall back on is what we're doing, [which] by most measures is not doing very well.

Still, politics is an issue not only in the large urban districts. Indeed, school board members in one of the smaller rural districts in our study, Pastoral Unified, were the target of intense political pressure aimed at getting them to reinstate the charter of a school that was financially and legally out of line. The board had revoked the charter when issues about the misuse of funds arose. But parents of students in the school, charter school advocates, and conservative state policy makers launched an onslaught of political pressure that led the board to reinstate the charter. One former board member explained how her fellow board members were "taken in" by all the lobbying and attention from the conservative state policy makers and charter school advocates.

I don't know . . . unless they felt flattery was enough to do it. And I know that they got standing ovations when they went to the graduations. And they got lots and lots of praise for their support of the . . . [charter] school. So I suspect, being the human beings that they are, this was something that they . . . [this was] real heavy stuff.

She told us that powerful state officials sent the board members letters asking them to reinstate the charter and that her colleagues on the board loved showing off these letters to friends and co-workers. "So I think it was that kind of thing. I don't—I don't know. It just was over my head. I could not understand how they could be taken in."

The reinstatement of the charter did include a new agreement requiring charter school students to take the same test as other students in the district. But, two years later, the curriculum director of the charter school informed us that the parents of two-thirds of the students in the school had requested and been granted waivers exempting their children from the exam, resulting in limited data on student achievement.

In this rural district and in the Madrona Unified example cited above, political pressures—either from the local school community or from the broader network of charter school supporters—sometimes overrode board members' concerns about the lack of evidence of higher student achievement at a charter school.

Yet in another urban district, Vista, whose board had more local political support from its constituents than did Madrona's, board members voted not to renew the charter of a conversion school that had failed to show substantial achievement gains. In reality, the Vista board's decision was also more about politics than academic accountability, because a group of powerful parents from the charter school wanted the school returned to district control and lobbied the board to not renew the charter. Still, the fact that the Vista school board voted to not renew the charter of a school that was doing no better or worse in terms of standardized achievement gains than other charter schools in the Vista district or than Madrona's renewed charter schools illustrates the importance of the political context of accountability in charter school reform. It appears that some school boards have more authority to hold charter schools strictly accountable than do others, in part because of political pressure from powerful constituents and advocates.

We also found that school districts were subject to a multitude of additional political pressures affecting the degree to which officials felt empowered to regulate charter schools. These pressures variously arose from other school districts, from the business community, from civil rights groups, and from demographic factors.

For example, several districts we visited, including Liberty Elementary School District and Pastoral Unified School District, felt pressure from neighboring school districts to regulate their charter schools, which enrolled a large number of students from these adjoining districts. This experience raised all sorts of regulatory questions for district officials in terms of whether or how they should intervene in the charter schools' recruitment and enrollment processes and to what degree they had the power to do so.

In other districts, such as the suburban Shoreline, district officials felt tremendous pressure from the business community to keep the charter "up to snuff" because much of the district's support from nearby corporations rested on the performance of all the district's schools, including the charter.

Still other districts, such as Madrona, felt pressure from civil rights groups to monitor equity in the charter schools. These groups applied political pressure to ensure that the charter schools did not become segregated relative to the rest of the district. In this district, however, competing pressures emerged from many White parents who had taken their children out of private schools to enroll them in charter schools and who sought to downplay desegregation requirements.

Finally, as the superintendent of Madrona Unified noted, urban districts in particular are bombarded with pressures relating to the types of students they serve, pressures that often shape how and to what extent districts are able to regulate their charter schools. He observed: "This system is deluged with problems of housing, problems of finance, problems with student achievement, problems of Ebonics, you name it. . . . So it becomes a question of where you can put your energy."

These findings on the political context of accountability demonstrate some of the ways in which the rational discourse of charter school accountability is mediated by the political context of the schools and districts we studied. These contexts have a very real and powerful impact on district officials who are struggling to implement a reform that they argue has been inherently ambiguous from the beginning.

LEGISLATIVE AMBIGUITY AND LEGAL LIABILITY

In addition to the political context of accountability and its impact on school district officials, virtually every official we interviewed said he or she found the California charter school legislation ambiguous. This was especially problematic when it came to the issue of liability because it meant that the districts assumed liability by default. The ambiguity coupled with the liability issues led many district officials to focus more heavily on fiscal as opposed to academic aspects of accountability. This focus on fiscal accountability occurred in part because that is the role school districts have played historically and in part because they were concerned about charter schools having a negative financial impact on the district.

In this section, we draw on data from our interviews with school district officials as they attempt to make meaning of the California charter school law and struggle with what they perceive to be many unanswered questions.

Ambiguity of the Law

Across the school districts in our study, we heard a common refrain criticizing California's charter school legislation for being ambiguous. Contributing to the legislative ambiguity is the fact that the term *accountability*—which figures prominently in discussions of charter schools—is used sparsely in the legislation. As Wells mentioned in Chapter 1, the law holds charter schools "accountable for meeting measurable pupil outcomes" and provides a method for schools to change from "rule-based to performance-based accountability systems." While this sounds good on paper, the crux of the problem, according to the district officials, is that the legislation does not explain what role the schools districts—as the main charter-granting agencies—play in all of this accountability.

The former school board president of the Madrona Unified School District argued that there are too many accountability and fiscal issues that the state has not defined and that have inherent ambiguities about who is responsible for what in charter school reform. A Vista Unified School District board member captured the essence of district dissatisfaction: "I'm thoroughly convinced that charter school legislation is a good example of how a legislature [can] take a good idea and run amok with it when legislators don't really have a clue as to how [a] school district functions."

The mismatch between the charter legislation and the ways in which school districts function relates directly to issues of accountability. While the legislation seeks to grant charter schools autonomy from districts, it falls short of spelling out the terms of accountability and liability that accompany this freedom. As a result, chartering districts are left to navigate this massive gray area. According to an assistant superintendent of the Mission Unified School District, "California's legislation is so ambiguous . . . districts in the state are really . . . floundering around. . . . And our district is no different."

Then there was the rural district we discussed before, Pastoral Unified, where the board of education revoked the charter of a school that had grown quickly and was not forthcoming with the district regarding how it recruited students or used public funds. Although the charter was revoked, it was re-instated due to the political pressure we described above. Part of the reason why the political campaign to reinstate the charter was so successful, school board members and district officials explained, was that the California charter school legislation did not give the district much leverage in trying to hold the school accountable. According to a board member, "Legally, the way the bill was written, you can do just about anything you want. . . . There are no checks . . . and balances at all. So they weren't illegal from that point of view. But from . . . being able to work with them, it was impossible."

A Madrona Unified board member summed up one of the central issues regarding the legislation this way:

> The frustration is that the [authors of the] charter school legislation didn't think through clearly what the role of local districts and govern-ing boards would be. On the one hand, there is the promise of total autonomy and freedom. You get to divorce yourself from the stupid school district and do your own thing. On the other hand, school districts remain legally responsible and accountable for what happens in the charter schools, particularly financially.

The ambiguous legislation also reflects competing beliefs about charter schools and thus different political philosophies about what types of relation-ships charter schools and their charter-granting agencies should have (see Wells et al., 1999). For example, when the large and urban Mission Unified School District assembled an advisory board to consider issues of charter school over-sight, the board quickly developed into two camps. According to an assistant superintendent, one group's advice was to "give them time, give them space . . . let them make some mistakes. . . . You're not going to know if it works if you [go] over there with a ruler and slap them." The opposing camp was more skeptical, however, suggesting that the district "watch them like hawks, [be-cause] you don't know what they are about to do." And while it was up to the district to determine the parameters for charter school oversight, the state, according to this district official, was "absolutely unhelpful in trying to work through any of that."

Not only was the Mission Unified's advisory board split on these issues, but the school board was equally divided. According to a district administrator, the five Mission Unified board members were also "all over the map" on the issue of charter school oversight. One board member, he said, wanted to nurture the charter schools, and another board member argued that charter schools need to figure things out by themselves. He concluded that "you can have almost any position on this topic and be fine, because there's nothing to tell you, you should or you shouldn't."

Also clear from our interviews, however, is that the legislation's ambiguity would not be quite so troubling to most of these officials if it weren't for their fear that if something went wrong with a charter school, the districts, as the charter-granting agencies, would be held responsible.

Liability Matters: Guarding Deep Pockets

In fact, legal liability—and its financial implications—was one of the most salient issues for the district officials in our study. Most of these officials assumed, lacking any legislative indication to the contrary, that their districts were legally liable if anything happened to the charter schools—for example, if a charter school went bankrupt or if a lawsuit was filed against the school. This assumption of liability profoundly influenced how these officials considered charter school autonomy from the district.

A Madrona Unified school board member noted:

> Unless you're physically going to lift the school up and move it out of our jurisdiction, we, I assume, will continue to have liability. If the facility was formerly part of the school district, if it's burnt to the ground, who will be responsible for rebuilding it? If there's an earthquake, who will be responsible for fixing it? What is the status of employees? If they take a leave from the school district and the charter goes under, they want their rights back, they want their seniority back, they want their retirement benefits back, they want all of that back.

These concerns about liability were echoed across all 10 school districts, but especially in the larger districts where the pockets of public resources are deepest. For instance, the Madrona superintendent stated that no matter how distant charter schools try to be from their districts, lawsuits against the schools invariably will move toward deep pockets.

I always worry with those charter schools, the first time some kid gets his head banged in, and there's a major injury, when he sues, what happens. Well, let me tell you, I don't care what they've said over at [the charter school], they're a part of Madrona Unified. [The plaintiffs] are suing big, deep pockets over here. So, we cannot simply say they're not part of us.

Thus, according to the district officials, on the one hand, they are expected to respect the autonomy that the California law grants to charter schools. On the other hand, they considered themselves legally responsible if charter schools participated in unethical or irresponsible behavior. Such understandings of the law only fueled the sometimes antagonistic relationships between the districts and the charter schools. For instance, in the Vista Unified School District, school board members' worries about liability contributed to their reluctance to grant charters earlier in the reform. Officials said that this concern continued to influence board members when evaluating individual charter proposals.

Moreover, our data indicate that publicly elected school board members, in particular, felt their constituents also held them responsible for charter school operations. Their broader public, they argued, would be angry if the school district had to "bail out" a charter school. According to the superintendent of the High Country Unified School District:

Ultimately, after everything is said and done . . . I read the legislation [as saying] that my school board ultimately is going to be held responsible and accountable for something which could really go terribly wrong and certainly would be held accountable in the eyes of the public if something were to go terribly wrong. This is because you are the ones who chartered it. It would be nice to have that removed.

In fact, many of the officials we interviewed stated that they would like the state to play a more central role in terms of the legal responsibility for charter schools—if not actually granting the charters then at least helping to develop the guidelines to do it. A Madrona Unified board member, for instance, argued that if charter schools are to be completely divorced from their school districts, then the state or some other entity should grant the charters, and the school districts should be held "one hundred percent harmless from anything that happens whatsoever."

Clearly, the district officials we interviewed—especially those in the large and beleaguered urban school districts—were frustrated by a reform that they described as asking them to take a gamble and loosen their reins on individual schools while at the same time be prepared to pay for any mistakes made by these more autonomous schools.

CONTROL AND FISCAL ACCOUNTABILITY

In many of the districts we studied, these liability concerns contributed to a situation in which district officials tried to maintain as much control over the charter schools as possible, at least in terms of the resources they received and their use of district funding. In part because of these liability issues and in part because of uncertainty regarding just how to hold schools accountable for academic outcomes, school district officials also tended to be more focused on holding charter schools fiscally, rather than academically, accountable. Thus, in many cases, neither aspect of the autonomy-for-academic-accountability bargain was being met because charter schools were not enjoying the kind of freedom from regulation that other schools endure nor were they being held to a higher standard in terms of student achievement.

Accountability and the Changing Role of the District

Although many district officials said they supported the concept of autonomy for charter schools, they also emphasized that their districts retained ultimate control over these schools. District officials argued that while charter schools were free to educate students as they pleased, they nonetheless had to maintain the confidence of their local school board to continue operating. For instance, the general counsel for the Edgewood Unified School District—a very poor urban district—candidly addressed the issue of charter school autonomy versus district control, announcing: "My role is to make sure that everyone knows that the board is still in control." He elaborated:

> While charter schools may, by statute, have some degree of release from [district] rules . . . the board of education still has an overseeing role to make sure that the terms of the charters are complied with. Now, while [charter] schools may get the ability to experiment and try new things, I think the control the school boards continue to have [over] the charter is similar to the control the school boards have for non-charter schools.

In fact, the controller of Edgewood unified noted that while charter schools can be either "independent" or "dependent" in their relationships with districts—depending mainly on the degree of fiscal autonomy they have—the

Edgewood board of education had decided that all of the charter schools in the district would be dependent. This meant that they remained more closely tied to the district in terms of their financial operation. More "dependent" charter schools generally remain a part of their districts in terms of payroll, insurance, and so forth (UCLA Charter School Study, 1998). Although we learned that this was not always the case in Edgewood, the controller said that it was. He also said that the school board members had decided that they would like to have the district management oversee all the charter schools. "I don't think they will approve anything that would be independent or away from the Edgewood Unified School. So, so far all the charter schools [are] under the umbrella of the school district."

The board president of Mission Unified School District also staunchly supported the idea that the district had ultimate authority over charter schools "The Board is the final authority on whether they stay in place [or] whether they're canceled. As long as they're public schools . . . the Board has final say."

District officials' assertions of control do not necessarily reflect a simple unwillingness to share power with charter schools. Rather, their views are refracted through a chartering system that links charter schools to their districts through a variety of processes, leaving district officials feeling not just legally, but also professionally, responsible. The Sunnyside Unified superintendent emphasized this link—and the shared responsibility that accompanies it. For instance, when a new principal was being selected for the charter school in her district, the superintendent determined that the selection would be made jointly by the school and district. She stated:

> The principal works for Sunnyside School District. It is not a private practice. . . . You cannot give away responsibility for which there is no accountability. So I cannot turn that over to the [charter school's] leadership team to choose the [principal] because they are not ultimately accountable for that person's success. I am.

In the Vista Unified School District, officials recognized that charter schools' unique relationships to their districts complicated the accountability process. The Vista superintendent suggested that, contrary to the spirit and rhetoric surrounding charter school reform, it was easier to hold traditional schools accountable for their actions than charter schools. "The non-charters are ours. There is no question about the accountability. They can go through a typical military or industrial reporting [system]." But for charter schools, he said, "the negotiations will obviously be different."

Despite efforts to control charter schools, there was some recognition on the part of district officials of the need for changing relationships between the charter schools and their districts. Many of the officials we interviewed said they struggled with these changing roles. Individual board members or district administrators were torn and conflicted about how they should treat charter schools. In some districts, these issues were more divisive, with different people on different sides—some bent on maintaining traditional, controlling practices and others ready to redefine their roles. In Vista Unified, for instance, one top-ranking official in the district administration noted that at least one of the school board members was not at all supportive of charter schools because she thought that too many district resources, especially administrators' time, were going to charter schools. But other board members were fairly supportive. As the main point person in the central office for charter schools, this administrator found herself in a delicate situation—in the middle of a divided school board and in the middle between that school board and the charter schools. She noted, "I basically walk a fine line. . . . the direction that I give a charter school is not . . . necessarily telling them what to do and how to do it, but providing just professional opinions, you know, and I say that to them, 'It's my opinion. . . .'"

The board president of Mission Unified School District talked about the tension between wanting to give the schools freedom and trying to fix things. She related this experience to parenting: "The hardest thing for our district has been once we get through with them, to keep hands off. To give help when it's needed but do it in a supportive way, instead of a restricted way."

An assistant superintendent in the Mission district noted that it was difficult for her to not get as involved in the charter schools as she does in the non-charter schools. She said, "I have trouble keeping my hand out of things." Still, she said: "If you ask some of the leadership of the charter what role they would like for me to play . . . when I asked them that question, they said, 'We don't want you to have anything to do with it.' So my role is not really very clearly defined."

Fiscal Accountability Is Easier Than Academic Accountability

Despite this need for control on the part of some district officials, the reality was that to the extent districts were able to hold charter schools accountable for anything at all, it was for how they were spending public funds—or fiscal accountability—as opposed to student outcomes—or academic accountability. In the final report of the UCLA Charter School Study (1998), we describe four major reasons why this happened.

First of all, California did not have a consistent state assessment system in place for the first 5 years after the charter school legislation went into effect. Thus, during this period (1992–1997) school districts chose which tests they administered and whether they required charter schools to give the same test. According to one state report, about 14% of charter schools did not administer any test during this time (SRI International, 1997).

Second, the concept of autonomy-for-accountability reflected an extremely simplified understanding of the multiple reasons why people engage in charter school reform to begin with and the extent to which they wish to be held accountable to one, state-defined set of student-performance measures. In other words, we learned that most charter school founders had their own visions of what schools should teach and what students should learn—for example, an ethnocentric curriculum or a project-based learning strategy—and the educational impact of those visions was not measurable by a single standardized test (UCLA Charter School Study, 1998).

A third and related reason why the accountability piece of charter school reform did not play out in reality as the theory would imply was that many of the defining purposes of charter schools we studied were non-academic in nature, such as discipline and safety. Thus, most of these desired "outcomes" did not lend themselves to traditional forms of accountability, especially student testing.

And finally, charter schools had multiple constituencies, including parents and supporters, to whom they felt they were accountable; generally, school district officials were not the most important constituents from the perspective of educators at the charter schools in our study.

As a result, in only one district in our study did a local school board revoke or fail to renew the charter of a school that was perceived to be not living up to the academic goals set forth in its proposal. Yet as we noted above, even in this instance, the non-renewal was not solely about the specified goals of the school's charter proposal or subsequent performance, but rather also about the politics surrounding the school—namely, that many of the most vocal parents no longer wanted the school to be a charter.

More typically, district administrators and school board members said they lacked adequate information to assess whether charter schools' academic or student-outcome goals were being met. We noted, for instance, in our final report that many of the charter school proposals were very vague when it came to descriptions of their academic goals (UCLA Charter School Study, 1998). In fact, several school board members stated their frustration over lacking any evaluation tools for the charter schools. According to one: "We still have not done a good evaluation of these schools to know whether they're more effective than they were before they were charters. I don't think, frankly, that they are. I mean that's my personal and gut feeling. But 5 years from now we'll probably know, and we'll probably say, 'Well, they're not doing any worse.'"

A member of the rural Pastoral Unified School District's board of education, which revoked and then reinstated the charter of the home schooling/independent study school mentioned earlier, explained:

I had some questions here about the program itself because it was so loose in the beginning that, we were asking about, "How do we know that students are achieving?" And they gave some standardized tests but it was strictly [voluntary]. So how valid is it? You know, the students who took it did really well but . . . why would you bring your kid in if you hadn't been teaching them?

Thus, we learned that district officials generally dealt with academic accountability for charter schools in much the same way they dealt with academic accountability for their other, non-charter public schools—with few sanctions and little direct involvement. For instance, an administrator in the Mission Unified School District noted that the academic accountability issue was a district-wide issue, not one that was unique to charter schools. He said, "There's no bottom line in this district at all. We don't have any real bottom line accountability academically."

In several districts, charter schools—particularly those that had been converted from existing public schools—seemed to be on the same page as the non-charter schools in terms of adopting district-level standards or participating in district–wide reform efforts. This meant that the district–charter school relationships around such issues as standards, curriculum, and student achievement were essentially the same as for non-charter schools. In the suburban Shoreline Elementary School District, for instance, one school board member discussed the connection between the charter school's academic program and that of the rest of the school district. She said that the charter school was "just the next step in being a quality district." Academic accountability was not a serious issue, she noted, because "we didn't have any sense that this was going to be something removed from us." Similarly, an assistant superintendent of Vista Unified stated that she saw charter schools in a very similar manner to the district's reforming schools.

Still, in other districts, where the charter school–district relationship was more strained, there was less direct district involvement in or communication about the academic accountability of the charter schools. For instance, in the Edgewood Unified School District, where, as we noted earlier, district officials tried to maintain a great deal of control over the charter schools in terms of legal and contractual issues, it appeared as though these officials were paying much less attention to the academic aspects of the charter schools. In fact, there was some confusion within the district about exactly what the charter schools were responsible for in terms of academics. For instance, when asked whether the charter schools used the same academic standards as the other public schools in the district, Edgewood's superintendent replied, "No. They determine their own standards."

Yet, the director of one of Edgewood's charter schools was under a different impression. She said that written into her school's charter was an agreement that the school would follow the district's grade-level standards. Furthermore, she said she also agreed to partially participate in the district's portfolio process, used to hold principals at all of the schools accountable. Although there were sections of the portfolio process that the charter school director decided to opt out of, she still intended to complete a portfolio and to submit it to the district as part of the school's "defense" for the renewal of its charter.

Uncertainty among district administrators about for what and to whom the charter schools were accountable in terms of academic outcomes was not uncommon in the 10 districts we studied. For instance, a board member in the Madrona Unified School District stammered a bit as he reflected on exactly what information the board had about the academic progress of students in the charter schools.

> They do the same testing regimen that we do, I think. They do additional . . . I thought we've had an annual report from them, I think. And I think even the two autonomous [independent] ones [charter schools] report everything. I mean, I think we know everything about them like we know about the other schools. I'm not sure.

Questions and concerns about the academic accountability piece of charter school reform were common. For instance, the special education director of the Mission Unified School District noted that he had "some real concerns because I don't know what the checks and balances are, I don't know what— when they say they're successful, what does that mean? We have no way of monitoring the integrity of the assessment system used for kids in the charter school."

In the suburban and relatively affluent Sunnyside Unified School District, the director of curriculum and instruction struggled with the question of academic accountability. She said that she did not know what the charter school's obligation was and that she was not certain what the charter school was required to do in terms of academic accountability.

> I don't know if it is hands off one hundred percent or if it is hands off except for standards. . . . My guess is that there will be some requirements even for charter schools to demonstrate that there is a certain level of proficiency, but at this point, I really don't know that. You know it changes frequently because it is such a political battle at this point. But the charter schools, I think, really were initiated to demonstrate new ways to achieve excellence and it seems to me that you can't

say, "Well, everyone else has standards but the charter schools don't have to have any standards."

District officials said they became even more confused about academic accountability the further the charter schools strayed from more traditional curricula, programs, and boundaries. Alluding to charter schools operating over the Internet, a Pastoral Unified board member noted, "You could have someone from San Diego [enrolled at another district across the state] . . . working on the computer. There are no boundaries."

Focusing on the Bottom Line and Accountability to a Broader Public

Due to the ambiguity of the academic accountability side of the equation and concern over liability issues, the control issues for districts were fiscal and contractual—as they are for most public schools. The Sunnyside Unified administrator quoted above noted that while the academic piece of charter school accountability was unclear, she was certain that the charter school in her district did have to meet some of the same fiscal responsibilities as the rest of the schools in the state. Similarly, the board president of Mission Unified said that the school board would mainly "step in" to interfere with charter school operations if there was a real misuse of funds. "Not just a different use of funds but a misuse of public money. Then you step in, and you don't worry about it."

These views represented a consensus of sorts in the districts we studied—namely, that despite all the unanswered questions about the academic accountability of charter schools, the issue of fiscal accountability was clear. Thus, related to all the legal, contractual, and liability issues mentioned above, when district officials maintained that they were ultimately responsible for charter schools, they typically meant that they were responsible for making sure that public money was not misspent. Rather than get bogged down in the minutiae of the lengthy California Education Code, one Pastoral Unified Board member argued that boards focus more on fiscal matters.

In this way, holding charter schools accountable for keeping their fiscal house in order rather than focusing on academic outcomes was in sync with many of the traditional norms and practices of school district central offices. As we mentioned, several interviewees noted that districts had never been very good at holding schools accountable for academic outcomes; whereas exercising fiscal authority—through the allocation of resources—had always been central to what school districts did.

The district officials' sense of the importance of this traditional role was heightened when it came to charter schools. Because district officials operated under the assumption that they would be held responsible for any debt their charter schools accrued, they were eager to establish clear financial controls over these schools. More than anything, they feared charter school bankruptcy. According to Edgewood's controller, "If they ever go bankrupt, because they report to us, we are responsible." To try to stave off such a scenario, Edgewood asked its charter schools to provide detailed reports on their income and expenditures. The controller even requested bank statements from the charter schools, to verify that district funds were faithfully deposited into the schools' accounts. According to the controller, "I require them to send bank statements [because] at least I would know that that money gets deposited in the bank. It's just all internal control."

The fear that charter schools would go bankrupt was most troubling to these district leaders because of what it could cost their districts and thus the burden it would place on all the schools and students for which they were responsible. Thus, these officials emphasized that their desire to be accountable to the larger public greatly influenced how they monitored and evaluated charter schools.

For example, a former school board president of the large, urban Madrona Unified School District commented that while many of the accountability and fiscal issues remained ill defined by the state law, his district would continue to press for a high level of fiscal accountability from the charter schools. He noted that one of Madrona's first charter schools had gone bankrupt, leaving the district with a huge debt (hundreds of thousands of dollars) to pay. He was committed to preventing that from happening again. He said the true tension surrounding charter school reform is "not between standards and autonomy, but between accountability for public dollars and autonomy."

STATE AND FEDERAL FACTORS/FORCES

In addition to the ambiguity they saw in the legislation and the impact that had on how they defined their working relationships with charter schools, district officials also expressed feelings of being caught politically (and logistically) between two powerful sets of competing demands: From "above," district officials said they were beholden to state and federal regulations requiring districts to monitor all of their schools. From "below," they faced pressure from charter schools wanting to be released from most regulations and oversight. District administrators, therefore, stated that they struggled not only to define their roles in relation to their charter schools, but also to ensure that the districts themselves remained fiscally and legally accountable to the external forces that monitored them—that is, the state department of education, federal government, courts, and teachers unions.

Accountability to State and Federal Rules and Regulations

The district officials we interviewed in the charter school study spoke of numerous state and federal regulations that are often vague, change frequently, and are sometimes in conflict with one another. These officials expressed feeling the heavy burden of regulatory responsibility while, at the same time, having little professional autonomy. As a board member in Pastoral Unified School District stated, school board members are often frustrated too by the plethora of state guidelines and regulations. These regulations lead board members to believe that they do not really have control over very many things—for charter or non-charter schools.

Some of the most restrictive regulations governing school districts, according to district officials, stem from state and federal categorical programs, such as Title 1 and bilingual education, and other highly regulated programs such as special education. While they recognized that programs funds for these constitute a significant portion of school districts' budgets, particularly those of urban and poor districts, and are thus an important source of district income, these programs come with what district officials consider to be some of the most stringent regulatory strings attached. These officials argued that they must ensure that all schools adhere to these regulations so that both the schools and the school districts themselves are in compliance. As Sunnyside Unified's Title I administrator noted, "I have to keep them [the schools] out of jail and me out of jail."

Charter schools had, in many districts, created deep fissures in this rigid regulatory structure: Both district officials and charter school personnel expressed that they were unclear about whether, or to what extent, charters must comply with the same regulations that apply to other, non-charter schools. As Mission Unified's special education director said of the special education regulations and charters:

> It's very difficult to deal with that kind of unknown with the charter, as opposed to . . . you know, things may be implemented differently in our [more than 100] schools, but at least you know there's a parameter procedure out there that people will work within, so you know how to deal with it. With charters it's kind of, you know, an unknown. They haven't been around long enough to know how to deal with that.

We also found that district personnel varied widely in the degree to which they tried to accommodate the charter schools' needs. In some districts, like Sunnyside Unified, officials worked hard to assist the charter school in aligning its goals with state and federal regulatory requirements. Other districts, we discovered, were less proactive in assisting their charters with regulatory compliance; many of these district officials handled the problems that arose with their charters on a case-by-case basis, often calling the state department of education as necessary to help them resolve various issues.

Several district officials we interviewed said they observed that charter operators themselves were confused about the extent to which they must comply with state and federal regulations—and that while some charter directors turned to district personnel to resolve questions about program compliance, others did not. According to one district administrator, some charter school operators picked and chose from various regulations. Thus, not only were districts charged with determining charter schools' regulatory responsibility, but they also had to communicate this responsibility to their charter schools— while at the same time monitoring whether these maverick schools were, indeed, complying with these guidelines. This was a burdensome task, according to the district administrators who were often in charge of monitoring the regulatory compliance of tens or hundreds of other, non-charter schools.

Accountability to Court Orders and Enrollment Policies

Five of the 10 districts we studied were operating under court-ordered desegregation or desegregation consent degrees. Officials in these districts generally agreed that charter schools should comply with desegregation programs, but most were unclear about who within the district was responsible for monitoring such compliance. Indeed, when we asked district officials who was responsible for ensuring that charter schools remained within desegregation guidelines, we received varied responses. Some district officials said this responsibility rested with the school board as the charter-granting agency, others placed responsibility with the school district's attorney, and still others said that responsibility was in the hands of those who worked in the district's desegregation office.

Indeed, as was noted in Chapter 1, the California charter school legislation requires schools to include in their charter proposals the means by which the school "will achieve a racial and ethnic balance among its pupils that is reflective of the general population residing within the territorial jurisdiction of the school district to which the charter petition is submitted." We found, however, that this requirement of the law was not being enforced by the school districts and that many of the charter school proposals did not even address these issues (see Lopez, 1997).

Furthermore, there was huge variation across the districts as to whether the charter schools were required to comply with desegregation programs and court orders. We found that this compliance depended, in part, on the type of desegregation program in place in the district and on the political context of the school and the district. For instance, compliance with such policies often required charter school students to have access to transportation. In only one of the districts we studied did the district provide free transportation for students (UCLA Charter School Study, 1998). Thus, the fact that the state law does not provide transportation funds for charter schools makes it very difficult for many of the districts to hold these schools accountable to school desegregation programs.

In one of the districts with voluntary desegregation programs, Madrona Unified, the assistant superintendent in charge of integration said that he felt pressure to ensure compliance with desegregation mandates because failure to do so would result in a loss of valuable desegregation funding from the state. He said, "The program is such that we receive funding on this basis, as we've described it to the court, we've described it to the controller's office, and it has to be maintained in that way."

Again, the charter school legislation in California appears to leave district administrators with few guidelines as to whether, and how, charters fit into desegregation plans. Meanwhile, district officials said they were under heavy pressure to ensure that all district schools remained in compliance.

CONCLUSION

Faced with a state mandate to grant charters to schools but little direction from the legislation on how to hold these schools accountable for academic outcomes, the officials in the districts we studied ultimately felt caught between the proverbial rock and a hard place. On the one hand, these officials faced tremendous pressure from state and federal government regulations, local constituents, desegregation court orders, and other external forces. On the other hand, they faced pressures from charter school educators and their advocates who demanded freedom from many of the regulations with which districts are legally bound to comply. It is hardly surprising, then, that many of these officials said they thought districts should be released from their responsibility for charter schools altogether.

The main implication of our findings is that the policy talk of deregulatory reforms that makes the autonomy-for-accountability trade-off seem so workable is, indeed, "wishful rationalism" (Simola, 1998). It appears that "freeing" schools one by one while leaving the larger public school apparatus in place results in tension, ambiguity, and even resistance among school district officials who see themselves as caught between the autonomous schools and the regulations of the public system. Within different district contexts the struggle looks different, but many of the underlying concerns—especially legal and financial liability—remain the same. State and federal policy makers need to reconsider the serious legal implications of "freeing" charter schools from all regulations and allowing them to function with an outcome-based accountability model, while the entities that grant and renew the charters remain governed by the regulations inherent in the traditional input-oriented accountability system. This is not necessarily an argument against laws that name local school districts as charter-granting agencies; rather it is a call for more thoughtful public debate and discussion on the various ways in which charter schools interact with and influence the existing public education system, especially their local school districts.

REFERENCES

Abelmann, C. H., & Elmore, R. F., with Evan, J., Kenyon, S., & Marshall, J. (1998, April). *When accountability knocks, will anyone answer?* Paper presented at the annual meeting of the American Educational Research Association, San Diego, CA.

Elmore, R. F. (1996). *Accountability in local school districts: Learning to do the right things.* Paper presented at the Edwin O'Leary Symposium on Financial Management, University of Illinois at Urbana–Champaign.

Elmore, R. F., Abelmann, C. H., & Fuhrman, S. (1996). The new accountability in state education reform: From process to performance. In H. F. Ladd (Ed.), *Holding schools accountable: Performance-based reform in education* (pp. 65–98). Washington, DC: Brookings.

Hargreaves, A. (1985). The micro–macro problem in the sociology of education. In R. Burgess (Ed.), *Issues in educational research: Qualitative methods* (pp. 21–47). London: Falmer Press.

Ladd, H. (1996). Introduction. In H. F. Ladd (Ed.), *Holding schools accountable: Performance-based reform in education* (pp. 1–22). Washington, DC: Brookings.

Lopez, A. (1997, April). *California charter schools.* Paper presented at the annual meeting of the American Educational Research Association, Chicago.

Massachusetts State Auditor. (2001, October 22). *Independent state auditor's report on the activities of the executive office of education's and the department of education's administration of the charter school program.* Boston, MA: Author.

Mehan, H. (1992). Understanding inequality in schools: The contribution of interpretive studies. *Sociology of Education, 65,* 1–20.

Miron, G., & Nelson, C. (2000). *Autonomy in exchange for accountability: An initial study of Pennsylvania charter schools.* Kalamazoo: The Evaluation Center, Western Michigan University.

O'Day, J., & Smith, M. (1993). Systemic reform and educational opportunity. In S. H. Fuhrman (Ed.), *Designing coherent education policy* (pp. 250–312). San Francisco: Jossey-Bass.

Raab, C. D. (1994). Where we are now: Reflections on the sociology of education policy. In D. Halpin & B. Troyna (Eds.), *Researching education policy: Ethical and methodological issues* (pp. 17–30). London: Falmer Press.

Radnor, H. A., Ball, S. J., & Vincent, C. (1998). Local educational governance, accountability, and democracy in the United Kingdom. *Educational Policy, 12* (1), 124–137.

RPP International. (2000). *The state of charter schools 2000: National study of charter schools, fourth-year report.* Washington, DC: U.S. Department of Education, Office of Educational Research and Improvement.

Simola, H. (1998). Firmly bolted into the air: Wishful rationalism as a discursive basis for educational reforms. *Teachers College Record, 99*(4), 731–757.

SRI International. (1997). *Evaluation of charter school effectiveness.* Menlo Park, CA: Author.

Sugarman, S. D., & Kuboyama, E. M. (2001, Summer). Approving charter schools: The gate-keeper function. *Administrative Law Review, 53*(3), 869–942.

UCLA Charter School Study. (1998). *Beyond the rhetoric of charter school reform: A study of ten California school districts.* Los Angeles: Author. [www.gseis.ucla.edu/docs/charter.pdf]

Wells, A. S., Grutzik, C., Carnochan, S., Slayton, J., & Vasudeva, A. (1999). Underlying policy assumptions of charter school reform: The multiple meanings of a movement. *Teachers College Record, 100*(3), 513–535.

Wells, A. S., & Slayton, J. (1997, April). *The role of school districts in charter school reform: Questioning the underlying assumptions of neoliberal ideology.* Paper presented at the annual meeting of the American Educational Research Association, Chicago.

Wells, A. S., Slayton, J., & Scott, S. (forthcoming). Defining democracy in the neoliberal age: Charter school reform and educational consumption. *American Educational Research Journal.*

Willard, D. J., & Oplinger, D. (2000, September 13). Whose choice? An introduction. *Teachers College Record Online* ID Number 10496. [http://www.tcrecord.org]

CHAPTER 3

Reinventing Government
What Urban School Districts Can Learn from Charter Schools

SIBYLL CARNOCHAN

Throughout the history of this nation's experiment with democracy, reformers have debated the value of more or less government, the best administrative structures for government agencies, and the appropriate scope and focus of government involvement in local matters (Arrow, 1963; Bailyn, 1960). In education, this debate has tended to revolve around the issue of centralization and decentralization of educational governance (Elmore, 1993; Tyack, 1993).

Charter school reform enters this debate over government's role in managing schools with a promise to strike a new balance between centralization and decentralization. Charter schools are public schools, in that they receive public funds and must report to a public authority, but they also have autonomy from district and state regulations and thus are free to set local goals and strategies. Charter reform fits within the larger movement to "reinvent government" (Osborne & Gaebler, 1993), granting local school communities considerable autonomy in decision making while maintaining public authority over the end-results—or outcomes—of their actions. In Chapter 2, this is described as the shift from input-based accountability to outcome- or performance-based accountability where more deregulated schools must demonstrate their success in terms of student achievement.

Still, despite the greater autonomy that charter schools enjoy, public authority over these schools, as noted in Chapter 1, is still vested primarily with the local school districts that grant most of the charters in California. Thus, charter schools, freed from many regulations, must negotiate new relationships with their districts. For instance, they may wish to adopt certain district programs or policies and reject others. Their districts, as the charter-granting agencies and the public entities responsible for holding charter schools accountable, may try to influence the degree to which charter schools can operate outside the regular public school system. As a result, charter school reform promises to change not only local schools but also the relationship between schools and their host districts.

Building on the themes presented in Chapter 2 about the ambiguity of accountability in charter school reform, this chapter argues that charter schools and their complicated new relationships with their school districts offer district administrators a new opportunity to evaluate their current governance structures. Indeed, the data presented in this chapter suggest that if school district officials would take charter school reform seriously and investigate why charter schools either embrace or reject their host districts, they could gain valuable insight into how their district policies and practices affect individual schools. Such an analysis is especially timely in an era of state-imposed standards and assessment, when districts are seemingly caught in the middle between these state accountability mandates and school-level demands for more autonomy from district control. In other words, this chapter helps district officials understand which aspects of the autonomy-for-accountability trade-off are most valuable to charter schools. In what areas or domains of their operations do charter schools want the most autonomy, and are these domains in which districts could grant schools a bit more flexibility?

To begin answering these questions, I draw upon data from three charter schools in the Mission Unified School District. Thus, this chapter enters into the larger decentralization debate by eliciting from one district's experience with charter reform, lessons that may be relevant to other districts. In doing this, it is important for me to note that a school "district" is not necessarily a unified entity since different people employed by a district can and do hold different positions and opinions. Therefore, I use the term "district" to refer to the agreed-upon policies of a school board as well as the perspectives expressed by district "officials" or those employed as district staff.

In this chapter, I first present a framework for understanding the relationships between charter schools and school districts. I also explain my selection of Mission Unified School District and the three charter schools within that district as my area of focus. Next, I present the most important findings from this district's experience with three charter schools, using qualitative data to look at when and why charter schools cast away or embrace the district. Finally, I reflect on the implications of these lessons for districts seeking to reshape their relationships with schools, for charter school policy generally, and for researchers studying decentralizing reforms. In all, this chapter seeks to push the policy debate over government's role in local affairs beyond the current stalemate that casts urban school districts solely as change-resistant bureaucracies and toward a conversation about new, more productive relationships between school districts and schools.

FRAMEWORK FOR ANALYZING CHARTER
SCHOOL–DISTRICT RELATIONSHIPS

As I mentioned above, this country has long debated the appropriate role of government in public schooling, and much of this debate has focused on whether control of schools should be centralized or decentralized. The historical argument suggests that in the early decades of the 1900s, administrative progressives succeeded in placing more control over what had been a very decentralized, locally controlled public educational system in the hands of centralized school district administrators (Callahan, 1962; Tyack, 1974). By the 1960s, the federal government began to play a much more influential role in education through legislation such as the 1964 Civil Rights Act and the Elementary and Secondary Education Act of 1965 and court rulings on desegregation and bilingual education. Thus, control over public education was centralized to an even greater degree (Tyack, 1974). And in the 1980s, we saw state governments playing a larger role than ever before in education (Mazzoni, 1995). But in recent years, political parties and theories that support divesting control from school districts—as well as the state and federal governments—and placing it in the hands of local educators, communities, or parents, have gained popularity and appeal (Chubb & Moe, 1990; Finn, Bierlein, & Manno, 1996; Nathan, 1994).

Some historians and researchers, however, have questioned the notion that *either* centralization or decentralization represents the "one best system" (Tyack, 1974). In Richard F. Elmore's (1993) words:

> If the historical debate tells us anything, it is that the central policy question should not be whether to centralize or decentralize authority, but rather what should be loosely controlled from any given level of government and what should be tightly controlled. In the practical world of political and administrative decisions, no absolute values attach to centralization or decentralization; there are only relative values, gained from balancing the interests of constituencies at various levels of aggregation around the central task—teaching and learning. (p. 51)

Elmore suggests, therefore, that research must frame decentralization not as "good or bad" but rather as a question of how decentralization works, in what circumstances, and why. Understanding decentralizing reforms, Elmore's analysis suggests, requires that the very concept of decentralization be disaggregated and not discussed as one single set of experiences for all schools and all children.

While Elmore seems to be speaking to the importance of disaggregating decentralization according to its source—whether it is a result of federal to state or state to district decentralization—this chapter looks at decentralization from districts to schools. For this reason, it calls for yet another layer of analysis, another set of tools for understanding how decentralization plays out in schools and school districts. Research on school-based management—one strand in the continuum of decentralizing reforms—presents us with an appropriate analytic tool. In a comprehensive review of literature on school-based management (SBM), Murphy and Beck (1995) discuss the fact that SBM affects different school-site "domains," that is, the "areas or functions that schools control" (p. 47). The authors conclude that SBM reforms tend to affect five school-site domains—goals, budgets, personnel, curriculum, and organizational structure. Thus, they argue that any analysis of decentralization should attend to the varying effects it has on these different domains. This chapter considers charter schools' experiences in terms of four of the five domains laid out by Murphy and Beck: school-site organizational structure (which the data in this chapter suggest is primarily an issue of governance structures), personnel, budgets, and curriculum. In the process of discussing these four domains, this chapter also illustrates the fifth domain articulated by Murphy and Beck, namely, the schools' goals.

There is yet another element, I would argue, to a framework that adequately conceptualizes the relationship between government and schools. If the merging of Elmore's and Murphy and Beck's analyses of decentralization suggests that it is critical to understand decentralization in terms of *what* is decentralized from *which* level of government, Joel F. Handler's (1996) work emphasizes the importance of considering *who benefits* from changes in the control of schools. Handler describes the issue this way:

> Deregulation and privatization is often justified as representing the removal of burdensome and oppressive state control, but for subordinate groups, it might only mean re-regulation under another master. However, this conclusion is not foreordained. Decentralization involves shifts in power relations. Is there now more space for subordinated individuals and groups? (p. 6)

In other words, Handler notes that decentralization can have varying effects as a function of local power relations. While it may bring greater authority to families and communities traditionally excluded from educational decision making, it also could subject such groups and communities to subordination to other community power structures or factions. What is critical in any attempt to understand decentralization, Handler suggests, is empirical investigation of who gains authority over what issues in particular contexts. Only through such analysis can we begin to understand the complexity of the relationship between decentralizing reforms and power relations.

Taken together, Elmore's, Murphy and Beck's, and Handler's perspectives suggest the need for a conceptual framework that acknowledges that decentralization is a complex reform strategy with different effects on different levels of government, different domains, and different constituents. This chapter uses such a framework, considering how charter schools and district officials in Mission Unified School District experience decentralization across different school-site domains, noting *when* and *why* charter schools reject district control or seek district assistance, and recognizing *who* seeks or rejects district control or assistance. First, I will explain why the Mission Unified School District is a good site for my analysis.

SELECTION OF THE DISTRICT AND CHARTER SCHOOLS

This chapter draws largely from qualitative, case study data collected for the UCLA Charter School Study described in Chapter 1 of this book. Following the methodologies of the UCLA study, the data for this chapter were collected from Mission Unified School District, one of the five large urban school districts in the study, and three of Mission Unified's charter schools. According to the process of "purposive sampling" (Merriam, 1988), I chose to focus on Mission Unified because it, for the following reasons, provides a unique opportunity to understand the relationship between school districts and schools. First, the urban Mission Unified is one of the state's largest school districts. Since much of the criticism of bureaucracy and government focuses on large and urban districts, it seemed critical to use data from just such a district.

Second, Mission Unified was in the middle of a continuum of varied school district responses to charter school reform (see UCLA Charter School Study, 1998). On one end of the continuum, some districts obstructed schools' attempts to convert to charter status or groups' attempts to develop new charter schools. On the other end of the continuum, some school districts not only supported charter schools but also helped to start them. Mission Unified had approved 10 charter schools by 1998, which was the per-district limit at that time. In this way, Mission Unified seemed to take a supportive position toward charter school reform. At the same time, some charter supporters criticized Mission Unified for exercising too much control over its charter schools. Thus, Mission Unified provided an opportunity to study a district positioned in the middle—neither wholly embracing nor entirely rejecting charter school reform.

Third and finally, Mission Unified began approving charters immediately after enactment of the state charter law in 1993. Thus, some charter schools in the district had been operating for several years at the time this study's data were collected. Therefore, the charter schools and the district had considerable experience in defining their relationship.

Given that Mission Unified provided a good setting in which to explore issues of decentralization, I focused on three charter schools within this district in examining the district–charter school relationships there. These three schools—Franklin Charter Academy, Foundation Elementary Charter School, and Jefferson Charter School[1]—were purposively selected to provide insight across a few categories. First, Franklin and Jefferson are "conversion" charter schools, meaning public schools that "converted" to charter status. Foundation is a "start-up" school in the sense that it was a new school started as a charter school. Start-up schools tend to be more autonomous from their school districts, while conversion schools—having a history with their districts—tend to maintain tighter ties to district procedures and policies (SRI International, 1997). Furthermore, as I explain in more detail later, both Jefferson and Foundation were supported by non-profit organizations that—to varying degrees—negotiated with Mission Unified officials on behalf of these schools. In the case of Jefferson, a long-standing advocacy organization partnered with the school when it became a charter school. I refer to this organization as Jefferson's "partnering organization." Foundation, on the other hand, was created by a non-profit educational management organization (EMO), which I refer to as the "EMO sponsoring organization." In this way, these schools provide insight into the range of school experiences and relationships with district rules and regulations.

Second, the three schools had been engaged in charter reform for varying lengths of time and with varying results. Franklin Charter Academy, a fairly large middle school serving 1,200 students in grades 7–9, received approval for its charter in the fall of 1995. Foundation, a K–3 elementary school with only 160 students enrolled, gained its charter and opened in the fall of 1997. Meanwhile, Jefferson, also an elementary school and serving several hundred students in grades K–5, actually had its charter revoked in 1996 about one year after it had been approved. Thus, the three charter schools provide slightly different time frames for their experiences with charter school reform. These longitudinal differences proved to be important in terms of each school's relationship with its district.

Third, in terms of their locations within the school district and their enrollments, both Franklin and Foundation are located in poor sections of the district, while Jefferson is located in a lower-middle-income neighborhood. Still, all three schools serve predominantly students of color—mostly Latino and/or African American students. Thus, as public attention increasingly focuses on the low achievement of poor students and students of color, the study of these three schools offers empirical evidence concerning the relationship between school districts and schools serving these students.

CHARTER REFORM IN MISSION UNIFIED SCHOOL DISTRICT

In part because of the distinctions among the schools, each of the three charter schools (or once-charter schools) discussed here had different experiences in the school-site domains affected by decentralization—namely, governance, personnel, budgets, curriculum, and goals. And yet, despite the varied experiences of these three charter schools, we learned that each school struggled to define or redefine its relationship with the school district in ways that were most supportive of its mission. In this way, the story of these three schools speaks to broader issues about what to decentralize and when.

School-Site Governance Structures: "Exchanging Dictators"

Under the California charter school legislation, each of the charter schools in this district operated under a somewhat new, more localized governance structure. Yet, as Table 3.1 demonstrates, the freedom to create new governance structures led to the creation of different governing bodies—usually called "governing boards" or "governance councils"—at the different charter schools. Thus, who had voice and input into the policies and procedures of the school varied across these sites. And while all three schools had parent representatives on their governing boards, one of them—Foundation—had no educators from the school who were voting members of the board. This lack of educator representation on the board resulted from the way in which this particular school was founded. Indeed, employees of the non-profit EMO that sponsored the school actually wrote the charter and designed the school. The educators were hired after the fact to implement the vision of these founders. The lack of educator voice in the governing process, therefore, was part of the school's original design.

Jefferson and Franklin, on the other hand, were conversion charter schools, which meant that at least some of the educators at each of these schools had supported and worked on the charter application and had ensured that educators were represented on the governing boards.

Despite these different governing board configurations, data from all three of these schools suggest that while charter school founders and operators value greater governing autonomy in theory, in practice this autonomy frequently is limited by local power struggles. For example, at both Jefferson and Franklin considerable school-site conflicts emerged as a result of new governance struc-

Table 3.1. Governing Board Members

Jefferson	Franklin	Foundation
Conversion charter school—no longer a charter school	Conversion charter school	Start-up charter school
• Representatives from the partnering organization • Teachers • Administrators • Parents	• Teachers • Administrators • Classified staff • Parents	• Representatives from the EMO sponsoring organization • A community member • Director of the religious institution where school is located • Parents

While Franklin and Foundation were both part of the larger UCLA Charter School Study, Jefferson was dropped from the UCLA sample of schools because its charter was revoked and, therefore, it was no longer a charter school.

tures. At Jefferson, this new governance structure involved the school's partnership with the local non-profit organization. In other words, when Jefferson converted from a regular public school into a charter school, members of its partnering organization suddenly had input into the policies of the school. According to the educators we interviewed, the partnering organization's agenda began to conflict with the school's agenda. The educators said they thought the partners were taking advantage of the school for their own political purposes. For instance, Jefferson educators accused members of the organization of using the school's fund-raising activities as a way to pay for some of the organization's staff by writing these staff members into grant proposals whether they could contribute to a particular program or not.

Furthermore, accusations of false promises and impropriety in the handling of the school's funds by the partnering organization, and mistrust between the staff of the school and that of the partnering organization turned into an unworkable situation. Finally, the educators at Jefferson pleaded with the school district to revoke their charter. One Jefferson teacher reported: "I often felt that it was like going from one dictatorship to another." By this she

meant that the school went from the district's "dictatorship" to the "dictatorship" of its partnering organization. As Jefferson's principal explained it:

> We thought [charter school status] was going to be a wonderful thing,
> and it could have been a wonderful thing, by the way, and still could
> be a wonderful thing. OK, we just got with the wrong partner, and
> I'm sure you've heard this from everybody. . . . It's like a bad marriage,
> you know, "marriage is a good institution," you know, if you have a
> lousy partner get out and live on and find somebody else.

Thus, while educators at Jefferson had believed that charter reform could
provide valuable autonomy over school-level decision making, the relationship between the charter school and its partnering organization granted the
educators little more autonomy—and considerably more conflict—than they
had experienced under the school district's watch. Interestingly enough, these
educators turned to their former "dictator"—the school district—to attain
autonomy from what they saw as a more oppressive governing relationship.

At Franklin, where there was no partnering organization, staff also reported
high levels of conflict. As a result of the school's engagement with charter reform, factions developed among staff, with some teachers supporting the charter idea and others opposing it. Because the creation of Franklin's new charter
school governance structure coincided with a highly divisive teachers' strike in
the district, the pro- and anti-strike factions of the faculty took opposing sides
on almost every decision the school's governing body attempted to make. Said
Franklin's principal, "So we are a charter and supposedly we have more flexibility but yet we are not able to do it." School-level conflicts, he reported, thwarted
the school's ability to use the autonomy provided by charter reform.

Parents of students enrolled in Franklin also expressed frustration with
the school's new governing structure, arguing that they had not gained greater
voice in the decision-making process as a result of the school's conversion to
a charter school. Commenting on the conversion of Franklin to charter status, a Spanish-speaking parent explained that she had been a volunteer at
Franklin for more than 2 years. She said she did not see the conversion to charter
status as beneficial for the parents because their views were not being taken
into account in the running of the school. She said:

> I mean the [charter school] program itself has not harmed us because
> it was to give us advantages to make our own decisions, but it has
> harmed us because of the people running it. They may think that
> because the school is autonomous then we can do what we wish,
> without even taking us [the parents] into account. In that way we have
> been harmed a lot.

This mother reported that she and other parents had considered inviting a district representative to parent meetings, in an attempt to get the school's governing board to hear their input. She expressed her belief that school-site autonomy exacerbated conflicts between certain school staff and Spanish-speaking parents like herself.

At the EMO-created Foundation Elementary Charter School, which was almost 2 years behind the other two schools in implementing charter school reform, few such dramatic conflicts emerged. Still, there were indications of potential tensions between the teachers and the new governing board, which, as I noted, had no teacher representatives. For example, teachers expressed frustration with a decision made by the governing board without staff consent. Basically, the board had purchased a set of instructional materials over the summer when few of the teachers were present. According to the teachers, they had agreed only that the materials would be used for the early grades but the board opted to purchase the materials for all grades in the school. Moreover, some teachers said they were uncertain about "who runs" the charter school and expressed frustration that they were not represented on the board. One Foundation teacher noted that she had valuable expertise in budgeting, legal requirements of schools, and the flexibility afforded schools through charter status, but that the board did not draw upon her knowledge. Teachers said that they approached the board to ask if they could have a representative on the board, but they were told it would be a conflict of interest. Thus, while few outright conflicts had emerged at Foundation at the time of data collection, when the school had only been in operation for about a year, the data indicate the potential for conflicts to emerge around teachers' authority within the school.

The experiences of these three charter schools point to the tensions that can arise in situations where schools gain autonomy over their governing structures. This is not to say that tensions may not have existed in these schools before they became charter schools, but the adoption of new, more decentralized governance structures under charter school reform seems to have brought power struggles to the forefront in two of these three schools. In the third school, such struggles appeared to be hiding just beneath the surface. In other words, the data suggest that schools that break away from their host districts and establish local governing boards may still be faced with conflict over decision making, conflict that threatens the schools' ability to make use of their governing autonomy. In fact, Jefferson's administrators and teachers ultimately asked that the school's charter be revoked, believing a return to district control preferable to battling with an external partner. These findings suggest that decentralizing school reforms such as charter school reform do not necessarily lessen tensions and conflict within the educational system; rather, they just allow for new tensions to emerge in different places and among different actors.

I return to these data on governance issues when I consider the implications of these schools' experiences for school districts. First, I discuss the data on schools' experiences with the other domains, starting with personnel issues.

Personnel

Autonomy over hiring was the most frequently cited advantage of charter status for the educators and operators of these three Mission Unified charter schools. This was also the case for many of the other schools in the UCLA Charter School Study (1998) and other charter school research as well. Yet, at the same time, these schools teach us that such autonomy also can lead to some potentially problematic issues for employees.

First of all, it is important to note that the three Mission Unified charter schools used hiring autonomy to varying degrees and for varying purposes. For example, two of the schools tended to use their autonomy to hire non-teaching staff, such as guidance counselors, school secretaries and office managers, grounds keepers, and parent coordinators. In these instances, freedom to hire staff seemed in part to be an issue of cost. Franklin's principal told us:

> For example, . . . this school has several charter employees who don't have to meet any kind of criteria for the district or from unions in terms of classified staff. I will give an example. I have a ground supervisor [who] works 8 hours, and he is here as a security person. And I would have to pay probably twice as much to get someone like that if I [were] following the rules of the district.

Thus, autonomy over personnel allowed this charter school to hire non-unionized, less costly employees for non-teaching positions. This was also true in many other charter schools in our larger study.

Furthermore, before the 1998 amendments to the California law, charter schools were free to hire uncertified or less expensive teachers. But interestingly enough, none of these charters used hiring autonomy for this purpose. Franklin, in fact, wrote into its charter that it would maintain district and union hiring procedures and levels of compensation for classroom teachers. Jefferson's staff, likewise, used its charter status to hire new teachers but did so with a commitment to protect whatever rights and compensation teachers had won through their bargaining unit. As one of Jefferson's teachers explained:

> [In the district you're] bogged down with all this bureaucracy and red tape which keeps you from moving, and so I loved things that with charter you can do. For instance, staffing. . . . It makes it much more

possible for you to get people to work in your schools [who] really want to be there and people [who] you want to be in there because you know that they have what the students need. . . . [With the district] you are more bogged down with the union. . . . And this is by no means to say that we didn't want teachers' rights honored because . . . I do believe that teachers have rights. . . . They have rights and I was never one for violating their rights but sometimes . . . the restrictions that are put upon you by a union are not necessarily anything to do with student learning, and that is the bottom line.

Thus, the educators in these two charter schools valued flexibility to hire personnel without abiding by district regulations and union seniority rules, but they continued to hire certified teachers and abide by the union's collective bargaining agreement for compensation and working environments for teachers. In fact, the UCLA Charter School Study (1998) found that in many charter schools in California educators saw hiring certified teachers as a real plus in selling their program to parents.

On the other hand, at the start-up Foundation Elementary Charter School, where governing board members conducted much of the interviewing and hiring, only one out of the seven teachers the school initially hired was certified. Still, despite the school's decision to hire non-certified teachers, Foundation did opt to pay its teachers according to the district's pay scale.

Meanwhile, although charter school officials said they saw the greater freedom to hire as critical to their ability to build strong schools, staff at two of the three schools reported problematic power issues around the hiring/firing processes in charter schools. For example, at Franklin, some teachers reported that they signed the charter petition, despite their own reservations, only due to fear that the principal would fire them after the school became a charter if they did not sign. One teacher explained: "[The teachers] were afraid that our previous administrator was going to get rid of those people who did not philosophically believe like he did, and they wanted to make sure that all of the safeguards that are in our contract are here." Ultimately the teachers in this school succeeded in incorporating their bargaining rights into the school's charter. Nonetheless, their experience suggests that autonomy over school-site hiring can have a chilling effect on teachers who fear being fired for reasons that may not pertain to performance, which is why unions and bargaining agreements exist in the first place.

A somewhat different issue emerged at Foundation. At this school, the teachers thought—but were not sure—that they were covered by the district's collective bargaining agreement. Members of the school's governing board, on the other hand, told us that, definitively, the teachers were *not* covered by the agreement, but rather were under contract solely with the charter school's governing board. The fact that Foundation's teachers thought they were members of the union when in fact they were not suggests that there is—at the very least—the potential for misunderstandings resulting from the hiring autonomy schools enjoy via charter school reform.

Thus, while charter school officials in these three schools said they valued hiring autonomy, such autonomy also generated problematic power relations for teachers and staff within charter schools. I consider the implications of these findings for school districts in a later section, first turning to the data on school-site budgeting.

School Budgetary Discretion

The charter school officials interviewed at Franklin, Foundation, and Jefferson all expressed a desire for greater budgetary control as one of their main reasons for engaging in this reform. When asked why she pushed for her school to convert to charter status, one Franklin teacher said: "Money. Being able to spend money without having to go through all of the loops and twists and all that kind of thing."

One of the most frequently mentioned reasons charter officials wanted greater discretion over their budgets was to allow them to purchase needed supplies and materials more quickly and efficiently. The need for more autonomy in this area seemed especially important to these charter school operators because relative to other areas of the district they were all serving poor neighborhoods and poor students—communities that often receive the least from their districts in terms of services. As a Franklin administrator explained:

> What happens in schools like an inner-city barrio school like this one, you know, you have heard or you may have observed that sometimes as far as the look of the school, some folks may feel that it is ignored. . . . Well, the [district's first charter school] secured its own landscape company and so that was a major departure. And so what happened was that the district had to give us our allocation for landscaping, and we contracted [with] a private landscape company that keeps these grounds in tremendous shape, and they work for us.

In other words, Franklin's administrators felt "ignored" by the district's facilities and maintenance department and sought charter reform as a means to address their own facilities issues.

Foundation, which also served low- to middle-income students of color, was housed, at the time of our visits, in a newly renovated site on the grounds of a religious institution. Both the religious institution and the charter school's

EMO sponsor contributed hundreds of thousands of dollars to renovate the school's facility. At Jefferson, officials cited promises of new facilities, such as a roving health van and other services, as some of their reasons for partnering with a local non-profit organization and pushing for charter status.

In fact, all three of these charter schools used budgetary discretion to clean up their grounds, to renovate classrooms, to build playing fields, or to undertake other facilities and maintenance projects that they thought would make their schools a better environment for students, families, and school neighbors. In other words, educators and officials in these schools sought budgetary autonomy to buy services they thought the district did not adequately provide. In this way, the budgetary discretion that charter school reform offered these schools appeared to be one of the most important aspects of going charter. Although, as I explain next, the freedom to choose curriculum was also important to the educators in these charter schools.

Choosing the Curriculum

In fact, some of the most salient autonomy issues for the educators and operators of these three charter schools were those related to school-site curriculum. This section addresses four practices related to such curricular autonomy, including autonomy over instructional materials and strategies, professional development, school calendar, and discipline policies.

Instructional Materials and Strategies. According to educators in these three charter schools, autonomy over instructional materials and strategies was one of the central reasons they engaged in charter school reform. In none of these schools, though, did educators throw out all of the district-chosen materials and strategies. Rather, they seemed to pick and choose, in some instances retaining district materials and programs, in other instances replacing them, and in many cases supplementing them with additional materials.

For example, Jefferson stuck with district's math and science program but implemented a new reading program with a heavy phonics component. Foundation supplemented the district's curriculum with materials from E. D. Hirsch's Core Knowledge program. Franklin, a school that served predominantly Spanish-speaking students, maintained much of the district's programs but sought to bolster its bilingual program.

What is most interesting about these charter schools' experiences with instructional autonomy, however, is that each established and sometimes maintained relationships with entities other than the central district to develop its instructional program. Foundation and Jefferson each had partnering or sponsoring organizations to which they turned for instructional assistance. Franklin worked on its curricular issues with a district official and a subgroup or cluster of schools within the district connected via student feeder patterns. As Franklin's principal explained:

> Because of the students that we share in this area, we . . . represent all racial ethnic backgrounds but there is a significant number of Hispanic, Spanish-speaking students. We started meeting together and being united as cluster principals about 2 years ago under the direction and leadership of our assistant superintendent. So we have a bond and we have a cluster vision and a covenant . . . [by which] we have chosen to lead our lives by and it is very close-knit. . . . We are not separate from them.

The data suggest, then, that while these schools embraced autonomy over instructional materials and strategies, each school also built new relationships to sustain and develop its instructional programs.

Professional Development. Regarding professional development, the charter school educators reported that they still participated in some of the district's professional-development workshops and that they found some of these workshops quite helpful. But they also noted that district-provided, professional-development programs were helpful only when they dovetailed with the particular needs of the charter schools' staff at the time. Reflecting on the district's staff-development programs and how they affected his school before it became a charter, a Jefferson school official said:

> Well, sometimes there are some decisions from the top down that may not be as helpful in what we want to do. For example, they might have a decision on staff development. . . . Here at Jefferson we may be on the page where our staff development needs to be reading or we have got a new math adoption, and we want to really get to that. So we would have had to [use] our staff-development day [as] dictated by the district rather than what we really needed.

In other words, the district's schedule for professional development did not always meet school needs and, for that reason, actually drained the school of time better spent elsewhere. As charter schools, these three schools were able to pick and choose when they would participate and when they would devise their own staff-development programs.

Thus, while these three charter schools wanted to benefit from some of the workshops and programs that the district ran, they wanted to do it in ways that met their particular needs. Describing his continued but altered relationship with district professional-development programs, Franklin's principal explained: "When . . . our district wants to do a training, for example, of a new math adoption, well, we choose to do it within our cluster and we choose to do it in a particular way where it is coordinated with our school sites [in the cluster]." Thus, charter schools in this district saw a need for continued professional development and support but they also wanted to re-form district services to better align with school-level needs. This finding implies that charter schools with full budgetary autonomy might well choose to buy some of the professional-development services of the district. But in buying those services, they would select the district products that best filled their needs.

Calendars. The discussion of professional development points to another curriculum-related issue raised by charter reform. All three of the charter schools studied in Mission Unified sought to vary their school calendars, making them distinct from the regular district calendar.

At Jefferson and Franklin, the weekly calendars were changed to allow time for weekly staff meetings and training seminars. Moreover, Jefferson had implemented a year-round calendar, hoping to improve student achievement by reducing the length of school breaks, in a district that no longer used year-round calendars. And during our study Franklin was in the midst of discussing a new school calendar that would have been better aligned with the vacation and travel schedules of its many immigrant students. Likewise, Foundation set a longer school day and was considering adopting a longer school year as well, with the goal of increasing students' time spent in instruction and accommodating working parents' schedules. All three of these schools, then, opted out of the district's more traditional school calendar—to different extents and for different reasons. While this is not unique to charter schools, the respondents at these three schools said that they could make such changes more easily as charter schools.

Discipline. There is a fourth issue related to a school's curriculum over which charter schools in this district sought greater autonomy, namely, student discipline. I have placed the issue of discipline within the domain of curriculum because in all three of these schools most staff and parents expressed their belief that students placed in undisciplined classrooms were distracted from any focus on learning. For many parents, this was a main reason for choosing charter schools.

In all three of the charter schools, discipline was addressed in part through the adoption of school uniform policies designed to lessen any disruption or competition associated with the way in which students dressed. In addition, Jefferson hired a new guidance counselor—a man, who was respected in the neighborhood made calls to students' homes. The Jefferson staff also renovated a room to serve as a kind of "time out" room where teachers could send disruptive students to talk to the counselor, do homework, and stay out of the way of students who were still engaged in the day's lesson. Foundation, in contrast, saw its small size as critical to maintaining discipline. In addition, the staff had adopted a "three-strikes" policy, by which students would be expelled from the school after three serious offenses.

Thus, all three schools used charter reform and independence from district rules to institute policies—whether uniforms, guidance counselors, or strong sanctions—to address issues of student discipline.

LESSONS FOR SCHOOL DISTRICTS

Having laid out the data on governance, budgets, personnel, and curriculum, I now outline the lessons school districts might take from the charter school experience in Mission Unified. While clearly the data from this school district are in many ways specific to the particular district-to-school relationships, local history, and specific policies within Mission Unified, it is also true that Mission's experience with charter reform raises a host of issues that confront other urban school districts.

Managing Self-Governing Schools

For districts seeking to learn from charter school reform, the data from these schools' experiences with decentralized governance structures present a complicated picture. On the one hand, these charter schools valued the idea of having autonomy over governance structures. On the other hand, the data suggest that these decentralized schools experienced high levels of conflict under new governance structures, with staff and communities often battling over who would steer the schools. While such battles may occur regularly in the everyday life of schools, charter reform seems to have brought these battles to the forefront of school staff's experiences, perhaps because the autonomy gained through charter reform raises the stakes of decisions made at the school level.

The data suggest, then, that districts and schools engaged in decentralizing reforms would benefit from the establishment of systems to assist schools with conflict mediation. In fact, this has become, to some degree, the role of the particular school district discussed in this chapter. One district official explained: "Our charter schools have this tendency to have problems, particularly internal people problems, and . . . probably . . . the most taxing and time-consuming part of all of our charters has been around the people issue— governance." Working to find new administrators when serious school-site conflicts emerge, providing human relations training, and functioning as a grievance board when schools wanted to "give back" their charter, Mission Unified officials spent considerable time managing the school-site conflicts that emerged in charter schools.

This situation presents a conundrum to districts. At the same time as districts grant charter schools autonomy over governance structures, they are also accountable to ensure that these school are educating students. Thus, district officials sometimes need to step in—especially when invited—to make sure that educators are not caught in the midst of conflicts that inhibit their ability to serve students. The Mission Unified experience suggests that districts—whether through their own offices or through providing some external resource—also must assist charter schools in managing such governance conflicts as they emerge.

Balancing Hiring Flexibility with Protections for Employee Rights

Again, charter school operators in Mission Unified and other districts highly value autonomy over hiring and firing for teachers and classified staff. At the same time, however, the data suggest that hiring autonomy can open the door to problematic power relations within schools, with teachers and other school staff worried about or unsure of their rights in the charter environment.

Districts, then, must confront the issue of how to balance the goals of school-site authority over hiring and firing with need to protect the rights of teachers and other school employees, including their right to know the status under which they are hired. This is clearly a complicated issue that districts and unions spend considerable time negotiating. The experience in Mission Unified calls for some type of halfway meeting point, where charter schools could hire any teachers they wanted—certified or uncertified, provided they had bachelors degrees and passed a criminal screening process. Then, these teachers could be required to work toward their state teaching certification and tenure with the district. Once tenured, charter school teachers cannot be "fired," although district officials could work with charter schools to assist some teachers in transferring to other schools if conflicts arose. Additional research that explores "model" bargaining agreements for teachers' unions would assist in the quest for agreements that struck the right balance between hiring and firing flexibility and employee protection in charter schools.

Budgets for Facilities Improvements

A related issue is the priority that these three charter schools, located in relatively poor neighborhoods, place on maintenance and facilities. It would be easy to extrapolate, based on these schools' experiences, that districts should simply grant schools discretion over facilities and maintenance funds so that schools can get quicker and better service than they experience with a district system. But this line of reasoning runs straight into questions of district employment policies. With budgetary discretion in this area, schools can and do hire non-unionized, "cheaper" individuals and companies to do their maintenance and facilities. Although government regulation in this area may be burdensome for individual schools, it was created for the historical purpose of providing negotiated wages and benefits for district employees.

As districts throughout the country grapple with the global issue of the role of unions, they must, at a minimum, find the money and will to provide schools in poor areas with better facilities-related services. In the absence of better services, poor schools will be likely to seek alternative strategies, including hiring responsive, non-unionized labor. Bonds passed in California in the late 1990s will supply a portion of the necessary funds in that state, but infrastructure maintenance and improvement is an issue that will continue to demand funds and attention from the many entities with fiscal and governing responsibility for schools.

Autonomy and Assistance for Curriculum Issues

Finally, districts can learn from the charter school experience with curriculum issues. Just as the UCLA Charter School Study (1998) concluded that charter schools rely heavily on external and alternative sources of support, so do the experiences of charter schools in Mission Unified suggest that charter schools seek assistance in the area of instructional materials and strategies and professional development. Thus, it seems that the call for autonomy often is coupled with requests for assistance. The data suggest that districts should consider increasing both autonomy *and* assistance for local schools, especially since these districts, as the charter-granting institutions, are ultimately responsible for holding the charter schools accountable for student outcomes.

Regarding instructional materials and professional development, districts should consider crafting policies and procedures that allow schools greater flexibility to meet the curricular needs and demands of their particular school communities. Districts might take it upon themselves (and some already have) to adopt a "cafeteria" approach to curricular services and policies, an approach that allows schools to select among an array of instructional materials and professional-development opportunities. At the same time, districts must improve the quality of the assistance provided to schools in the domain of curriculum and allow schools to choose services that are tailored to the kinds of assistance schools need at a given time. Thus districts might consider engaging in a detailed analysis of school-level needs and rebuild district services around the results of such analysis.

With regard to calendars and discipline, districts also must strike the appropriate balance between flexibility and oversight. With calendars, districts should allow more flexibility for schools to meet students' needs for variations or extended programs, while at the same time continuing to monitor schools' practices in this domain. With discipline, again there is a need for balance. While districts need to support schools' attempts to emphasize student discipline, they clearly have a role to play in ensuring that students' rights are honored. That is, districts need to ensure that students' due process rights are protected when charter schools expel students.

In all of these instances, the advent of charter reform does provide districts with the information they need to begin to broaden the array of services and strategies they provide to schools. The ongoing struggle for districts, then, is to find a balance between the need for flexibility and the need for oversight and assistance. Clearly, this arrangement would make life harder for district staff, since they would be required to work with more instructional programs in schools with different professional-development schedules, calendars, and needs. But it seems that such a trade-off—a more complex managerial task for the district but more appropriate services for schools—clearly would be worthwhile.

IMPLICATIONS FOR POLICY, RESEARCH, AND THEORY

In this section, I move beyond the lessons for school districts to a broader discussion of the implications of this district's experience with charter schools for charter reform policy writ large and research on decentralizing reforms beyond charter reform.

Reinventing Districts with Charter School Reform

Stepping back from the question of how districts can learn from charter schools, I consider whether charter reform itself offers districts a viable strategy for reinventing themselves. The data do suggest that charter reform can play an important short-term role in improving schools, illustrating the kinds of changes schools can make as a result of charter reform—improvements in facilities, faster purchasing, new school calendars, hiring staff to fill school needs. And since the students who are enrolled in schools today will not benefit from long-term changes in school practices, short-term solutions are important, particularly as they point to the hopes and needs of staff and students in high-poverty schools.

But analyzing the issue from the district-level perspective reveals that charter reform may not produce the kind of long-term solutions districts need to change practices on a system-wide basis. For charter reform, as the data from Mission Unified suggest, brings with it the autonomy schools need but does not guarantee that charter schools will receive the assistance that they also need—for example, technical assistance, professional development, or conflict mediation. If charter reform does not support school-level needs in these areas, it certainly does not provide guidance or assistance to districts— the charter-granting agencies that are responsible for these more autonomous schools—as they struggle to upgrade and update their own operations. Districts themselves need technical assistance, professional development for staff, and advice on such issues as labor–management relations, curriculum development, and improving infrastructure of facilities, technology, and the like.

Moreover, while charter reform may prod some districts to seize the opportunity to learn about school-level needs and goals, it also may exacerbate what one district official called the "we–they" phenomenon. At times charter advocates cast the district bureaucracy as "bad" and autonomous schools as "good," and as a result charter reform actually can make it more difficult for districts to build the kinds of district–school relationships necessary to achieve long-term goals. In some ways, charter reform seeks to "get around" school districts rather than get them up to speed (see Chapter 2).

In summary, districts can and must use charter reform as an opportunity to evaluate and change district practices and policies. But districts will have to look beyond charter reform to find the support and strategies to make the changes indicated by charter reform.

Reconceptualizing Research and Theory

Stepping back from the policy implications of these data to reflect on their implications for research and theory, two issues emerge. First, the data suggest that theories of and research on decentralization need to disaggregate decentralization not only in terms of the levels of *autonomy* afforded in particular school-site domains but also in terms of the kinds of *assistance* schools require and sometimes gain via particular decentralizing reforms. For as this study's data reveal, autonomous schools such as charter schools do seek assistance at the same time as they embrace autonomy. Second, the data confirm the importance of looking at decentralization not solely in terms of the domains affected but also in terms of how decentralization interacts with school-site power relations and issues of accountability. Again, it was only when this study began to look at charter school reform in terms of who benefits from autonomy and in what ways, that it became clear that this reform can result in alienation among some constituencies, whether unionized classified employees or, as at Franklin, some Spanish-speaking parents. These findings also force us to think about the autonomy-for-accountability trade-off in a slightly different light. For instance, when it comes to charter schools and other decentralization reforms, we might think about not just academic or fiscal account-ability, but also accountability in terms of governance and who really has voice within these more decentralized settings. In this way, these findings also raise important equity concerns.

One is reminded of Elmore (1993)'s reflection: "Debates about central-ization and decentralization in American education, then, are mainly debates about *who* should have access to and influence over decisions, not about *what* the content and practice of teaching and learning should be or *how* to change those things" (p. 40, emphasis in original). Perhaps charter school reform rep-resents a step beyond many other decentralizing reforms, in the sense that char-ter schools' experiences do tell a story about *what* kinds of changes the current district-led system might undertake. At the same time, charter school reform does not—in fact, refuses to—suggest *how* the system might make those changes.

NOTE

1. While Franklin and Foundation were both part of the larger UCLA Charter School Study, Jefferson was dropped from the UCLA sample of schools because its charter was revoked and, therefore, it was no longer a charter school. Still, several interviews were conducted with the leaders of Jefferson, which allow me to include it in this chapter.

REFERENCES

Arrow, K. J. (1963). *Social choice and individual values.* New York: Wiley.

Bailyn, B. (1960). *Education in the forming of American society: Needs and opportu-nities for study* (Vol. 3). Williamsburg, VA: Institute for Early American His-tory & Chapel Hill: University of North Carolina Press.

Callahan, R. E. (1962). *Education and the cult of efficiency: A study of the social forces that have shaped the administration of the public schools.* Chicago: University of Chicago Press.

Chubb, J. E., & Moe, T. M. (1990). *Politics, markets & America's schools.* Washing-ton, DC: Brookings.

Elmore, R. F. (1993). School decentralization: Who gains? who loses? In J. Hannaway & M. Carnoy (Eds.), *Decentralization and school improvement: Can we fulfill the promise?* (pp. 33–54). San Francisco: Jossey-Bass.

Finn, C. E., Bierlein, L. A., & Manno, B. V. (1996). *Charter schools in action: A first look.* Washington, DC: Hudson Institute.

Handler, J. F. (1996). *Down from bureaucracy: The ambiguity of privatization and empowerment.* Princeton, NJ: Princeton University Press.

Mazzoni, T. L. (1995). State policy-making and school reform: Influences and influentials. In J. D. Scribner & D. H. Layton (Eds.), *The study of educational politics* (pp. 53–73). Washington, DC: Falmer Press.

Merriam, S. B. (1988). *Case study research in education: A qualitative approach.* San Francisco: Jossey-Bass.

Murphy, J., & Beck, L. G. (1995). *School-based management as school reform: Taking stock.* Thousand Oaks, CA: Corwin.

Nathan, R. P. (1994). Deregulating state and local government: What can leaders do? In J. J. DiIulio (Ed.), *Deregulating the public service: Can government be improved?* (pp. 156–174). Washington, DC: Brookings.

Osborne, D., & Gaebler, T. (1993). *Reinventing government: How the entrepreneurial spirit is transforming the public sector* (2nd ed.). New York: Penguin Books.

SRI International. (1997). *Evaluation of charter school effectiveness.* Menlo Park, CA: Author.

Tyack, D. (1974). *The one best system: A history of American urban education.* Cambridge, MA: Harvard University Press.

Tyack, D. (1993). School governance in the United States: Historical puzzles and anomalies. In J. Hannaway & M. Carnoy (Eds.), *Decentralization and school improvement: Can we fulfill the promise?* (pp. 1–32). San Francisco: Jossey-Bass.

UCLA Charter School Study. (1998). *Beyond the rhetoric of charter school reform: A study of ten California school districts.* Los Angeles: Author. [www.gseis.ucla.edu/docs/charter.pdf].

CHAPTER 4

Public Funds for California Charter Schools

Where Local Context and Savvy Meet Formula

JULIE SLAYTON

One way charter school legislation theoretically "sets schools free" from state and district regulations to compete in the educational marketplace is by altering state funding structures to send public education funds—calculated on a per-pupil basis—directly to the charter schools. Such a system bypasses much of the state and/or local district bureaucracy and allows the money to follow the student, forcing both competition and efficiency. It sounds fairly straightforward—a matter of simply multiplying the per-pupil funding level by the number of students enrolled. What could be more simple?

Drawing on qualitative data—interviews, observations, and documents—I examined the language of the charter law and its translation into the actual funding experiences of schools in four of the 10 school districts from the larger UCLA Charter School Study. I learned that the implementation of charter school legislation in California, as it pertains to the public funding of these more autonomous schools, is anything but straightforward or simple. In particular, this chapter focuses on the very salient finding that charter schools receive varying amounts of public funding in large part because of the political context of their school districts, including the attitude of board members toward charter schools, and the savvy and knowledge—or lack thereof—of charter school administrators (for additional findings, see Slayton, 1999).

Thus, the more well-connected—especially with school district officials—and well-informed charter school administrators we studied used their knowledge of the law and available resources, or their ability to apply political pressure, to ensure that their schools received all of the public funding to which they were theoretically entitled. Furthermore, some of these well-connected educators were able to draw additional revenue or benefits from their host districts. Meanwhile, other less well-informed or less politically powerful charter school administrators were unable to claim the same level of support from their districts. This finding demonstrates that despite the rational language of the California charter school law—and many similar laws across the country—its meaning, as it relates to funding, is interpreted differently in different political contexts. Depending on who leads the charter school and who is on the school board, very different funding relationships and realities between charter schools and their sponsoring districts exist. In this way, this chapter also furthers the theme of the ambiguity of charter school–school district relationships and accountability systems, as discussed in Chapters 2 and 3 of this book.

This finding has serious implications for school districts and charter schools on the one hand, and for policy and lawmakers on the other. For instance, we learned that this is not simply an issue of charter schools in different school districts receiving different amounts of public support. We found that sometimes charter schools within the *same* school district can and do receive different amounts of public support. Indeed, these findings raise concerns about whether charter schools are being funded equitably in relation to each other or in relation to other public schools. This first look suggests they are not.

Thus, the first section of this chapter provides a description of the funding guidelines of the California charter school law. In the next section, I present data from four school districts and five charter schools in those districts from the UCLA study, focusing particularly on their funding practices as they relate to the basic per-pupil funding and categorical programs. And in the final section, I present conclusions, questions, and concerns raised by the data.

CHARTER SCHOOL FUNDING

The savvy and knowledge of charter school administrators in California is of great importance in determining funding levels for their schools because of the way the charter school law was written by the state legislature and then interpreted by the California Department of Education. While this chapter discusses this issue as it pertains to one state law, the complexity of charter school funding formulas is not unique to California.

As part of the 1992 Charter School Act, the California legislature set forth what appears at first glance to be a very straightforward method for funding charter schools. The legislation states that a charter school is entitled to funding based on its regular average daily attendance multiplied by the per-pupil amount of the sponsor district's base revenue limit, which is the maximum amount of general state and local funding a district can receive. The base revenue limit is different for districts serving students of different grade levels because of the different expenses associated with educating students at different points in the K–12 system. Thus, an elementary district generally will receive a lower base revenue limit, a high school district generally will receive the highest base revenue limit, and a "unified" school district—comprising elementary, middle, and high schools—generally will receive a base revenue limit that falls in between.

Thus, according to the statutory language, it appears that a charter school in a unified school district is entitled to the unified school district's base revenue limit regardless of whether it is an elementary, middle, or high school. Yet, as the data below suggest, this interpretation of the legislation has not been adopted universally. Moreover, the variation in the application of the legislation across and within districts raises concerns about equitable funding for charter schools, especially those serving poor and minority students. Although amendments to the California law passed in 1998 changed the specifics of how charter schools are funded beginning with the 1999–2000 school year, much of the legal ambiguity discussed in this section remains, as do the issues related to unevenness and inequity across charter schools.

In addition to a school district's base revenue limit, charter schools are eligible to receive funds from a list of state categorical programs for which their students qualify. The legislation identifies the following categorical programs: California state lottery, state summer school, minimum standards funding, certain block grants, class-size-reduction funds, and charter school funding from the California Department of Education or other sources. With regard to special education funding, the legislation requires that a student entitled to special education services receive the state and federal funds that would have been provided for that student to receive those services at a non-charter school. But the problem with these expensive categorical programs, such as special education, is that funding provided by the state and federal governments for these programs typically do not cover the entire costs of providing services, especially in the area of special education. As a result, districts supplement special education funding with general-purpose revenue. This supplement is referred to as an "encroachment" on the general budget. Some argue that charter schools, as every other public school, should pay their share of this encroachment, but, as I note in this chapter, that is not always the case.

The legislation does not include other types of revenue that non-charter schools receive from their districts. For instance, charter schools are not automatically entitled to local bond, sales, or parcel tax moneys nor do they, as a matter of course, receive school construction or capital funds, or a school facility. Nor does the legislation address whether charter schools are eligible for other state programs, including some categorical programs, such as transportation, mentor teacher, desegregation, and GATE (Gifted and Talented Education). Charter schools can negotiate with their school district for any funds not identified in the legislation (Premack, 1997).

In addition, the original California legislation did not address whether and how much charter schools must pay their districts for providing oversight or services to the schools. Indeed, the first law, which was in effect when we completed our study, did not account for oversight costs or services that previously had been provided by the charter schools' parent districts. These costs and services include, but are not limited to, such things as budget oversight, building maintenance, use of district facilities, insurance, staff development, business office services, and legal services.

Meanwhile, as was noted in Chapter 2, districts continue to be responsible for providing information to the state regarding *all* of their schools and they are most likely liable for the actions of the charter schools in their districts. Thus, from their perspective, they need to retain some form of oversight requirement. Additionally, as was noted in Chapter 3, in some instances charter schools choose to retain district-provided services instead of seeking outside providers. In other instances, districts require that charter schools retain some services for a fee. This ambiguity leaves it up to the districts and their charter schools to negotiate how much, if anything, the charter schools will pay for the districts' oversight or services. The 1998 amendments to the California charter school law attempted to clarify this process by limiting the amount a school district could charge a charter school for oversight to 1% of the charter school's revenue or 3% if the charter school had a rent-free facility. Still, some ambiguity remains in terms of which district services are included in this limit.

Indeed, much of the uncertainty related to charter school funding stems from the fact that, although the original legislation indicates that the California Department of Education will send charter schools their funds directly, Department of Education officials, in 1993, opted not to fund charter schools in this way. Thus, in most cases charter school funds, like non-charter school funds, flow through their sponsor districts' accounts and are then passed on to the charter schools (Management Advisory 93-10, 1993). According to Premack (1997), this decision was made because the original California charter legislation lacked the necessary mechanisms to send funding directly from the state coffers to the individual charter schools.

Thus, California Department of Education officials recognized that a negotiation process would exist between the school district and the charter school either at the time the charter was granted or at a later date. For instance, a Management Advisory (93-10, 1993) issued by the department noted that the charter school and the district also might "make binding agreements to allow their parent districts to increase or reduce funding from their allocations." Reductions might be agreed to in order "to pay for specified services from parent districts or in reflection of the fact that elementary schools within unified districts typically spend lower amounts per pupil than do high schools" (p. 2). Increased allocations may be made to reflect higher per-pupil expenses for high schools within a unified school district.

As the data below demonstrate, this negotiation process has translated into different levels of funding for charter schools within and across unified school districts throughout the state. Moreover, it is in the negotiation process that the savvy and know-how—or lack thereof—of the charter school administrators play a significant role in determining the amount and type of public funding each charter school will receive. For instance, this savvy and know-how play a role in whether a charter school pays oversight and service costs to its district, whether a district provides a facility for its charter school or schools, and whether a charter school pays for any of the school district's additional special education costs.

FROM POLICY TO PRACTICE: UNEVEN AND INEQUITABLE CHARTER SCHOOL FUNDING

We learned that sponsoring school districts entered into funding agreements that were often very different across individual charter schools and different from those of other sponsoring districts. This section will present findings based on data from the 1997–98 school year from four of the 10 school districts covered by the larger UCLA Charter School Study and five charter schools within these four districts. These four districts and five charter schools were selected because they share certain basic commonalties that allow for both some within-district and some cross-district funding comparisons. Four of the five charter schools—one middle school, one high school, and two elementary schools—are from the larger UCLA Charter School Study. The fifth school, an elementary school, was selected because it provided an excellent opportunity to compare two fiscally independent charter schools within the same district.

The most important similarities among the four school districts are that they are all large, urban, unified school districts. They also all serve large populations of poor and minority students. Additionally, all five of the charter schools examined were fiscally independent schools. Unlike fiscally dependent charter schools, fiscally independent charter schools negotiate individual funding agreements with their sponsoring districts. These agreements give the charter schools complete control over their resources and lay out the terms of the funding relationship between the sponsoring district and the charter school. This similarity allowed me to compare the kinds of agreements each school entered into with their sponsoring districts and the consequences of these agreements for the charter schools.

For each district, I will present an analysis of the data that are relevant to understanding the overall funding relationship between the charter schools and their sponsoring districts. I will address each district and its charter school or schools individually, first providing background on the school/district context by describing the school–district relationship and then the qualifications of the charter school administrators responsible for their schools' funding. Next, I will present financial data for each of the districts and their charter school or schools. The financial data presented vary from district to district and sometimes from school to school within the same district. Furthermore, the varied application of the charter school law—due to the different local political contexts of the charter schools and the different levels of expertise and know-how of the charter school leaders—created significant differences in the level of funding each of these five charter schools received. I argue that such variation raises important equity concerns regarding charter school funding.

Central Unified School District

During the 1997–98 school year, Central Unified School District (CUSD) served a racially and ethnically diverse student population within a racially and ethnically diverse city. CUSD had only one charter school operating. Unlike the other schools discussed in this chapter, Wilson Elementary School was a "conversion" charter school, which means it was already operating as a public elementary school before converting to a charter school. The principal at Wilson, Michael Dellinger, had a Ph.D. and had been a principal in the district before coming to Wilson so he was already familiar with many of the district policies and services. Dellinger led the effort at Wilson to convert the elementary school to a charter school in 1993. In the early years of the school's existence as a charter school, Dellinger opted to keep Wilson fiscally tied to the school district—or fiscally "dependent" on the district—which meant that in terms of funding and accounting, the charter school's relationship with the district was not dramatically different than it had been prior to converting to a charter school. According to Dellinger:

> Originally we didn't want to be in the business end. We wanted to focus on the academic program . . . and we didn't want to have to deal with millions of dollars. I didn't want to have to deal with millions of dollars and I had no experience in dealing with a million-dollar budget.

Meanwhile, Dellinger studied his school's budget, working closely with district personnel to learn the technical aspects of the budgeting process while remaining fiscally connected to the district. After several years of operating the school in this way, Dellinger had a great deal of budgetary experience and understanding and had created an incredibly detailed budget spreadsheet, which he used to identify all of the school's sources of revenue and all of its expenditures. He felt ready to operate the school as a more fiscally independent entity—separate from the district—in order to have the ability to make decisions about how to spend the school's entire budget instead of just a small portion of it. So when the state proposed a "direct funding pilot" that would allow a group of charter schools to receive their funding directly from the state, and therefore become completely fiscally independent of their school districts, Dellinger applied. In order to participate in the pilot, charter schools, their districts, and their counties had to come to the table to negotiate all financial issues regarding these schools. Although the direct funding pilot stalled over liability concerns, Dellinger moved forward with the district to pursue financial independence anyway, and Wilson became a fiscally independent charter school in 1996.

As I demonstrate below, Dellinger had the knowledge and information necessary to ensure that his school received the greatest amount of resources it could. And not only did Dellinger demonstrate his expertise when it came to budgets, but he was also politically savvy in his dealings with the district. Thus, despite some initial conflict between the school and both the district and the local teachers union over the specifics of the school's teachers' contract, Dellinger developed positive relationships with many key administrators in the district. For example, he had a very close working relationship with the district's director of budget services, who characterized this relationship as "wonderful." In fact, Dellinger had developed this relationship up front, in 1993, when he and his staff first proposed the charter and set forth how the school budget was laid out. The district's director of budget services reviewed this proposal "to be sure that there was no cost impact that was above and beyond what any other school was getting." The school was also fairly well supported by the district's school board. And, over time, Dellinger improved the school's relationship with the union.

The 1997–98 school year was the first year that Wilson had complete control over its budget and received its money from the district without any financial control still in the hands of the district. That year, the school received the "base revenue limit" per-pupil amount plus lottery funds, California class-size-reduction money, bilingual/EIA (Economic Impact Aid) education funds, school-improvement-program money, federal Title I funds for poor students, parent-involvement money, and instructional materials funds. In terms of the base revenue limit money, Wilson was receiving about $3,569 per pupil for the 1997–98 academic year. This was a "differentiated" revenue limit, which meant it was the same base revenue limit as for other elementary schools in the district but less than that for middle or high schools. As Dellinger stated,

"The school does not receive any additional money . . . [beyond what] the students in any other schools generate." Although other elementary charter schools in other school districts receive the "unified" or average revenue limit for the entire district instead of the lower elementary rate, Dellinger stated that it was "not worth the battle to say we should get the unified rate." On the other hand, Dellinger stated that he felt that the budget had the potential to be continually flexible in terms of what the school worked out with the district—that the school eventually might receive the unified rate.

With regard to funds beyond basic revenue and categorical funding, the school had the following experience. While Wilson did not receive locally collected tax revenue, Dellinger indicated that he believed the school eventually might receive money generated from developers' fees and local bonds. The school did pay an overhead administrative fee to the district for supervisory oversight and services provided by the district. This fee was 5.78% of total expenses. This fee paid for the district to continue to handle the school's payroll and other services such as accounting, purchasing, internal auditing, completion of state-required reports, liability insurance, and the advice and support of the Board of Education, superintendent, and district's general counsel. Because Wilson was a conversion school, the school did not have to seek a facility. Instead, the school paid 2% of its expenditures for rent and billed back to the district for things that were not repaired in a timely manner, such as broken windows, leaking roof, and malfunctioning air conditioning. Thus, while the school paid $57,000 for rent, one year it was able to bill back over $52,000 of that to the district for maintenance.

Furthermore, unlike most charter schools, Wilson had a large special education program that included 65 students with orthopedic disabilities from other schools in Central Unified and from other school districts in the area. Instead of sending the special education funds for these students to the charter school, the district continued to cover the costs of providing services to these students. The school did pay its share of the per-student special education "encroachment," or the difference between the actual cost of special education and state and federal funds the district received to pay for these services. This was more than $75,000 a year. (The school also paid its share of the district transportation encroachment.) Dellinger stated that he was not interested in receiving special education funding directly from the district because it would be too expensive for the school to maintain its own independent program, given the size of the special education population. He noted:

> We could not operate this facility if we got all the special education funding, [because] the old formula just doesn't [provide enough money]. Most of these kids do not . . . all of [them] do not live in this attendance area. So it's a district responsibility. If anything . . . we

could charge the district actual cost. But it's easier just to say, district, you keep the current operation. We won't change anything with special ed [because] to operate this facility you have to look at the whole general fund from the district [because] money generated from other kids [is] supporting this. It's a very . . . expensive operation.

In short, through his familiarity with the school's budget, Dellinger was sure that his school was receiving all of the money to which it was entitled. He had developed an extremely comprehensive budget, knew his way around it, and knew exactly to what he was entitled. The Central Unified budget director described the way she had worked with him on the budget: "Michael will come in with his total package. His categorical funds, his state instructional allowance money, his general funds money, special ed money. He will come in with the whole big picture at one time, and we will talk about it and work with that." Thus, Dellinger was able to ensure that his school received resources from as many sources as it was allowed to under the law. Clearly, his relationship with district budget officials and his knowledge of the law and his budget gave him a huge advantage over many other charter school administrators when it came to fiscal issues.

Edgewood Unified School District

Edgewood Unified School District (EUSD) presented a very different context for charter school reform. During the 1997–98 school year, while the general population of the city of Edgewood was racially diverse, the student population in EUSD was predominantly African American and Latino, and poor.

At the time of our study, Edgewood Unified had three charter schools, all middle schools. All three were required by the district to operate as fiscally independent institutions. In other words, the charter schools themselves had virtually no say in what their financial relationship would be with the district. Instead, the Board of Education and the district administration issued a set of guidelines and requirements that charter school petitioners were to follow.

In this section, I focus specifically on Edgewood Unified's Community Charter School. The principal of Community Charter School during the 1997–98 school year, Darla Henderson, was a bilingual teacher and then an elementary school principal in a nearby school district before becoming Community's principal. She did not have a great deal of experience in or knowledge about school budgeting before coming to the charter school. She said that at her previous school, business services and facilities constituted only 10–15 % of her job, while at Community they were her central focus. Moreover, did she not have outside sources to turn to in order to get information or ask questions, nor did she find the district administrators particularly helpful.

Meanwhile, district personnel consistently characterized the district's relationship with its charter schools as supportive. The superintendent at that time said, "We have a very positive relationship with all of our charters. In fact, in some ways, they are a part of the family." Yet, other evidence suggested that the district had a more distant relationship with its charter schools. In fact, when asked where the charter schools fit in her vision of the district's future, the superintendent said that charter schools were not directly part of her overall vision for the district, although she was open to providing them with whatever support they needed. The educators and parents at the charter schools, however, said that the district was not very supportive at all. In fact, Community's principal said she did not think that charter schools were even on the district's radar screen.

The district's guidelines for charter schools also seemed to indicate that the board and central administration wanted very little to do with charter schools. For instance, the guidelines required, as noted above, that all EUSD charter schools be fiscally independent and become a non-profit corporation, or a completely separate legal entity from the district. In addition, the guidelines required each school to locate its own site and be responsible for the acquisition of all equipment, materials, and support services. There was no obvious district support, financial or otherwise, to Community or the other charter schools. Moreover, the funding relationship for Community, as with the other two charter schools, was based on the initial set of 1993–94 negotiations between the district and Community's first principal. This basic funding relationship, set forth in a Memorandum of Understanding (MOU), changed very little before or during Henderson's one-year tenure at the school.

Many of the educators at Community Charter School were fairly ambivalent about the school's relationship with the district. According to Henderson, the school could probably get more services from the district than it did but the educators chose not to, for several reasons. First of all, they were concerned they could not afford to pay for them because, according to Henderson, "if we start using too many of their services they're going to want to revise the MOU. . . . And like I say, we can't afford to pay for some of the things that they may want to offer us." Moreover, there was resistance among many of the teachers at the school, a "fear of being sucked back in" to the district. While Henderson had been interested in taking "the best of what the district offers and maintain[ing] our independence," many of the teachers said that it was not that easy to take what the district offered without succumbing to more district control. This tension made it difficult for the charter school to negotiate with the district.

In terms of what Community Charter School did receive from the district, like the other two charter schools in Edgewood Unified, Community received a "unified" base revenue limit, or the average per-pupil funding for the district. But it was difficult for our research team to determine exactly what that base revenue limit for the district was because every source of information from the district or the schools provided a different answer. For instance, the MOU between the charter school and the district stated that the district's base revenue limit was $3,544 for the 1997–98 school year. Thus, this was the amount that Community Charter School should have been receiving per pupil. Yet, our efforts to confirm this figure with district officials proved fruitless, as different sources gave us different information about the amount of money Community received.

The proposed school district budget for the 1997–98 school year did not set forth the base revenue limit for the district. According to the assistant superintendent for business services, the base revenue limit for 1997–98 in the Edgewood district was expected to be approximately $3,200. A former government relations person for the district stated that the schools in the district got "somewhere around $3,700 per student. That is a base. Not including the add-ons for categorical. I think it is closer to 36 or 37 [hundred] to be honest." Furthermore, the California Department of Education documents indicated that the unified base revenue limit for Edgewood for 1997–98 was $3,651.26. Thus, depending on the source, Community was either under- or overfunded for each student compared with students in other schools in the district.

Meanwhile, Henderson was unable to provide any additional insight into her school's funding. She said she did not have a complete understanding of what she was entitled to under the law, but she said she believed the district was not giving her all of the funds to which she was entitled.

> I tried to find out [the average base revenue limit per pupil]. At one point I called the County Office of Education at the time when the budget was not finalized in Sacramento, and they thought at the time it was going to be about $4,000, so I was going, hey, where's the rest of this money. And I still feel that way, but I think they readjusted their figure to be somewhere around $3,700–$3,800. It's still a significant chunk of change that we are missing, and a critical one. I mean that, if we're talking about, $32,000, $35,000 dollars, that would make the whole difference.

She went on to describe the school's budget as "pretty bare bones." The absence of available information contributed to Henderson's belief that she was entitled to additional funds. The combination of the lack of information provided by the district and the lack of knowledge on the part of the charter school administrator put her and her school at a disadvantage in relation to other charter schools in this and other districts. With a complete understanding of the district's base revenue, Henderson could have been sure that she was receiving what she was entitled to based on the district guidelines. On the other hand, in this particular case, given the district's rigid relationship with its charter schools, more knowledge most likely would not have helped her to negotiate for a higher base revenue limit. Additionally, the absence of consistent data across sources made it impossible to ensure that the basic funding the school received was the funding to which it was entitled.

In addition to setting forth the specifics of the base revenue limit, the MOU between Community Charter School and the district provided information on exactly which categorical funds the school was entitled to receive. These included mentor teachers, staff development, Title VI, and EIA (Economic Impact Aid). Community also was to "receive funding from the California state lottery" and from "new" or "one-time" funding sources, such as class-size-reduction money, available to schools or school districts from the state. Additionally, while not stated in the MOU, the school budget reflected that the school received limited-English-proficient funds, school-improvement-program funds, and state-compensatory-education money. According to Henderson, the state-compensatory-education money was given to all the charter schools by the district in lieu of federal Title I compensatory funds because the "bureaucratic requirements" of the federal funds "would be huge." Meanwhile, the requirements for state funds were less laborious. Henderson noted, "And that's a very kind thing for them [district officials] to do. I don't know if they did it intentionally or what, but I'm really [grateful] if that is the case."

As discussed at the beginning of this chapter, there are several additional components of a charter school budget—beyond basic and categorical funding—that can be negotiated. For instance, charter schools can negotiate to receive local tax revenue and capital or school construction funds, which charter schools are not entitled to under law but some districts still provide. One the other hand, districts may negotiate to have charter schools pay administrative oversight and services costs or the additional, non-reimbursed special education costs—or "encroachment."

Edgewood, like most other districts in California, does not provide locally collected tax revenue to its charter schools. The district also does not provide any of its charter schools with facilities or money for facilities. The founders of Community Charter School were forced to seek out a location and rent both the property and the buildings in which the school operates. Henderson explained: "And then, as I said, the facilities, having no access to any of what they, any special funding [the district] may get from the state in regards to facilities, that's a problem. I mean bond measures that [the district] get[s] and we haven't been able to access." In fact, for the 1997–98 school year, the charter school spent over $60,000 on rent for a small parcel of land in the midst of a dusty industrial park and some portable classrooms.

Reflecting on Community's fragile financial and physical health, Henderson expressed frustration with her lack of expertise and the ambiguity of charter school reform.

> And, you know, it's my belief that probably we would be entitled to those things, but it's a combination of us not knowing or having expertise to find out what that stuff is, and then the fact that we are actually fiscally independent of them, that means that we're basically, we have to rely on their good graces in terms of anything that they want to give us.

With regard to special education funding, Community Charter School did not receive the money directly from the district. While the original charter proposal for the school, submitted to the district in 1993, specified that Community would receive special education money, the most recent budget for the school showed no special education allocation. Similarly, the MOU for 1997–98 did not state that the school would receive special education funds or services, although during that school year the district did send a district-employed special education teacher to the charter school on a part-time basis. But the school's budget did not identify any expense or income related to special education.

Regarding supervisory oversight and service costs, according to district charter school guidelines, before the 1998 amendments to the California charter school law, the district could charge the school up to 15% of the school's total expenses. Yet, it is not clear from district and school documents, budgets, or interviews with district and school personnel whether the school paid the district for supervisory oversight. The school did not pay the district for insurance, and according to Henderson, Community spent a great deal on private insurance. "We have to go to a carrier, we spend close to $10,000 a year on [insurance]. So that's a problem."

The finding identified at the outset of this chapter was clear from the data on Edgewood: The lack of savvy and knowledge of the charter school administrator was one of the primary reasons that the school received less support and fewer resources than other schools examined in this chapter. It is clear that the principal's lack of political savvy and lack of information about school funding and basic funds she was entitled to under law meant that the school was unable to draw additional support and resources from the district. Furthermore, the political context of this district and its approach to working with—or not working with— charter schools contributed to the community's dilemma.

Madrona Unified School District

During the 1997–98 school year, both the general population and the student population of Madrona Unified School District (MUSD) were ethnically, racially, and socioeconomically diverse. Because of the district's large size, there were pockets of extreme affluence and pockets of extreme poverty within Madrona's borders. At the time of our study, Madrona had 15 charter schools operating. These schools ran the gamut in terms of their size, origins, student demographics, and degree of autonomy from the district. Four of these schools were fiscally independent, while the rest were fiscally dependent.

The district had only two start-up charter schools. One was Academic Charter School, which, like most other start up charter schools, was fiscally independent. Academic Charter School had two co-directors, Scott Kent and Whitney Jefferson, both of whom came to this reform with some helpful expertise. For instance, both men had received their masters degrees in education, and both had learned a great deal about school finance and school budgets. They had taken advantage of various materials that were available to them, including a "book on accounting procedures and account codes" available from the state, and books from the County Office of Education "on how to do the budget and accounting." Kent said that the people at the County Office of Education had provided helpful guidance as he and Jefferson set up accounts and decided how to use different funds. He also said that he and Jefferson could not have handled their budget initially without the help of the County Office of Education and a business consulting firm they connected with through a private donor.

Both of the school's co-directors characterized the school's relationship with the MUSD as quite positive. Kent said:

> I think for the most part it is positive. . . . I think there could be a little bit more buy-in, in terms of what we're trying to do among some district staff. But I think, . . . over the time of our relationship it's grown a lot stronger. I think a lot of the early stuff was uncertainty of whether we were capable of doing what we were setting out to do. But I would say that our relationship with the district is stronger than it ever was. That with our new site, even, they are seeing a greater contribution that we can make toward their efforts.

Jefferson went even further when talking about the district's relationship with the school. He said that the Madrona school board required the founders to raise $200,000 in private funds before it would approve the school's charter application. He said that the board members and district officials did not believe that he and Kent could raise that amount of money. He said that this perception was confirmed when he talked to the district's charter school liaison. When the two founders did raise the money, Jefferson noted, "it really engendered [the district's] support afterwards, because they were like, 'oh these guys really are good. They're not just pie in the sky young folks who are just talk. They are people who are committed to what they want to do and who are actually doing it.'" In fact, he said that the district had been "very supportive" of their efforts. He added, "It's a breath of fresh air to the profession to see this kind of thing just happen. And I think their support . . . has come along with that."

Like Wilson, Academic Charter School received a differentiated revenue limit as an elementary school in MUSD. Thus, while the unified school district's base revenue limit for the 1997–98 school year was projected to be $3,521.55, the charter school's projected base revenue limit was $3,351 per pupil, reflecting the lower elementary rate. This is consistent with district documents, which show the school's actual per-pupil funding to be $3,346.

In addition, according to Kent, the school received the following categorical funds: Economic Impact Aid, Title I, bilingual education money, school-improvement-program funds, and state lottery money. According to the school's charter proposal, the founders requested that the school also receive other categorical funds, including funding for class-size reduction, migrant education, educational technology, instructional materials, special education, staff development, school improvement, and gifted and talented education. According to Kent, Academic received some of these funds, but the school's budget did not reflect the specific categorical funds received. Instead, categorical funds were lumped together with "other state revenues." On the other hand, district documents state that the Academic received lottery money as well as funding for several categorical programs, although not necessarily the ones the school had wanted. For instance, district documents showed that the charter school received funding for some of the programs it had specifically requested, including class-size reduction, economic impact aid, and school improvement program. But it also received money for a state reading program, travel funds for the charter schools national conference, and a mentor teacher program.

At the same time, there was not a great deal of concern on the part of the co-directors over categorical funding because, Kent said, the school had such a small student body—fewer than 150 students—that these programs, funded on a per-pupil basis, would not generate much revenue. But he thought that as the school grew and categorical funding increased, it would become more of an issue.

Meanwhile, Academic, unlike any of the other four charter schools discussed in this chapter or most other charter schools in the state, did receive local tax revenue. According to the charter school's 1997–98 budget, Academic received over $400,000 in local revenue from the district—more than $2,800 per pupil. This local funding combined with the base revenue limit—

before adding on the categorical funds, which totaled about $150,000—brought the per-pupil public funding for Academic to more than $6,000, significantly higher than the other charter schools discussed in this chapter.

As for supervisorial overhead and services from the district, according to Academic's charter proposal, the school was to be charged "at the district's state-approved indirect rate for any services provided." Kent said that this rate was 3% of the school's budget. It was unclear from district and school financial documents whether or not the district actually had subtracted the supervisorial oversight costs from the school's revenue. But according to Kent, the district actually failed, for whatever reason, to take this money. He was unsure of whether this was just an oversight on the part of the district. On the other hand, the district did require the school to have and pay for liability insurance. In fact, Academic spent about $12,000 a year on insurance.

In terms of facilities and rent, after a few years of renting space from a local church, Academic Charter School moved into a converted manufacturing facility. According to several people we interviewed, including the former owner of the plant, the site was worth more than $5 million. Academic paid $1 a month for the use of the facility, which had been donated to a foundation housed within a local university for the charter school to use. Thus, the university, not the charter school, owned the building, which meant the charter school could occupy the space without dealing with any of the headaches of owning and maintaining the plant. Thus, this virtually "free" space coupled with its significantly higher per-pupil funding made the financial situation at Academic a stark contrast to that at Community Charter School in particular.

As for special education funds, Kent said that the district provided services for special education students on a case-by-case basis; thus, the school was not receiving funding, but services. He did note that the charter school was "still kind of working through that one." Still, it was unclear, from school and district data, whether the school paid a portion of the district's special education "encroachment" costs.

All in all, it is safe to say that Academic Charter School did better than most other charter schools—in our study and beyond—in getting the public funding support it needed. Still, as Chapter 5 illustrates, what makes the financial picture of this particular school even more amazing is that, unlike the other charter schools discussed in this chapter, Academic Charter School was able to garner a huge amount of private funding. In fact, only about 60% of its total operating revenue came from public funds because the co-directors engaged in major private fund-raising efforts to provide the additional funds the school needed in order to operate. Thus, while it appeared that Academic had a relatively positive relationship with the Madrona Unified School District with respect to its funding, the charter school did not depend solely on district revenues to survive. On the other hand, when Kent found out that the district had not been completely forthcoming when it came to information regarding new or one-time funds that were available to all schools in the district, he immediately remedied the situation. He said:

> A couple of times . . . we did find laws or memorandums from the state department that said we were entitled to something that we weren't getting and shared that with the district. Within . . . by the next revenue payment, which are monthly, it was there. Or even before, in some supplementary payments. So they've been wonderful in passing through the money that is supposed to come to us.

Yet, Academic co-directors' solution in such cases did not work for all of Madrona's charter schools. In fact, by leaving it to the individual charter schools to divine what additional monies they might have been entitled to, the district created a situation in which some charter schools had an advantage over others. Those schools that had personnel who knew where to look for additional resources could and did come back to the district and request funding to which they were entitled. Kent and Jefferson were two such administrators. They used the resources they knew were available to them to structure their budget and to request those funds they thought they deserved. Other charter schools, such as Community and other nearby Madrona charter schools, lacked personnel with the time, knowledge, or connections to stay on top of these issues and get more money for their charter schools.

Vista Unified School District

During the 1997–98 school year, the general population and student population in Vista Unified School District (VUSD) was extremely diverse racially, ethnically, and financially, with pockets of affluence and poverty. The district had three charter schools, one high school, one middle school, and one elementary school.[1] The high school, Directions High School, and the elementary school, Learning Tree Charter School, are the focus of this section. Both Directions and Learning Tree were financially independent, start-up charter schools, while the other charter school in the district was a financially dependent conversion charter school.

The school administrator responsible for funding at Learning Tree was Martie Connor, the school treasurer. While she came to her job almost a year before the 1997–98 school year, she was not formally trained in finance and had no other training that would have necessarily prepared her for her job of negotiating with the district. In fact, when asked about changes she would like to see made in the school's financial agreement with the district, she replied, "I really couldn't say off the top of my head what we can bargain for even. Yeah, that's an area I find very difficult." Additionally, although she was very interested in doing so, Connor had not yet talked to any other charter school people involved in their school's finances or met with anyone who could have provided her with support.

With regard to the district's relationship with the school, one Vista Unified school board member characterized Learning Tree as "a mess, a first-class mess." Similarly, the district's chief financial officer said that the school board did not have a very good opinion of the charter school. In fact, Connor confirmed that there were people on the school board who were not supportive of the school. She said, about starting the charter school, "We went to the Unified School District, and they basically had no way to not let us start, even though they weren't very excited about it. But legally they had to let us start. We had all the required signatures and the legal backing, so they finally provided us with this building." On the other hand, another board member said that the school had a couple of advocates on the board who helped convince the superintendent to give the school a site, which he did.

Unlike Connor, Ken Morris, principal of Directions High School, was described by a district administrator in the following way: "This gentleman is a former teacher, a lawyer, a bright guy, well-connected, wealthy, da, da, da, the whole bit." In addition to being an attorney, Morris obtained a masters degree in education specifically to learn what he thought was necessary to start a charter school. Additionally, he brought together a very sophisticated and well-connected group of individuals to serve on the charter school's board of directors, advisory board, and governing council. Morris drew from his personal and professional connections to compose these groups, which were made up of Vista Unified school board members, lawyers, educators, and business and medical professionals. In addition, one of the board members was an attorney who also acted as general counsel for the charter school and who participated in negotiations with the district. This board member stated that he worked with the principal at the outset of starting the school on the "political side." For instance, he assisted Morris in helping to persuade the district's Board of Education to support the charter school.

This political clout and savvy on the part of Directions' board members was not nearly as prevalent on Learning Tree's governing board. Also, unlike Learning Tree, Directions clearly had a very good relationship with the district. Many Vista school board members spoke of the school as one that should succeed. Moreover, the attorney on the charter school's board pointed out that the school had done everything it could to position itself so that the district would "open their arms and say, 'We'd like to have this opportunity.'"

Furthermore, Vista Unified had MOUs with both Learning Tree Charter School and Directions High School that outlined the sources of revenue to which the schools were entitled. Yet there were differences between the MOUs that led to significant differences in the level of funding the two schools received from the district. On the one hand, Learning Tree's MOU specified that it should receive the district's "revenue limit rather than a reduced revenue limit, which it might receive by virtue of the fact that [it] is an elementary school in a unified school district." According to the MOU, then, the projected base revenue limit for the 1997–98 school year was $3,212.81 per pupil. On the other hand, the district's proposed budget for 1997–98 projected the district's overall base revenue limit to be $3,568 per pupil. According to the VUSD chief financial officer, Conrad Wolfe, the elementary charter school received a per-student base revenue limit of $3,400.

Conner, the charter school's treasurer, could not clarify the confusion regarding the school's base revenue limit. In fact, her understanding was that her school received $1,775 per student. In her attempt to determine her funding, she had calculated it based on her understanding of the base revenue limit per student, the school's current number of students, and the number of days in the school year. Connor also said that she would "love to know more" about the breakdown of the money she received every month but that she had not been successful in getting that information from the district and it was "just hard getting everything figured out." Meanwhile, Wolfe, Vista Unified's Chief Financial Officer, who had told us that Learning Tree was receiving about $3,400 per student, insisted that the school was receiving all the revenue it was entitled to under the law.

There was no mention in the MOU between Learning Tree and Vista Unified of the categorical funding to which the school was entitled according to the California charter school act. When asked about the categorical money the school received, Connor said she thought that the funds she received had categorical money included. She said, "He [Wolfe] sends stuff periodically, I get notice served that says, 'You got this amount,' and I don't know if it's increased. And it's very confusing, and that's something that I have been trying to understand. . . . He sends me stuff that says, category this and category that and the amount, and I'm hop[ing] that it's just put into the payment." On the other hand, Connor was aware that the school received class-size-reduction funds automatically because Learning Tree was a public school.

Connor was unable to identify any other categorical monies that Learning Tree received, yet, according to district documents, the school was eligible to receive state-compensatory-education funds for the 1997–98 school year. Similarly, according to other district documents, the charter school did receive funds for both school improvement and economic impact aid for limited-English-proficient students during the 1996–97 school year and most likely continued to receive those funds as long as it enrolled students who were eligible for them. Beyond these limited categorical funds, neither documents nor interviews identified any other categorical funding for Learning Tree. Connor indicated that she hoped to hire a grant writer for the school so that someone could monitor the monies the school was receiving and those to which it was entitled.

With respect to the other potential source of revenue discussed above— locally collected tax revenue—Learning Tree's charter proposal and MOU with the district specifically indicated that the school was *not* entitled to revenue from the city's sales tax.

In terms of facilities, unlike the other start-up charter schools discussed in this chapter, Learning Tree was given a district-owned school facility that was not being used. Still, the facility was in need of significant repair when Learning Tree took it over. As one teacher put it, "This was a dilapidated building, completely a mess. We got it 6 weeks before school started and poured into it and painted it and put tile in it and did a lot of work on [it] just to open it up, so we were kind of like running out of breath."

Initially, Learning Tree paid for numerous repairs to the building in lieu of paying rent to the district. But by 1997–98 the school was paying approximately $27,000 a year in rent, with an anticipated 4% increase per year. The charter school continued to deduct repairs for the buildings from the rent, although the district would not pay for repairs to the portable classrooms the school had acquired to accommodate increased enrollment. Connor speculated that the reason the school was not allowed to deduct repairs from the rent of the portable classrooms was because they were new.

In terms of district oversight and services, Learning Tree was required to purchase a variety of services from the district. For the most part, these were services that someone in the district's administration had determined the school needed and thus billed the school for them. Among these services were business and legal services as well as insurance coverage to protect the district, the Board of Education, and the students. Connor said, "Yeah, and actually they just deducted from last month's payment about $2,000 for insurance, insurance of the board and student[s]. . . . It's like $1.50 or something per student, and then whatever the board fee was and some kind of business transaction—it's just automatically deducted." Meanwhile, Learning Tree continued to pay its own liability and workers' compensation insurance.

Finally, Learning Tree was required to pay, pursuant to its MOU, its share of the district's special education encroachment. But there was nothing in the school's budget that reflected that the school actually paid its portion of that cost. In fact, when all was said and done, Learning Tree paid only about $1,468 for these services and did not pay an additional administrative overhead fee back to the district. Thus, the total fee the school paid to the district did not even equal 1% of the total allocation to the school by the district.

In comparing Learning Tree's agreement with the district with that of Directions, we see in the MOUs that the two charter schools had very different relationships with the district. Thus, while Learning Tree received the district revenue limit, Directions' MOU set forth that the school "shall receive a base revenue limit funding that reflects [the district's] difference in per-pupil spending at different grade levels." When asked what this meant, Vista Unified's financial officer, Wolfe, said the school was receiving the greater funding for a high school in the district rather than the unified school district base revenue limit. According to Directions' principal, Morris, the school's base revenue limit was $3,568 per pupil for the 1997–98 school year. As mentioned above, this is the same number estimated by the district as its overall base revenue limit. Still, Morris said the school got a "fair amount extra"— between $200 and $300 per student—because it was a high school. Wolfe said that Directions received this elevated base revenue limit was because Morris had threatened to take the issue before the Vista Unified school board if Wolfe did not agree to the increase. Wolfe said, given the political support Directions had among school board members, he did not think he had any choice but to grant the charter school the increased base revenue limit.

Furthermore, unlike Learning Tree's MOU, the Memorandum between Directions and the school district set forth that the school was entitled to receive revenue from various state and federal sources. These included the California state lottery, state summer school funding, categorical block grants, class-size-reduction funds (if applicable), charter school funds, and any other appropriate or mutually agreeable sources of funding. Thus, the categorical funding the high school was entitled to, according to the California law, was clearly stated in the MOU between the high school and the school district.

Another difference between the two Vista Unified charter schools' MOUs is that Directions' Memorandum does not explicitly state that the school is *not* entitled to local bond, sales, or parcel tax revenue, although both Morris and Wolfe said that the school was not receiving those funds. As with Learning Tree, Directions was required to pay for a variety of services provided by the district, including additional insurance coverage, attendance reporting, business services, and legal services. Directions paid the district a total of $1,895 for most of these services, with the cost of additional insurance still to be determined at the time the MOU was signed. Directions was not required to pay an additional administrative overhead fee to the district. Morris said he hoped to stop paying for legal services provided by the district because his school had legal representation provided by his old law firm on a pro bono basis.

With respect to facilities, Directions High School was housed in a private university located in the district. The school paid the university about $25,000 a year for use of the facility. Through its partnership with the university, the charter school had space for its administrative offices and classrooms as well as access to the university's computer labs, auditoriums, and libraries.

Additionally, Directions' MOU, like that of Learning Tree, required the school to pay its share of the special education encroachment. Yet only Learning Tree was required to pay its pro rata share for a consent decree addressing previous segregation in the district. And finally, Directions' MOU spelled out the categorical programs through which the charter school received funding, whereas Connor of Learning Tree knew very little about what categorical funds she should have been receiving. Because the Learning Tree MOU was not clear on this issue, Conner had to rely on the various notices she received from the district. In this way, Directions' MOU clearly gave this charter high school advantages over Learning Tree.

One thing is obvious from the data: The level of political sophistication, knowledge, and connections varied greatly between the administrators of these two schools. While Connor came to her job as treasurer of the charter school the year before the 1997–98 school year, she was not formally trained in finance and had no other experience that would necessarily have prepared her for her job or negotiating with the district. Moreover, aside from a lack of knowledge about school funding generally and the provisions of the law specifically, Connor did not appear to have any political support in the district. Morris at Directions was in a very different position. Not only was he an attorney with a masters degree in education, but he had a very sophisticated group of people supporting him, including members of the Vista Unified Board of Education. This support was at least part of the reason why Wolfe agreed to provide the school with a higher base revenue limit. It was also Morris's experience, knowledge, and support network that helped him to more clearly describe in his MOU with the district which categorical funds the school would receive. All of these factors led to a much more comfortable and supportive public funding situation for Directions than for Learning Tree.

IMPLICATIONS, CONCLUSIONS, AND QUESTIONS

One finding clearly runs through the data: The political connections, savvy, and knowledge—or lack thereof—of a charter school administrator plays a central role in determining how much public funding a charter school receives. Given the varying levels of knowledge and understanding at the charter school level and the ambiguity of the state funding guidelines, it is not surprising that there was great variability in public funding received by the different charter schools in this sample. Also, in line with this finding is a report (SRI International, 1997) that found that the financial knowledge base of the school leader made a profound difference in the level of resources that an independent charter school received. In each of the four districts discussed in this chapter, the independent charter schools with administrators who had greater expertise regarding finance were receiving, or appeared to be receiving, more of the funding to which they were entitled by the funding legislation. In fact, savvy charter school administrators were able to use their knowledge and information, and in some cases political leverage, to negotiate for more than the other charter schools in their districts and than other charter schools in other districts. As one district administrator said, "What happens is political, I'm sure you understand what the outcome is, . . . you err on the side of the charter school." Policy makers concerned with equity in school funding should be interested in this issue because the application of the law is clearly creating inequitable funding across the state.

In addition, the data in this chapter also raise an important question regarding the financial viability of some charter schools that are unable to raise extra private resources to support their operations. Revenue limits are not sufficient for, nor intended to cover, facilities costs at non-charter schools (SRI International, 1997). In fact, school districts rely on a variety of sources, including bonds and developer fees, to cover facilities costs, and local sales tax to provide educational programs. For start-up charter schools, the lack of guaranteed start-up funds and the lack of money to pay for their facilities were very salient issues. In only one of the four districts discussed in this chapter, Madrona Unified School District, did the district provide charter schools any local revenue they raised. This lack of support was most noticeably damaging in Edgewood where it contributed to the uncertainty of the school's financial viability on a yearly basis. This sentiment also was reflected in the opinion of an official in Vista who felt that without the support of an outside private organization to provide facilities and facilities support—including state construction funds—independent charters were not financially viable. Similarly, as discussed above, Kent, co-director of the Academic Charter School, stated that his school could not operate at its current site without private funds. Documentation and implications of charter schools' increased reliance on private resources are the central focus of Chapter 5 of this book.

Yet, clearly this lack of public support for charter school facilities was experienced unevenly across the different sites. For instance, as Table 4.1 summarizes, the charter schools in this sample paid very different amounts of rent for very different facilities.

Thus, Community Charter School paid more than $60,000 a year for a dusty plot of land in an industrial park and the portable classrooms that constituted its "facility." In addition to this rent, the school had to install run-

Table 4.1. Facilities' Cost

Charter School	Cost of Facilities to Charter School
Community Charter School	$60,000 plus
Academic Charter School	$1 a month
Wilson Elementary School	$57,000 a month
Learning Tree Elementary School	$27,000 minus cost of improvements
Directions High School	$25,000

ning water and a sidewalk to keep students out of the mud when it rained. Community had to pay for its rent out of its base revenue limit and categorical funding. This contributed to the school's inability to purchase new instructional materials and pay teachers' salaries that were competitive with the district. On the other hand, Academic Charter School paid virtually no rent for a facility that was valued at more than $5 million. Relieved of the burden of paying rent each month while receiving federal, state, and local funding, and able to raise a lot of private funding from wealthy benefactors and corporations, Academic could purchase virtually any instructional materials the teachers desired and paid salaries that were competitive with the district.

In addition to the financial strains that the charter schools themselves experience, another question that still must be addressed is whether charter schools pose a financial risk or raise equity concerns for the school districts in which they exist. Charter schools are required by law to be so-called "revenue neutral." In other words, in theory, they are not to cause an increase in revenue required by the district to operate them. Despite this legislative criterion, one district administrator raised the concern that charter schools present an economic drain to the school district. He argued that charter schools increase the number of teachers in a district without necessarily increasing the total revenue limit generated by the students in that district. In other words, the same number of students enrolled in a district are spread across a larger number of schools and classrooms, which means the same district budget must pay for a larger number of teachers. Presently there are too few charter schools, start-up charter schools more specifically, to be able to see whether they are causing a financial drain on their sponsor districts. But to the extent that the total number of charter schools continues to increase, this concern becomes more palpable.

Thus, there are a whole host of important issues and concerns related to the public funding of charter schools that policy makers, district officials, and charter school operators need to consider—not only in California, but across the country. As other chapters in this book illustrate, despite any seemingly straightforward or rational language in the charter school law, the daily experiences of people working in and around this reform are quite varied. To the extent that these variations are in part dependent on the political context of a given school district and the knowledge and political connections of charter school administrators, we need to consider the long-term implications of this policy on the ideal of equal educational opportunities.

NOTE

1. As noted in Chapter 2, Vista Unified did not renew the charter of what had been the fourth charter school in the district.

REFERENCES

Management Advisory 93-10, California Department of Education, December 21, 1993.

Premack, E. (1997). *California charter school revenues: A guide for charter schools and sponsor districts.* Sacramento, CA: Author.

Slayton, J. M. (1999). *School funding in the context of charter school reform: Legislation versus implementation.* Unpublished doctoral dissertation, University of California at Los Angeles.

SRI International. (1997). *Evaluation of charter school effectiveness.* Menlo Park, CA: Author.

CHAPTER 5

Public Schools, Private Resources

The Role of Social Networks in California Charter School Reform

JANELLE SCOTT and JENNIFER JELLISON HOLME

In Chapter 4, Slayton demonstrated that charter schools receive various levels of public funding from their districts due to several factors, including the ambiguity of California's charter school legislation and the knowledge and expertise of the charter school principals. Whatever level the charter school's public funding may be, it is generally insufficient to completely support this reform, especially within new, "start-up" charter schools. Thus, in this chapter, we look at charter schools' need to supplement their public funding with private resources. Specifically, we discuss the strategies employed by start-up charter schools—those that are newly created, as opposed to converted public schools—to accumulate and sustain private resources. Using these strategies as lenses, we see that charter schools in different social contexts are unable to accumulate the same levels of private support despite their common need to do so. In other words, there appears to be a strong relationship between the geographic, political, economic, racial, and educational environments within and around these start-up charter schools and their ability to raise the private resources they need.

We argue that this relationship exists because the processes charter schools use to garner private resources are circumscribed by the social status and the social networks of their local school communities. In fact, we contend that the high-status networks—personal and professional connections to people with money and political power—are even more critical to private-resource accumulation than the particular strategies used to acquire resources. Thus, understanding the social context of the schools is critical to understanding why the same processes or strategies of private-resource accumulation net such disparate results for different charter schools. More specifically, we see vast, disturbing inequities emerging within and across charter school reform—inequities that mirror the wealth and poverty of the communities that house these schools. We conclude that policy makers should attend to these inequities by targeting start-up funds and technical assistance to charter schools in low-income communities. In the absence of such government efforts to further support charter schools in poor neighborhoods, we argue that some (perhaps many) charter schools in low-income communities will be forced to partner with private, for-profit or non-profit educational management organizations (EMOs) because of the financial support these groups offer. More will be said about this in the conclusion of this chapter.

The following three questions framed the inquiry for this chapter:

1. By what processes do start-up charter schools secure private resources?
2. Which schools are most successful in generating private support and why?
3. What are the implications of the varying levels of private support for educational inequality?

In an effort to answer these questions, we examined data from the larger UCLA Chater School Study and found that several strategies were used across these sites. We then used these strategies in analyzing data from six start-up charter schools located in four urban and one suburban school district in California. As we will discuss in greater detail, these strategies include having aggressive school administrators; selecting high-status, wealthy, and influential school governance council members; forming partnerships with corporations, universities, or law firms; grant writing and fund raising from various private sources; and drawing from various in-kind resources, such as parent volunteers.

We focus on these strategies to demonstrate that private resources are not limited to monetary sums, but also can include more subtle forms of support that are difficult to quantify. Furthermore, these strategies are not mutually exclusive; in fact, they are sometimes complementary and overlapping. Nor are they unique to charter schools; many non-profit organizations also employ them. What is noteworthy, however, is how the very same strategies taken on with similar determination, energy, and commitment in the context of public charter schools can yield such divergent results.

STARTING A NEW CHARTER SCHOOL

As other chapters in this book point out, charter schools are allowed to operate as fiscally "independent" entities or remain more "dependent" on their district for administrative resources or services. Start-up charter schools, which are often fiscally independent, rarely receive facilities or capital expenses from their districts. These independent start-up charter schools in California and elsewhere generally pay for their rent or mortgage out of their daily operating budgets.

So-called conversion charter schools, or those that convert from existing public schools, generally remain more dependent on their sponsoring districts and thus face fewer resource-related difficulties. We know, for example, that conversion charter schools usually continue to operate in the same buildings for little or no rent, maintain most of the same staff, and utilize district services such as food, transportation, and payroll (UCLA Charter School Study, 1998).

Thus, one of the most formidable challenges to starting and maintaining a new, start-up charter school is securing adequate resources (Corwin & Flaherty, 1995; RPP International, 2000). Given these fiscal challenges to starting charters, it becomes important to understand how start-up charter schools manage to surmount them. In this chapter we focus on *how* the schools secure private resources and *why* different schools have access to different resources. In order to do this, we examine charter schools in their social, economic, and political contexts. We argue that these contexts circumscribe the networks available to charter schools, and the forms of capital—economic, social, or political—upon which they can draw in their efforts to make their schools successful.

NETWORKS: THE TIES THAT BIND

As we examined the strategies start-up charter schools used to acquire resources and tried to make sense of why the same processes led to such widely different results across schools, we turned to social network theorists. In contrast to those who see individual actions removed from social relations, network theorists examine the more dynamic ways in which people both shape and are shaped by their social networks. For example, Granovetter (1985) writes:

> Actors do not behave or decide as atoms outside a social context, nor do they adhere slavishly to a script written for them by the particular intersection of social categories that they happen to occupy. Their attempts at purposive action are instead embedded in concrete, ongoing systems of social relations. (p. 487)

This understanding of actors enables us to examine the ways in which charter school educators' actions are embedded in social relations, including the wealth or poverty of their local communities.

To acquire and sustain the private resources they need to survive, many charter school communities draw from social networks. To understand how people network, Granovetter (1973) discussed the concept of "strong" and "weak" social ties. Strong ties are those that an individual has to family and close friends. Weak ties are more distant connections to co-workers, business associates, or other peers from school. Granovetter (1983) suggests people use weak ties as bridges between strongly tied social groups. Weak ties, then, can connect groups made up of strong ties, further strengthening individual access to information, relationships, and other resources. Individuals who rely only on strong ties may be more isolated socially, disconnected from opportunities for mobility or expanding their experience. This reliance solely on strong ties is particularly problematic for poor and politically disempowered people whose family and friends are also mostly poor and disempowered. On the other hand, Granovetter (1983) notes that weak ties tend to be particularly important to the social mobility of poor people. He writes: "Weak ties provide people with access to information and resources beyond those available in their own social circle; but strong ties have greater motivation to be of more assistance and are typically more available" (p. 209). Thus, the potential impact of weak ties on poor people's lives and opportunities for mobility is quite large.

We found in our examination of start-up charters that the social location of such schools determines the types of ties that envelop them. For example, schools located in high-status communities have strong and weak ties to many resources, and are therefore able to tap easily into financial, social, and economic capital in their community, as we will demonstrate later. Yet the strong ties, or social networks, of schools located in poorer areas and serving poorer students, fail to link such schools with similar resources, in part because they are not available in the immediate community. Therefore, we find these schools must expend comparatively more effort using what weak ties, or more distant connections, they have, to obtain the resources they require. For instance, we found that generally charter schools in poor neighborhoods either were supported by wealthy, private individuals or organizations from outside the nearby community or simply got by with less.

As noted, one of the most important functions of social networks is the way in which they connect individuals or institutions to resources. According to Pierre Bourdieu (1986), two of the most important types of such resources are economic capital (financial resources) and cultural capital (high-status knowledge). Possession of these two types of capital, Bourdieu argues, enables individuals, families, or groups to maintain or increase their power in society

(Swartz, 1997). Bourdieu maintains, however, that these forms of capital are not merely to be held, but are strategically used and "cashed in" by individuals or groups seeking to improve their social standing (Bourdieu & Wacquant, 1992; Lareau, 1989).

In relation to Granovetter's theory of social networks, it is useful to consider the differences between high- and low-status communities in the possession of cultural and economic capital, and the ways in which strong or weak social ties grant access to these types of capital. A consideration of these disparities in access to cultural and economic capital across communities is particularly important in the United States where a long history of segregation and discrimination in both housing and education resulted in significantly greater degrees of economic capital (wealth) and cultural capital (educational attainment) for White families than for families of color (Oliver & Shapiro, 1997). These disparities in capital, furthermore, have multiplied over time, as economic and cultural capital provide access to one another (Bourdieu, 1977).

Charter school reform has been laid down upon this highly unequal economic and social landscape; as such, differences in charter founders' and operators' social networks, which grant access to important resources, must be considered when analyzing start-up charter schools' resource needs and strategies for garnering these resources. As we will show, founders and operators of start-up charter schools located in high-status communities generally have many close connections (or strong ties) to individuals in those communities who possess a tremendous amount of resources that they may grant to the charter school. However, founders and operators of charter schools located in economically impoverished communities rarely possess these strong ties to well-resourced individuals or institutions; rather, they must use their weak ties (i.e., distant acquaintances) or in fact forge ties (i.e., by approaching businesspeople or foundations) in order to tap into resources far outside their communities to individuals or organizations that may have drastically different educational or organizational visions for the schools.

Educational policy makers and researchers rarely mention these disparities across charter schools. Yet, we believe it is important to illuminate ways in which pre-existing inequalities across communities, and unequal access to resource-rich social networks within these communities, have been magnified by charter school reform.

OUR SAMPLE OF START-UP CHARTER SCHOOLS

In this chapter, we analyze data from six of the nine start-up charter schools in the UCLA Charter School Study. The three start-up schools from the larger sample that were excluded from the analysis were combinations of home-schooling and independent study programs. None of these required a large building with classrooms and seats for all their students, full-time teachers to staff each class, or the furniture and supplies of a regular school. The resource needs of the other six start-up charter schools were clearly much greater—particularly in the area of capital expenses. Examining these six start-up charter schools, therefore, allows us to document the ways in which such schools meet their tremendous resource needs.

Despite their similarities, the six schools were different from each other in many regards—in particular, their social locations and the students they served. For instance, these six schools were located in communities that ranged from affluent to very poor. The schools also differed in the length of time they had been in operation. All were within their first 5 years of operation, but some had been open for several years while others were relatively new. We recognize that newer schools may have different resource issues and concerns than schools that have been able to work through them over time. We are confident, however, that the open-ended, semistructured interviews utilized in this study allowed the respondents to reflect upon their experiences and that temporal differences emerged from the data. Wherever possible, we have drawn from interviews of stakeholders with comparable roles at their respective schools, namely, principals, founders, governing board members, donors, and volunteers.

The following brief descriptions of each of the six start-up charter schools in our sample provide a sense of the local contexts in which these schools were founded and the social networks that envelope them. One of these schools was introduced in Chapter 3, and three of them were discussed in Chapter 4.

Foundation Elementary Charter School. As described in Chapter 3, this start-up, independent school served a low-income and working-class population within the large, diverse, and urban Mission Unified School District. The charter school's partnership with a private educational management organization (EMO) played a large role in shaping its curricular and instructional philosophy while also providing administrative support and resources, including locating and renovating the building in which the school was housed. The staff described the school as having attentive teachers, small class sizes, and challenging curriculum.

Academic Charter School. As introduced in Chapter 4, Academic was a charter elementary school in an impoverished neighborhood in a large urban school district—Madrona Unified—serving mostly low-income students of color. Academic Charter also managed to attract substantial corporate and foundation support, including the donation of an industrial building complex in the community, for which it paid basically no rent. In addition, Academic raised more than a million dollars in direct financial donations, mostly from corporations and wealthy individuals. The school's leaders also forged partnerships with local universities and a national school reform movement, through which they received in-kind support for their school.

Community Charter School. Also a focus of Chapter 4, Community Charter School was located in a poor, urban school district—Edgewood Unified School District—that served mostly students of color. The founders of this middle school envisioned serving students who supposedly got lost in the district's large middle schools, schools they described as being violent and impersonal. The charter school had a rocky start in its first 4 years, facing facilities challenges, high staff turnover, and lack of resources. Community basically consisted of bungalows—or portable classrooms—in an empty lot in an industrial park, surrounded by anonymous warehouses.

Directions High School. Described in Chapter 4, this urban charter school served an ethnically diverse student body, although it had more White students than most schools in the Vista Unified School District. Still, there was not a clear majority of any one racial group among the students. Directions boasted an impressive array of supporters, from district officials to major corporations, as well as the benefits of several private partnerships. This support enabled the school to secure a building location in a private university. They expended little for capital costs, with the exception of the $25,000 annual rent for use of the building.

Shoreline Charter School. This elementary charter school was located in a wealthy suburban community and, like most other schools in the suburban Shoreline district, served mostly White middle- and upper-middle-class students. The school was started with the involvement and support of leaders from the school district, and it was one of the first charter schools in the state, approved and opened when no start-up funding was available. Yet, as we will describe later, the school has received substantial financial and in-kind support from the professional connections of its parents and corporations in the surrounding community.

Heritage Charter School. This was a very small school, serving approximately 60 students, with two full-time teachers. Heritage enrolled students of color from a different racial/ethnic group than those in Community, although, like Community, this middle school—also in the Edgewood Unified School District—arose out of some community members' concerns about a perceived lack of responsiveness by the district toward their children. There had been significant financial difficulties at the school, even though it enjoyed the support of a community group. Still, the building the school rented was in poor condition, needing repairs, particularly heating and plumbing, which failed from time to time. According to the lease on this building, Heritage was responsible for all maintenance. Thus, when plumbing or heating problems occurred, the educators at the school had to try to fix them or pay for someone else to. Given this responsibility, the rent they paid for the space seemed exorbitant.

EXAMINING STRATEGIES FOR ACQUIRING RESOURCES: THE USE OF NETWORKS

In the course of the UCLA Charter School Study, we learned that starting and operating a charter school demands a substantial amount of economic, social, and political resources. Consistent with the framework discussed in the first part of the chapter, we also learned that the nature and amount of resources were correlated with the social location of the charter school. In other words, charter schools in high-status and wealthy communities had an easier time garnering the resources they needed. Yet, the charter schools' success in getting these resources was also dependent on the status and wealth of their "acquaintances and networks," which were generally related to their social location but, as we will see, were not completely predetermined by it. In other words, our analysis shows that even in relatively low-income communities, charter schools can be well connected—that is, some of them have wealthy donors and are partnered with affluent and high-status institutions. But what is also apparent from our analysis is that these low-income schools are so much more dependent for their survival on people and institutions with whom they have very weak ties. And in instances where those ties do not exist, the poor schools are even poorer.

Despite the differences in status, location, and wealth of the charter schools, we found that all six of them used remarkably similar strategies in their efforts to acquire resources. We now turn to a detailed discussion of these strategies, using examples from schools where particular strategies were most salient. It is also important to remember that these strategies were not mutually exclusive, and the charter schools often employed all or combinations of them at any given time.

School Leadership

In a finding that overlaps with the issues discussed in Chapter 4, we learned that in three of the six start-up charter schools discussed in this chapter, the principals used their personal and professional connections to garner private financial and in-kind resources for their schools. These leaders generally wrote the charter proposals, hired the staff, and rounded up the resources required for the charter's opening, while garnering the help of key educators, community members, and donors to ensure the charter's continued success. These leaders invested a tremendous amount of time and effort into networking for their schools, while often expressing frustration that the time spent on fund raising could be better spent at the school site itself, working on curriculum, instruction, or meeting with constituents.

While no one involved in school reform could doubt the enormous degree of creativity, persistence, and determination involved in starting a charter school, the acquisition of resources—one of the most difficult tasks in starting a charter school—requires more than these personality traits. Rather, a leader's ability to garner critical financial support is often dependent on his or her connections to individuals who have resources or who know where to find them.

In two of the start-up charter schools discussed in this chapter—Heritage and Community—we found that this type of leadership was conspicuously absent; these were the same start-up charter schools that experienced serious problems in leadership turnover, both losing two principals in the first several years of operations. Not surprisingly, these two charter schools—both serving low-income communities—had some of the most serious troubles in garnering resources. In one start-up charter school, Foundation, the leadership issue was less significant, because the school had partnered with an EMO, and thus the charter's financial survival was less dependent on the networks of the school's leader. In this section, we discuss the leadership at Directions, Academic, and Shoreline charter schools.

Ken Morris, the founder of Directions High School, who was introduced in Chapter 4, was from an affluent and influential background and was a lawyer by training. He was forthright about the relationship between his personal background and his ability to get his school off the ground: "I mean, I'm able to bring certain connections to the table, I come from a relatively privileged background, and the whole legal, and the whole business connection has enabled us just to take the time to get the whole community connection." Yet even this relatively privileged educator recognized the limitations under which many start-up charter schools operate. He said, "I need to be spending time talking to families and teachers and parents, not raising money. And to me it's short-sighted to expect schools to be high quality if you don't give them the resources to plan." In addition, like many urban school districts, officials in his sponsoring district expressed concern about charter schools serving all students, particularly poor and minority students who had been the least well-served. With some irony, Morris noted that this caveat placed restrictions on the number of charter schools starting up that would be able to do so.

The district—their approach is good because it makes sure that any charter schools that you start in the city are committed to the students who need it most. But the downside is, it's very hard to do so, and if I had been less privileged, I'm not sure I would have been able to do so. It took every ounce of energy . . . every ounce of energy that I have, and connections, and everything else. And maybe you don't need to do all the things we're doing, and all the partnerships and everything, but we think it's worth it, and I think it's tough.

In contrast to charter schools that struggle on a daily basis to meet basic educational expenses such as teacher salaries, instructional materials, and rent, Morris noted of his charter school, Directions: "In some ways it's almost . . . we have so many . . . so many resources. It's hard to know what to do. . . . And so we make sure that we don't do too many projects."

As discussed in Chapter 4, Academic Charter School had two co-directors, Scott Kent and Whitney Jefferson, who together founded the school, wrote the charter, and located the funding required to get the school running. In the beginning, neither of these former elementary school teachers had any personal networks with foundations or corporations. Instead, they canvased the low-income neighborhood in which they were hoping to start the school for resources. Through these initial efforts they secured the donation of a community center to house the school.

In addition to the acquisition of this temporary facility, Academic's co-directors also needed $200,000 in start-up funds to prove to the school district that they could get the charter off the ground. Initially, the directors successfully secured a large grant from a national corporation. As Jefferson observed, the initial grant evolved into an ongoing commitment from the bank to the school, enabling the school to secure both monetary resources and financial expertise from the corporation's executive ranks.

We actually have one of their vice presidents serving on our board of trustees. Another way in which a traditional school won't be able to pull in people, these power-hitters . . . to serve on their board of governors to help direct fiscally and legally their organization. So we get to draw on all these private resources from a local school-type basis.

While both co-directors taught at the school initially, as the school grew they transitioned to strictly administrative roles, making the school very administrator-heavy, with a far higher administrator/teacher ratio (2:6) than most small schools have. However, Jefferson noted that he spent at least half his time fund raising and promoting the school, rather than performing more traditional principal roles. Jefferson's constant efforts at fund raising were crucial to the school's survival. As he noted, "We've been real fortunate to be able to have found the money thus far. But you know, this is a finite opportunity . . . we're not gonna always be able to find the money."

Shoreline Charter School was unusual because it was started by a business-savvy superintendent, Stuart Damon, and members of his school board. Damon brought the charter idea to his district, arguing that it would provide a vehicle to draw in students—and their funds—from outside the district, as well as provide a site where innovative instructional practices could develop. Thus, Damon was central in writing the charter, getting it approved, and securing funding for the charter through grants from local foundations. He already had powerful social networks in his local community, with legislators in Sacramento, as well as within the educational profession. Over time, however, this leader became less central in ensuring the financial success of the charter, as wealthy parents and community members took over the school's fund raising and resource gathering once the school was in operation.

As demonstrated in Chapter 4, savvy and well-connected leaders are critical to the ability of charter schools to obtain the public funds they need. It appears this same finding is true with private resources as well.

Governing Board Membership: Selection and Composition

Every charter school is required to set forth in its chartering application the structure of its governance (see Chapter 3). We found that regardless of social location or stated intentions, most charter schools selected individuals for their governing boards because of the connections, expertise, or resources these people could bring to the school. In this section we describe the process by which Directions, Heritage, Community, and Shoreline charter schools created their governing boards.

At Directions High School, the school's founder and principal, Ken Morris, selected the governing board members prior to the approval of the charter by the school district. On the board were leaders from the business, legal, political, and educational communities, many of whom were his former legal colleagues or other acquaintances. He commented on the value of his board member choices: "Basically, whenever we have an issue that relates to their area, we call them and get them involved. We will have quarterly meetings . . . it's really more whatever issues each of them represent, we use them for their expertise."

The board was responsible for school policies, school budget, resource solicitation from potential donors, and monitoring school personnel. For instance, members of the governing board with business backgrounds assisted with the school's application for non-profit corporation status. This application process can be quite lengthy and involved. In this respect, Directions Charter School was fortunate to have legal experts on its board.

Shoreline Charter School employed a rather unique process to select its original board members from a larger group of the school's founders. Because there were a limited number of slots on the governing board and many members of the founders' group were interested, all who wanted to be on the board sat in a circle and deliberated until enough people volunteered to step down. According to founders' group members we interviewed, this process of selection ensured that the people with the most to offer in terms of expertise, resources, and connections were put on the board, because those less valued were not encouraged to stay in the circle.

In the end, Shoreline Charter School's governing board members included a physician, a successful entrepreneur, and the spouse of a school district board member. One governing board member described the school's motivation for weeding through prospective board members.

> We want people who have some education background. We want people who have some business background in terms of knowing how to run an organization that has a budget. People with some political skills. . . . So we want people who can represent various constituencies but who can represent them and bring some special skills or relationships or background.

In fact, we heard from several people connected to Shoreline Charter School about the benefits of choosing the board members based on their connections. For instance, one parent talked about the characteristics of the board members in this way:

> And there are people who were, who were recruited, who were commandeered, really, people wanted them. There was a doctor, a medical researcher, a Ph.D. scientist. There's some consultant to Fortune 500 companies who's a parent, who's still got a child in the charter, who's on there. That's what's amazing is how the quality of a group like that attracts other quality people and there's a natural evolution and a transfer of power.

The connections that the governing board members brought to the school helped the school secure not only management expertise but also ties to the businesses in which the board members worked.

At Community Charter School, governing board members were selected in similar ways, yet the selection process did not result in a board that was as well connected. The board comprised parents, members from community-based organizations, teachers, and the principal. There were significant struggles over what exactly the functions of the governing board would be. In fact, it was not clear during the time that we studied the school what the board actually did. For example, the governing board was supposed to select and evaluate the principal each year, but according to one teacher who was on the board, "I'm not sure if they are going to set up another committee to evaluate the principal, I'm not really clear on that. We've never had to do that, so, it will be an experience." She noted that due to high staff turnover at the school, only two staff members remained who had been at the school since the beginning. "So a lot of committees do change, in terms of governance, because the board changes. And because teachers also leave, then that changes."

Thus, Community's governance structure was still emerging, and we spoke with at least one parent who thought that there was a lack of parental participation in policy matters. The principal, Darla Henderson, acknowledged the lack of clarity about the governing board's function and scope. She said, "The charter document was kind of vague in terms of the governance structure and so forth. There are different perceptions about who's making what decisions and about what the priorities of the school are or should be."

Yet, as Community struggled to garner more resources, the staff began to think about a more strategic selection process for governing board members. As one teacher noted:

> We're learning better to pull in community people as board members and advisors to help us with those other [areas of] expertise that you can't expect in any one key [person], even. So I feel we have matured. And this is our fourth year, and we're looking outward to pull in that kind of help. I think, we seem to all of us, [to be using] our connections in a way to pull in people who can contribute to the school, to be a resource to the school, to the educational area or provide in-kind contributions, hopefully in the fund-raising area.

Although the charter proposal for the Heritage Charter School stated that its governing board would be elected, the board was a selected group. Many came from the community the school served, but none at the time we visited were parents with students in the charter school. Furthermore, it was not clear to what extent parents were involved in the school at all. According to the principal, Henry Losoya, the board's task was to establish school policy while he administered the day-to-day operations. He explained the lack of parental participation on the board, noting:

> For the most part the everyday parent knows what's good for the child but . . . they don't understand a certain procedure or manner or how

to run a school. You can't run a school haphazardly; it can't be done. So that could be one of the problems if parents don't have an educational background nor the experience in school.

Yet we know that parents wanted to be more involved in the school. For instance, one parent we interviewed said she was disturbed by the composition of the board. She said the board often met at times when most parents could not attend and that many of the parents felt left out of the decisions made by the teachers and the board members. She lamented, "We were all parents with full-time jobs, none of us could have become a board member in the fashion that they were and do as much work. We just wanted to be included." She told us that at one point, tensions became so serious that she asked a mediator to come in to help negotiate between the parents and the board. After attending one session, however, no board members came to any follow-up meetings. She explained that the entire board, which "sort of seated themselves," was made up of people from the community who were educated, but, "my personal feeling is, I don't think you should have a board with just educators because, you know, then you get a perspective that's very slanted and not diverse."

Furthermore, despite the attempt by those who founded the Heritage Charter School to select a governing board composed of the best educated members of their community—a strategy that other charter schools in high-status communities employed—this did not enable Heritage to become a fiscally secure school with ample resources. In other words, the school's strong community ties did not connect it to other groups that could provide support.

At least one district official we spoke with doubted whether the school would survive without the assistance of wealthy individuals. Principal Losoya said he was aware of the school's precarious position, yet he believed that the school would produce private resources from within the community and become self-sufficient. He commented, "There may be some who don't have that access or the contacts or the people . . . someday, maybe, we can have our own basic foundation for ourselves."

Academic Charter School had several governing committees and a board of trustees. The role of the board of trustees was to ensure that the school was managed well, especially from fiscal and legal perspectives. The board of trustees also assisted with fund-raising efforts. While there were parents and teachers on other committees, only one parent and one teacher served on the board of trustees. In fact, most of the board members were high-level executives in corporations or other high-status institutions.

One of Academic's co-directors, Jefferson, said that the ability to govern the school without district interference was liberating. He observed that traditional schools would have trouble establishing a board of directors to whom they could turn over business matters if they were connected to a school district. Yet with a charter school, he said, he was able to bring in "these power-hitters. . . . So we get to draw on all these private resources from a local school-type basis. . . . We make a decision . . . it's implemented that next day."

Foundation Elementary Charter School had a governing board with no teachers or administrators and only one parent. The governing board, which was the main policy-making body at the school, comprised mostly representatives from the educational management organization and other high-status institutions. Board members were appointed by leaders of either the EMO or the church that housed the school. Foundation's principal, Shane Damian, noted that the head of the EMO was the governing board member in charge of community and business partnerships. A governing board member, who was the representative from a nearby college, was in charge of the educational arena, that is, the curriculum, according to Damian, to "really keep us in line, academically, you know." Thus, although the school appeared to have strong community support, with parents expressing their satisfaction, there was little school community presence on the board.

Partnerships

In some cases, charter schools sought out partnerships with universities, corporations, educational management organizations, or other institutions. Often various members of these school communities utilized both strong and weak ties, as well as their own social capital, to make these connections. In other cases, particularly when the schools lacked high-status ties, the partnering organizations sought out the charter schools. Thus, we learned that all six of the charter schools formed formal and informal partnerships with foundations or other organizations. While some of these schools formed durable partnerships that proved fruitful in terms of resource acquisition, other schools flailed about, searching desperately for a connection that would stabilize the school.

As we noted, Morris, the lawyer and principal and founder of Directions High School, established a partnership with a nearby university, through which the school received its very well-equipped facility. Morris noted that the school received certain resources by being located in the university. For instance, he noted, "It's like you have student services, you have facilities that have natural collaborations . . . that enable you to do things districts never do. Aside from the fact [that] we're in a beautiful building."

The legal counsel for the school, a firm to which the founder is connected personally, also handled negotiations with the school district, fighting for what they argued was a fair revenue limit for the school (see Chapter 4). The founder planned to use this resource to appeal to the school board for additional monies.

As discussed in Chapter 3, the charter proposal for Foundation Elementary Charter School actually was written by the non-profit educational management organization, which sought out this particular community as a place to start a new charter school. This EMO brought support to the school on all levels: it paid for renovations to the building, it hired and evaluated staff, and it supplemented state funding for various educational expenses. Thus, although there appeared to be little participation in school governance on the part of teachers, administrators, or parents, it was unlikely that this school could even exist without the partnership with the EMO because the community served by the school had limited resources. The trade-off appeared to be community control for existence.

In part, the partnerships Academic Charter School formed were also the result of the school being selected by wealthy patrons, corporate sponsors, and a university. While the school's founders and co-directors initially sought support and partnerships, over time their initial connections led to additional partnerships. For instance, through its early partnerships, the school received curriculum support, its large campus, and substantial media attention. This media attention, in turn, fostered the interest of donors, further assisting the school in resource accumulation. In addition, the school was part of a national reform movement, which brought curriculum support to the school.

Jefferson said that part of the reason Academic attracted so much attention and support from wealthy patrons was the novelty of charter school reform. For example, he explained, "I have seen more people that are interested from other organizations and from institutes of higher education . . . in my first year of charter than in the 4 years that I was at my traditional school. Charter schools are given a lot more attention." As the only start-up charter school in a district where most of the other, so-called "converted" charter schools were located in wealthy communities, Academic Charter School became even more of a novelty.

The school was selected by a group of well-connected, wealthy individuals who decided they wanted to offer support to an inner-city school engaged in reform. The businessperson who donated the building to the school said his desire to improve public education emanated from his frustration with what he saw as the large, unresponsive public school system and the proliferation of private schools in this country. He sparked a collaboration among a group of powerful associates, and they decided to support the charter school.

This collaborative, made up of members of prestigious institutions, several corporate sponsors, as well as members of the entertainment industry, donated huge amounts of resources to the school. As indicated in Chapter 4, during the 1997–98 school year, 40% of Academic Charter School's total revenue came from private donations. Several members from the collaboration currently serve on the board of trustees as well.

As a result, the school received a new building, valued at several million dollars, for free. And, according to the businessperson who donated the building, more resources were to follow. He explained, "The seed gift amounted to $10 million . . . and we need about $50 million because we've got 200,000 square feet of buildings there." He planned to help the school convert some of the space into a gymnasium and expand to become a K–12 school.

The donor's collaborative established a non-profit foundation housed at a local university, to which the building was donated. As was pointed out in Chapter 4, the charter paid the foundation a nominal rent per year for it. Therefore, the school did not own the building, which meant it avoided some of the maintenance and liability costs associated with ownership. Gifts to the school also were filtered through this foundation.

Meanwhile, parents of Academic students were required to donate 3 hours of volunteer work a month to the school, but the parents did not provide the school with the types of monetary or material resources that the schools partners provided.

While most schools in our sample had some degree of parental participation, this participation yielded different results. Parental volunteerism on the part of high-status parents, such as those at Shoreline, connected the school even more to resources in the business community. Working-class and poor parents, however, did not have access to these communities and thus contributed more hands-on work—for example, cleaning and maintenance or classroom assistance—to Academic, Heritage, and Community charter schools. It was these schools that were much more reliant on partnerships with larger institutions and outside donors for survival. In the next section, we examine the use of fund raisers and grant writing.

Grant Writing and Fund Raising

Efforts were made by several schools to generate funds through grants or fund raising. We found that while some schools received substantial supplementary funds through these efforts, others were less well-endowed. In particular, we learned a great deal about these activities at Directions, Foundation, Shoreline, Heritage, and Academic charter schools.

At Directions, the charter school's partnership with a private university brought it many of the resources it needed. As noted, the main benefit of the partnership was the school's facility. In addition, a new building was being renovated for the school to use. While most charter schools would have to cover these capital costs themselves, Directions' principal noted, "It's also nice that we don't really have to fund raise to do it. The [university] is doing it."

Similarly, Foundation Elementary Charter School benefited from the resources it received from its partnership with an EMO, especially in the area of capital improvements. Thus, leadership at this school did not yet feel the need to write grant proposals. For instance, the principal said, "We don't have the private grants and things we want yet. [The EMO] is funding the initial start-up for us right now."

Shoreline Charter School, on the other hand, utilized parents—most of whom were highly educated and possessed a great deal of social capital—for important tasks such as grant writing. These grant-writing parents were quite successful. In fact, the grants the school secured provided everything from business services to technology. For example, a governing board member was employed by a prestigious computer corporation that made computer hardware available to schools through a competitive grant process. This particular governing board member evaluated the grant proposals for this program. In fact, he noted that he actually "put together" the team of people at the company who reviewed the proposals. And while he removed himself from the evaluation of the charter school's application, his insider status certainly did not hurt the charter school's chances. Not surprisingly, Shoreline Charter School did receive one of these grants, which paid for many of the school's computers.

Indeed, Shoreline Charter School's impressive array of computer hardware, software, and technical support was testimony to this governing board member's facilitation. According to a district administrator, the charter school had more resources than traditional schools in the district, perhaps more than they needed. She commented, "They definitely have a lot more equipment than our regular schools do . . . computers, they're networked. It's gotten to the point now that the donations are not helpful at all. Their equipment is so new, and most of the donated things can't even be used."

In addition to the strong ties that the Shoreline Charter School parents possessed, the school was intimately connected with the district, which also helped in the area of grant writing and fund raising. Several people who were involved in the school were also well connected to—and sometimes married to—people in the district administration or the school board. The Shoreline superintendent and a district school board member collaborated to write the charter proposal. They also secured grants in excess of $100,000 to help start the school. Interestingly enough, a school board member observed that the charter school improved the overall image of the district to potential donors. She said that the charter school was the reason "we got the attention of the business community." She added that some district-wide grants had come in "because the charter was . . . a trusted commodity by grantors." She said that the district as a whole was seen as a "quality district," and the charter had become further evidence of that to the outside community.

Meanwhile, impoverished Heritage Charter School was in desperate need of the resources grants and fund raisers could bring. Yet the school had limited success in this area. This charter school was started by a founders' group, some of whom were connected via a community-based organization. Indeed, several individuals from this founders' group were actively involved in the school. One, in particular, took a leave from her job for several months to serve as the school's principal when it needed one unexpectedly.

The founders' group, which was funded in part through support from the community-based organization, in turn helped to launch the charter. One founder noted, "In one way we were more fortunate than other groups trying to start charter schools. We had resources in the beginning . . . a $25,000 start-up . . . [to] buy our copier, buy our fax . . . coffee maker."

Although the school was indeed fortunate to receive the start-up money, by its second year of operation it faced severe financial difficulty. Due to an error in record keeping, it was found to owe the district close to $70,000 mistakenly received when the school overestimated its student enrollment. The school, however, did not have anyone with either the time or the business acumen needed to handle financial affairs. It contracted out with a private financial manager, but one district official argued that this contractor overcharged the charter school for the services.

Despite these hardships, Losoya, Heritage's principal, was optimistic about the possibilities.

> But with charter schools we can . . . get grants and we can go to
> private foundations and businesses and we can solicit for money.
> We can get entrepreneurship. You know, to increase the level of
> funding . . . , for example, if . . . [the school] was getting, let's say,
> $3,500 per child from the district. If that's all we had, we could do
> education at a bare minimum. . . . Just the basics. The bare bones. . . .
> But if you go beyond that, we can get grants, donations, foundations,
> etc. . . . And once we get that in we can determine what the students
> need in order to achieve their potential.

Yet even as he was optimistic, he remained cognizant of the school community's lack of available networks. He noted: "You've gotta have people. You've gotta have a goal. You've gotta have a mission. You have to have community and state support. You have to have all of that. . . . People. Resources. Things we don't have right now."

In fact, his role as school principal was multifaceted by necessity. During one of our visits, he had to climb through the heating ducts in an effort to repair a broken heater. (When he was unable to fix the heater, he and other governing board members sat bundled in overcoats, shivering during their meeting that night.)

Losoya described his duties as follows:

> Due to short-handedness, I suppose, and that we are a new school, I'm
> doing a lot. . . . I mean I'm a secretary, I'm a [receptionist], I'm a cook,
> I'm a janitor, so believe me there's a difference. I try to do . . . the com-
> puter. I'm doing everything. I'm writing grants. I go out and do PR.

Meanwhile, a teacher at Heritage reflected on all the problems associated with the poverty of the school.

> Our biggest challenge right now is finding a site. This is not a good
> area. It isn't. We need to find a site that's safer for our students, plus
> we need our own gym. We need to meet those needs for the students
> as well as, we need to work on a lot of things. Our problem now is . . .
> we are so limited with money, and people are literally betting on us
> closing. It's kind of hard, but we're hoping that some rich, wealthy
> person will say, Hey, I'll give you a couple of million dollars. And then
> at least some of our challenges will be met and settled, and somehow,
> it doesn't look like it.

What this Heritage teacher did not know was that this is what happened
to Academic Charter School. Indeed, as we noted, while Academic also served
poor students of color, it was in far better financial shape than Heritage or
Community because it had received numerous private donations. In addition
to the support that Academic received from wealthy donors and corporations,
foundations were also interested in supporting this "inner-city" charter school.
Potential donors were given tours of the school, after which they often volunteered to fulfill a need. Describing the touring, a parent remarked:

> Now this is a big tour and they see all of this and then the potentials in
> it. And most times, they do give us something. We've had, we've
> gotten money from, [donors] who gave us $25,000 to put carpet on
> the floors . . . To as much as, anonymous donors who have given us a
> million dollars over 4 years.

The connections the original contributors had to other potential donors helped
to keep the school financially supported through significant donations.

At Community Charter School, there was no time or staff to pursue grants
and fund raising. Some teachers and former directors were successful at attracting small grants from corporations and foundations. But, overall, Community
Charter School, like Heritage, was greatly in need of resources. One teacher

discussed the importance of attracting people to the charter school who could use personal connections to get desperately needed resources. She said:

> You really need people who are very familiar with fund raising and looking for that money. And sometimes you just—who has the time to do that. You have to hire people who are actually proposal grant writers who are familiar with the system, so that means you have to have money for that particular grant writer . . . there have been donations here and there but not to that great extent.

Thus, in some instances, the charter schools did not need to exert much effort on fund-raising and grant-writing tasks because of the connections they had to those who had the money. In other schools, the staff and community were desperate for resources, but due to heavy workloads and social locations, they did not have the time, expertise, or connections to raise the amounts of money they needed.

Parental and In-Kind Support

We found that many of the start-up charter schools in our study benefited greatly from high levels of parent involvement. In most of the schools we visited, parents donated significant amounts of time and effort to the schools and provided both classroom and administrative assistance. In fact, four of the six charter schools discussed in this chapter had mandatory parent contracts that required parents to spend a minimum number of hours volunteering at the school. Yet we also found that the types of resources and support parents were able to provide varied dramatically across communities. Generally, charter schools in high-status communities were able to draw on the abilities and expertise of professional parents who were highly skilled in grant writing or teaching courses. Meanwhile, charter schools in low-status communities had parents whose involvement in the school more often consisted of performing unskilled tasks related to grounds keeping and maintenance. If these poorer parents were involved in fund-raising activities at all, they tended to seek small donations from local businesses. In this section, we look at parental support in Shoreline, Heritage, Community, and Academic charter schools because of the contrasts within this group of schools.

Shoreline Charter School required a high level of involvement from its parents. The parental-involvement contract, which parents had to sign before their children enrolled in the school, specified that parents must volunteer 80 hours per school year for one child and 120 hours per school year for more than one child. As noted, this school served mostly children of professional parents—doctors, lawyers, university professors, computer scientists, and so forth—and these parents frequently fulfilled their contract requirements by teaching, for example, courses in genetics, math, music, or foreign languages. One teacher described the parent-involvement program, noting that it provided pro bono expertise that most public schools could not afford.

> I have a couple parents who have just been godsent. One is an amateur astronomer. She has her degree in physics and she does computers now. . . . She did our Mars webpage. . . . One of the founding parents . . . has a microbiology background. . . . She brought in all her lab equipment. [Another parent] taught . . . an advanced math class for 3 years. I didn't have to deal [with it] at all. He and I met, and he taught me a ton. A lot of what I do now and how I approach my mathematics curriculum is because of [that parent's] influence.

Not only did many of these parents use their expertise to help the school, but as high-level professionals, many of them had more control over their schedules, allowing them to donate time during school hours. One parent, who was also a member of the governing board, noted:

> We are fortunate enough that . . . most of our community is affluent enough that there are parents who either are working but are in a high enough position where they have flexibility or parents who don't have to work full time or who have flexible hours because they are self-employed who can make themselves more available than would happen in a district where the people were not so affluent.

Shoreline's parents also served as liaisons between the school and various local corporations (often where they were employed) or donated other kinds of services such as catering or construction services. And, as mentioned earlier, many parents helped write or evaluate grants.

At Heritage Charter School, where there were no parent contracts or volunteer requirements, parents donated time and expertise to the degree they could. However, they were not able to satisfy their school's tremendous resource needs. Parents who had the time to donate did so most often as classroom volunteers, acting as tutors and classroom aides. Yet, as one parent noted:

> Our families aren't in that economic bracket where one parent can work and the other one doesn't have to. We do have a few parents that are here during the day, . . . and those parents are not necessarily from wealthy families, some of them have very low incomes but they're able to come volunteer and still secure their income. But I just feel like, we don't have the time to really become part of the school because we have to work during the day.

Thus, while parents and their contributions were valued at Heritage, there were cultural and socioeconomic barriers that prevented meaningful involvement. In addition, some parents felt intimidated by the prospect of being involved. One parent commented on this phenomenon.

> We need to make parents aware that they have that option and then more aware of how important it is to take that option. . . . I don't think we have a group of parents that are used to thinking of themselves as making a difference in the school if they're there. We are primarily a working-class economic bracket where you don't even think of yourself as a potential educator or tutor. We don't think of ourselves that way, so we don't think that we'd be valuable in the classroom.

Meanwhile, Heritage's teachers attempted to satisfy the school's tremendous resource needs by donating their own resources; one teacher mentioned that the teachers often bought food to feed students who came to school hungry. According to Principal Losoya: "For the most part we clean our own rooms and that type of stuff. We don't have a cook. We don't even have a lunch program. So, at first we were taking out of our own pockets to go and buy food to make sandwiches for the kids." Some parents, the principal noted, had written small food service grants for the school in recent years and had gotten some food donated to the school.

Community Charter School, located in the same impoverished school district as Heritage, faced many of the same problems in terms of obtaining the kind of parent volunteerism and donations that Shoreline had. Parents at Community Charter School were required to volunteer at the school 4 hours per month, and the parents had donated a great deal of time to the school in terms of cleaning and maintaining the physical plant, installing sidewalks, and performing janitorial tasks. Yet there was a clear need at this school for more large-scale fund raising that charter schools like Shoreline do through their parents' networks and support.

Community Charter School took advantage of some of the cultural resources in its community and had volunteers come in and teach a variety of courses, including art, history, and literature. Generally, however, this charter school had been struggling financially since it first opened. This strain, as Principal Henderson described it, prevented teachers from utilizing parent time in a more effective way.

> One of the problems that we have had here is that we are a start-up school, and you know, we have had very little support. We have really [gone] from crises to crises, and a lot of our time has been spent

putting out fires rather than moving ahead. And one of the ways that we haven't been able to really reach out is to reach out to parents as much as we would like to.

At Academic Charter, in-kind donations were a large component of the charter's operation. However, as described earlier, most of these donations were from corporations, and not the local community, which was fairly poor. Like many other charter schools, parents at Academic were required to volunteer at the school a minimum of 3 hours per month, and like at Community, at Academic this involvement often took the form of grounds keeping and janitorial services, such as cleaning. Some parents, however, helped the school solicit local organizations and businesses for funds, and several led tours around the campus for prospective funders. But the parents at Academic Charter School clearly lack the connections to major corporations and donors that Shoreline parents have.

Parents at Academic Charter School, like at Heritage and Community, found it difficult to volunteer often, because they had less flexibility in their work schedules to come and help out at the school during the day. Yet, as one Academic parent described, some parents found ways to volunteer despite this difficulty.

> You know, there is a certain group who come in the morning who work with breakfast and the clean-up after breakfast and those are the ones I feel who have time in that early morning to do that. We have one parent who finds time to go and buy the things that we need for the after-school children. . . . We have parents who will come and just help. Like, for example, my wife . . . she will come once a week and she usually goes down to the primary office, and helps straighten up things there, orders supplies that they need for their supply room.

These disparities in access to private resources also exist in non-charter schools, as the amount of resources any school receives is often dependent on the type of community—poor or affluent—it serves. However, we found that such disparities in resources are magnified in start-up charter schools, which are, as other researchers have documented, particularly resource-needy (see Chapter 4, this volume; RPP International, 1997).

IMPLICATIONS AND RECOMMENDATIONS

As we observed the spectrum of activities in which charter school communities engaged in order to gain the private resources they needed to thrive, we saw vast inequities emerging across schools. While inequality is not unique to charter school reform, what is unusual is the exclusivity and isolation developing across many charter school communities located in wealthy and poor neighborhoods, even as these schools are joined under the same umbrella of charter school reform. The networks in these communities—and the types of social or economic capital these networks provide for schools—enable some schools to maintain or create their privilege, while other schools fall even further behind.

Furthermore, charter school reform is unique in that it leaves partially "publicly funded" schools starved for resources to pay for fundamental things, such as buildings and equipment. At every start-up school we visited, respondents called for more start-up funding from the federal and state governments and individual schools districts. All start-up charter schools need a tremendous amount of resources.

Thus, charter schools exist within a policy framework that leaves them no choice but to scramble for private resources. We have witnessed the tremendous disparity in the resources gathered between charter schools that begin in low-status communities versus charter schools that are started by more privileged and powerful individuals and serve more diverse communities. We worry that many well-intentioned educational reformers have embraced the potential of charter school reform while forgetting the resource inequities that the reform fails to address (Wells, Lopez, Scott, & Holme, 1999). Due to decades of public neglect, many California schools are racially, politically, economically, and socially isolated, literally cut off from networking opportunities. Charter school reform in such communities means either starting a school that lacks many fundamental resources or partnering with an outside organization that may or may not allow low-income parents and students to have a great deal of voice in how the school is run.

We suggest that if policy makers, school district officials, educational practitioners, and researchers want to redress the inequities we saw emerging from charter school reform as it currently is constructed, they consider our recommendations. First, we suggest that start-up funds be targeted to charter schools in high-poverty communities—for example, schools in which most students qualify for free or reduced-price lunch and/or Title I funding. Furthermore, these start-up funds should come in grants, not loans. At the same time, community-based, as opposed to EMO-founded and run, charter schools should be given priority in receiving these grants. In other words, this money should be used to fund truly grassroots charter schools as opposed to those run by either for-profit corporations or other non-profit educational service providers.

Second, district officials should ensure that charter schools in poor communities are made aware of the public and private resources for which they may qualify. Technical assistance should be offered to these communities, which may not have the connections or expertise needed to apply for such resources.

Finally, policy makers, practitioners, and researchers must wrestle with the implications that the blurring of private and public spheres might have for the future of public education. Further research could shed light on how one of the central arguments for charter schools—creating innovative learning environments that also empower communities—is circumscribed by schools' access to resources, both public and private. Start-up charter schools, due to their smaller size and other constraints, are unable to subsist on public monies alone. Facing this reality means accepting that charter school reform is part of the trend toward privatization in public education (Wells & Scott, 1999).

Related to this issue, researchers and policy makers should consider the relationship between resource inequity and the proliferation of educational management organizations in charter school reform. There are myriad implications of the growing involvement of EMOs in public school management. Thus far, the research on EMOs by outside evaluators is still emerging (see Richards, Shore, & Sawicky, 1996), but it has raised serious questions about accountability, effectiveness, access, and equity (Miron, 2000; Toch, 1998; Winerip, 1998).

Clearly, the successful implementation of charter school reform requires heavy reliance on private resources and the private sector. While we have provided an initial look at one aspect of this trend, further research is needed to document the various forms privatization can take, and what the effects will be on *all* school environments.

REFERENCES

Bourdieu, P. (1977). Cultural reproduction and social reproduction. In J. H. Karabel (Ed.), *Power and ideology in education* (pp. 487–511). New York: Oxford University Press.

Bourdieu, P. (1986). The forms of capital. In J. G. Richardson (Ed.), *Handbook of theory and research for the sociology of education* (pp. 241–258). New York: Greenwood.

Bourdieu, P., & Wacquant, L. J. D. (1992). *An invitation to reflexive sociology.* Chicago: University of Chicago Press.

Corwin, R. G., & Flaherty, J. F. (1995). *Freedom and innovation in California's charter schools: Selected findings.* Los Alamitos, CA: Far West Laboratory for Educational Research and Development.

Granovetter, M. (1973). The strength of weak ties. *American Journal of Sociology, 78*(6), 1360–1380.

Granovetter, M. (1983). The strength of weak ties: A network theory revisited. In
    R. Collins (Ed.), *Sociological theory* (pp. 201–233). San Francisco, CA: Jossey
    Bass.
Granovetter, M. (1985). Economic action and social structure: The problem of
    embeddedness. *American Journal of Sociology, 91*(3), 481–510.
Lareau, A. (1989). *Home advantage: Social class and parental intervention in elemen-
    tary education.* London: Falmer Press.
Miron, G. (2000, April). *What's public about Michigan's charter schools: Lessons in
    school reform from statewide evaluations of charter schools.* Paper prepared for the
    annual meeting of the American Educational Research Association, New Orleans.
Oliver, M., & Shapiro, T. M. (1997). *Black wealth/White wealth.* New York: Routledge.
Richards, C., Shore, R., & Sawicky, M. (1996). *Risky business: Private management
    of public schools.* Washington, DC: Economic Policy Institute.
RPP International. (2000). *The state of charter schools: National study of charter schools,
    Fourth-year report.* Washington, DC: U.S. Department of Education, Office of
    Educational Research and Improvement.
RPP International & the University of Minnesota. (1997). *A study of charter schools:
    First-year report.* Washington, DC: U.S. Department of Education, Office of
    Educational Research and Improvement.
Swartz, D. (1997). *Culture and power: The sociology of Pierre Bourdieu.* Chicago:
    University of Chicago Press.
Toch, T. (1998, April 27). Education bazaar. *U.S. News and World Report,* pp. 35–
    46.
UCLA Charter School Study. (1998). *Beyond the rhetoric of charter school reform: A
    study of ten California school districts.* Los Angeles: Author. [www.gseis.ucla.edu/
    docs/charter.pdf]
Wells, A. S., Lopez, A., Scott, J., & Holme, J. J. (1999). Charter schools as postmodern
    paradox: Rethinking social stratification in an age of deregulated school choice.
    Harvard Educational Review, 69(2), 172–204.
Wells, A. S., & Scott, J. (1999, April). *Evaluation of charter schools.* Paper presented
    at the agenda-setting conference, of the National Center for the Study of School
    Privatization. Teachers College, Columbia University, New York.
Winerip, M. (1998, June 14). Schools for sale. *New York Times Magazine* pp. 42–
    48, 80, 86–89.

CHAPTER 6

Creating Charter School Communities

Identity Building, Diversity, and Selectivity

ALEJANDRA LOPEZ, AMY STUART WELLS,
and JENNIFER JELLISON HOLME

Charter school reform was designed to allow groups of people to create educational communities grounded in their shared values and beliefs about schools—whether these beliefs related to parent involvement, discipline, or curricular themes. According to California law, charter schools are intended to "provide parents and pupils with expanded choice in the types of educational opportunities that are available within the public school system." In this chapter, we discuss what this autonomy to create a school grounded in a shared set of values means to the people who engage in this reform and what the implications of their actions might be for student access to their schools and the public educational system in general.

What we have learned is that perhaps the most salient manifestation of charter schools' autonomy to create school communities is the freedom they have to allow their shared values and beliefs to shape their understanding of which students and parents "fit" into a school community and thus who should attend. Furthermore, charter school operators have much more power than most regular public school educators to act on these preferences. That is, through the use of several mechanisms that shape charter schools' recruitment, admissions, and disciplinary processes, charter school operators can exclude students who do not fit the culture or norms of the school. Thus, alongside the community-building and mission-shaping aspects of charter school reform, lie a set of more difficult issues related to student access. For instance, our data suggest that charter schools are making as many—or more—choices about which students and parents will attend, as parents and students are making choices about which charter schools they would like to attend.

As explained in Chapter 1, much of the rhetoric in favor of school choice policy focuses on the market metaphor of school reform in which schools compete for students and thus thrive or fail based on their market ability to attract "customers." Within such a "marketplace" individual schools theoretically strive to distinguish themselves as serving particular market niches, and parents respond to this market diversity by finding the right educational niche that best serves their children (see Brantlinger, Majd-Jabbari, & Guskin, 1996; Cookson, 1994; Gewirtz, Ball, & Bowe, 1995).

Indeed, charter school founders, operators, and constituents at different sites commonly expressed a desire to establish and maintain an image or identity of distinction for their educational communities in order to create niches in the educational marketplace. But in reality, the identity-building process is often more about the choices that charter schools are able to make in terms of who attends than it is about giving parents and students more choice.

In this chapter, we describe charter school operators' efforts to form distinct school communities grounded in shared values and beliefs—what we refer to as "identity-building" efforts—in terms of how they distinguish themselves within the context of their school districts and local communities. Furthermore, we consider how these distinctions relate to which students and parents are "desirable" in the eyes of charter school operators. We also consider how, despite the fact that many charter school operators say they greatly value "diversity" in their schools, their distinctions about who is "desirable" and who is not are often related in subtle, cultural ways to the social class, race/ethnicity, and/or primary language of the students. And finally, we describe how charter schools, unlike most regular public schools, are able to act on these distinctions by using specific mechanisms to structure who attends and who remains.

In this way, the community-building efforts that charter school reform fosters often stand in direct opposition to rhetoric about valuing "diversity" (Holmes, 1992). In other words, many of the shared "values" and "beliefs" that shape charter schools are strongly influenced by deep cultural and structural barriers. For instance, parents who can afford to be involved in certain ways, or give more resources to the charter schools, are more highly valued simply because they have time and money. Furthermore, parents who historically have succeeded in school and thus have been treated well by educators probably have a more positive orientation toward involvement in schools than parents who have had fewer such positive experiences in the past (Lareau, 1989).

Given these cultural and structural issues and the fact that we live in a very unequal society, it is difficult to create "homogeneous" school communities without creating further separation along racial/ethnic, socioeconomic, linguistic, and other cultural dimensions. Indeed, Wells, Holme, Lopez, and Cooper (2000) demonstrate that early evidence from various states with large numbers of charter schools suggests that this is indeed the trend—charter schools are more segregated by race and social class than the already segregated public schools.

In the sections that follow, we first describe how charter school founders and operators build "cultural communities" of people with similar moral values and beliefs. This shared sense of "morality," which in turn contributes to the schools' identity-building efforts, defines charter schools in opposition to other public schools and, thus, as deserving of recognition. Second, we give examples of the mechanisms by which charter school operators are able to structure their school communities—by controlling who gets in and who stays in—so that most students and parents share similar values and beliefs about schooling. And finally, we relate these findings to issues of racial/ethnic and social-class segregation and isolation—within charter schools and the larger public educational system.

We excluded from our consideration the three charter schools from the UCLA study that were home-schooling and/or independent study operations as not helpful in our efforts to explore the ways in which charter school reform gives people greater flexibility to shape, structure, and bound who participates in these educational communities and who is valued within them. For this chapter, then, we focus on data from the 14 "in-house" charter schools in the UCLA study that exemplified places where people shared a schooling space and negotiated relations on an everyday basis.

CULTURAL COMMUNITIES AND INSTITUTIONAL IDENTITIES

Castells (1997) talks about communities as "cultural communes" that include three main features: First, they appear as reactions to prevailing social trends; second, they are defensive identities that function as refuge and solidarity to a hostile, outside world; and third, they are culturally constituted, that is, organized around a specific set of values whose meanings are marked by specific codes of self-identification. According to Castells, these factors create a community of "believers." We have certainly seen this occur in charter schools. Charter school identities emerge as reactions to contemporary social trends such as the emphasis on more decentralized, local control over schools in a way that allows people to pursue their own ideals about schooling, often in opposition to other public schools. Furthermore, "culture," as it relates to shared beliefs and values about education, tends to play a large role in the creation and maintenance of charter schools.

Related to this notion of cultural communes is Clark's (1992) work regarding institutional identity in higher education. He writes about the development of an "organizational saga" that brings people together and helps them stay together by creating a sense of uniqueness and loyalty. He notes:

> The most important characteristic and consequence of an organizational saga is the capturing of allegiance, the committing of staff to the institution. . . . Deep emotional investment binds participants as comrades in a cause. Indications of an organizational legend are pride and exaggeration; the most telling symptom is an intense sense of the unique. . . . An organizational saga turns an organization into a community. (p. 235)

Charter school founders, educators, and parents in our study talked a lot about their uniqueness, compared with other schools in their districts and neighboring communities. By viewing themselves as unique, they succeeded in binding people together and securing loyalty to the charter. As Ford (1995) argues, "A cultural community has autonomy in that it can exert influence over individual members, construct morality, values, and desires, and provide an epistemological framework for its members" (p. 461). Similarly, we found that charter schools provided a framework of moral values and beliefs for their members and instilled an institutional identity for the educational community as a whole. Central to this identity are the types of students and parents these charter schools serve.

In their study of school choice in the United Kingdom, Gewirtz and colleagues (1995) discuss how families, as consumers, are categorized by school officials into two groups: *desirable* families and *undesirable* families. Desirable families are those with well-behaved students with high measured "ability" and well-educated and wealthy parents. Undesirable families, on the other hand, are those with students who are perceived to be "less able," those with special needs or behavioral problems, and parents viewed as not valuing education.

In this way, charter schools, as schools of choice, convey—through promotional literature, mission statements, and recruitment strategies—certain preferences and understandings about who is a good match as they engage in identity-building efforts and try to secure a niche in the educational marketplace. As Gewirtz and colleagues (1995) explain, "Whilst the market might foster a greater degree of responsiveness to parental desires and preferences, it is only the preferences of particular groups of parents which effectively 'count'" (p. 143).

Similarly, we learned that desirable parents' values and beliefs about schooling affect charters in several ways. For instance, in creating a charter school, founders, educators, and parents may coalesce around some shared set of values and expectations about schools, including how students should behave and how parents must demonstrate their commitment to the school. The more alike the founders, educators, and parents are in terms of their understandings of these issues, the easier the process is. And the more powerful and desirable the parents with the most financial and in-kind resources, formal education, and access to networks become, the more say they have in deciding who else gets in.

Many sociologists of education argue that those who have the power to define the identity and culture of schools are generally those with shared and valued forms of social and cultural capital—at least within the local context. For instance, Brantlinger and colleagues (1996) discuss how middle-class parents' values factor into the creation of school boundaries, particularly in terms of social class and, thus, who is welcomed and who is not.

> [There is the shared belief] that low-income parents and children do not value education . . . reverberated through narratives (e.g. "kids don't see school as important," "getting good grades does not matter for them," "parents don't value education," "they have modest aspirations"). . . . Bourdieu (1984) observes that affluent people assume that poor people prefer the lifestyles to which they are condemned by lack of funds. (p. 580)

The middle-class mothers these authors studied set themselves apart from poor families, defining themselves in opposition to the poor families and legitimizing their own position at the same time, by describing themselves as "smart, moral, and deserving of superior status and a larger share of material resources" (p. 581). The authors noted: "Though many of the middle class mothers were attracted to socially inclusive, integrated ideals of education, they were intent on having advantaged circumstances for their own kids" (p. 589).

In our study we found that middle- and upper-class parents were more likely than working- and lower-class parents to be involved in the "chartering" process, since they often had some expertise in the areas of proposal writing, budgeting and money management, and legal issues. Furthermore, these more powerful parents had better access to social networks and, in many instances, the free time of a stay-at-home parent. All of these "assets" were highly valued by founders' groups in the process of trying to attain charter status. Even in low-income communities, those who were most privileged, or had the most social and cultural capital relative to other parents in the area, tended to have the most control over what took place in charter schools, how they were created, and who attended them.

CHARTER SCHOOL DISTINCTIVENESS AND IDENTITY BUILDING

As noted above, charter schools have greater autonomy than most regular public schools to create their "distinct" educational communities. This ability to create communities and niches was more meaningful for new, start-up charter schools than it was for converted public schools that already had students enrolled, although even some conversion schools, over time, strove to develop a more distinct "clientele." For instance, in many states, charter schools are able to institute policies and practices that require a certain level and type of parental and/or student involvement.

Furthermore, charter schools have the ability to gradually become more selective over time—in terms of who attends and who is valued. This occurs as operators and parents more clearly define their shared educational values and beliefs and establish school goals, guidelines, requirements, and policies that help maintain and enforce those values. This also occurs because often in the early stages of the life of a start-up charter school, founders and operators are forced to recruit parents and students to fill the school. Our data show that over time, as they cultivate an identity, establish a shared set of values, and market their distinctiveness, charter schools are able to become more selective about which students and parents are considered desirable.

In the following sections we illustrate some of the identities around which charter schools were created as cultural communes or communities. We realize that many of the values shaping these school identities also are held by others not involved in charter schools. But it is important to emphasize that charter school reform allows people greater autonomy to structure who attends and who is most valued in their school communities. This is especially problematic, we argue, when perceptions about others' values and beliefs about schooling are uninformed and instead tied to status-related characteristics like race/ethnicity, class, language proficiency, neighborhoods, and so on.

Oppositional Identities: Different from Other Public Schools and Other Parents

For many charter school founders, educators, and parents, at least some aspects of their schools' identities are defined in opposition to other public schools. In this section, we offer examples of what the charter school founders, educators, and parents are moving away from, or the ways in which they want to be seen as "distinct" from other public schools.

In the schools we studied, merely having a charter set the educational community apart from other schools, giving them a new identity regardless of whether they did anything differently from other schools in their districts. Being charter schools gave them an enhanced sense of efficacy that they could be "different," recognition for any innovative or reforming efforts they made, and pride in the educational community they felt they helped to create. As with other schools of choice, people believed that they were better than others because the schools and the students were chosen (Cookson, 1994; Driscoll, 1993). For instance, affiliates of several of the charters in our study described themselves and their schools as "new," "novel," "unique," and "special." A director of one of the schools we studied noted:

> There's some advantage to just being different because people then recognize, "Well, geez, that's [a charter school], they're different." Even when they're not completely sure what it is, if you're being successful—and I think we are—and if people recognize you as being different, then . . . you have some advantage in gaining their support.

At another charter school, the principal explained:

> Well, I think the charter is . . . who we are. . . . I mean, it's given us an identity. It's given us a focus. It's given us the . . . I don't know—the impetus to, to be different. And I don't mean totally different. I'm not talking, apples and oranges, but shades of red. We're a different shade of red.

Whether real or perceived, the differences between charter schools and regular public schools were couched in slightly different terms, depending on the context. Thus, for some, the distinctions relate to issues of safety and security; for others, the issue was parent involvement. And while issues such as safety often can be interpreted as proxies for race and class, sometimes race and class themselves were discussed as issues of distinction. Thus, the topics of distinction varied to some degree depending on the local context, but the theme of distinction was robust across all these sites.

Defining Who Does *Not* Belong: Student and Parent Behavior

One aspect of this oppositional identity in terms of charter schools' distinction from other schools is their ability to define who does not belong within their educational community, often in terms of student and parent behavior. They also have the autonomy—more so than other public schools—to make sure that the people who do not belong, do not end up there, either by counseling people out, asking them to leave, or expelling them (these mechanisms are discussed in more detail in the following section). For instance, at one rural charter school, a parent said, "If you don't want to abide by rules, fine. Go to school somewhere else. And that's one thing I like about the charter program."

This parent also explained that at the charter school he did not "have to worry about people associating with kids [who] have bad manners, bad language." Similarly, some people we interviewed in this community talked about the charter school and its student behavioral contract, which allowed the educators there to "disinvite" students who broke the rules or who were not perceived to be committed to the charter school and motivated to make it work.

One former school board member from this district described the charter school's position this way:

> If you're just lackadaisically doing nothing and the parents are not involved in helping you understand that you need to do better, and so forth, then it is possible for us to say, this isn't the place for you. You can go any place and sit and dream. Go dream. It's okay with us. And we've got this long waiting list of people who want an education.

Another school board member talked about the charter school as similar to a private school because it does not have to deal with families that are not supportive. She noted, "There are still those families there. In reality, we will never be free of all of them, because that is what a public school is. The really bad ones, we would feel comfortable in getting rid of."

At this same charter school, the student review panel examined cases of students who were failing academically. Most teachers we spoke with at this site praised the student review panel for turning discipline around at the school. Students who did not show enough effort could be excluded. As one educator at the school explained, "Let me emphasize [we're] not taking kids out who *can't* do . . . we have a lot of help available for those children [who] need help. It's the issue of the student who *won't*, who's wasting our time together."

Another educator at this school expressed similar sentiment about parents and students who were not "trying" hard enough: "If you're not making an effort . . . then we've got a limited number of seats and there is someone out there [who] wants to take advantage of a good system . . . you take your child, and he can go sit anywhere." Furthermore, she noted that the charter was about "making the students responsible." Thus, she argued that for the student who was unresponsive and did not take advantage of opportunities or who was interfering with other students' opportunities, "we would be in a position to say, 'You're reaching the day when you're going to be disinvited. And we have another place for you to go . . . [other] schools that have agreed to take you.'"

An urban elementary charter school located in a low-income community had fairly strict parent-involvement and student conduct contracts. Educators at that school "counseled out" students who were not behaving in accordance with these contracts. At one of the school's governing board meetings, staff and parents who were present voted to approve a strict attendance policy whereby students could be asked to leave the school if they were tardy to or absent from school more than a certain number of days in one semester. It is important to note that this charter school, like many others, did not provide its students with any transportation to and from school. Thus, parents had to either drive the students every morning and evening or rely on mass transportation.

Still, many of the educators and most of the parents on this board said that the charter school was not for everyone, and if parents could not live up to the expectations, they needed to find another school. In this way, even though the school was in a low-income neighborhood, it probably was not serving the most needy students from that area of the school district. In fact, many of the parents we interviewed lived far from the school in a more working- and middle-class neighborhood of the metropolitan area. As one person we interviewed put it, the parents who heard about and chose this charter school were not those at the "bottom of the barrel" in terms of involvement in and support of their children's education. Likewise, a teacher at this charter school pointed out that a child who was disruptive would not do well in that educational community.

At another elementary charter school in a suburban community, several people said that the Spanish-speaking parents were not as involved, and thus many of the English-speaking parents were "tired of doing everything themselves." A teacher commented that the Spanish-speaking parents were more intimidated and uncomfortable than other parents. He described how even though one Spanish-speaking mother came in to help in his class, it was more work for him to explain to her how to help than to just do the work himself. He said, "So I'm sure that's part of it—the feeling of maybe this is going to take more time to try to communicate with them. And it's especially a problem with my Spanish not being that good."

Another teacher at this school agreed: "You have some parents who really want to come in and try who are more work than they are help." Although this phenomenon is not unique to charter schools, charter schools, unlike other public schools, have the freedom to make requirements of students and parents—particularly in terms of behavior and school involvement—and these requirements affect admissions decisions.

Furthermore, as we noted above, often even when charter schools are created in low-income communities, we found they tend to serve students who are relatively privileged—that is, have the most-involved parents, the greatest access to financial and in-kind resources, and so on—compared with others in the same community.

At another urban charter school, which also served a low-income population, the parent contract is strictly enforced, helping to define who does not belong at that school. In fact, six families were asked not to re-enroll one fall because they had not fulfilled their required "volunteer" hours. Similarly, a parent at a suburban charter school told us that she was forced to take her children out of the school, in part because she could not fulfill the parent-involvement requirement. She said, "The main thing was the time commitment, I did not have the time." This parent also pointed out that the parents who were most involved at the charter school were the stay-at-home moms. "They are very lucky. I wish I could do that, but I can't right now. It makes you wonder if charter schools can work in an inner-city area where all the parents have to work."

In this way, problem students were not always explicitly "thrown out" of the charter schools—sometimes they were gently "pushed out" or encouraged not to return, or their parents decided that the charter schools were not going to help them. At one suburban elementary charter school we studied, a parent talked about the parents who had actively taken their children out of the school because they were not doing well. A teacher at this school described the process whereby families reconsidered their "fit" with the school.

> I think the first year, we attracted a lot of dissatisfied consumers—parents and children who were unhappy with their other school and so they didn't come to us because of what we offered so much but because of what they were needing. And invariably . . . the people who came to us dissatisfied left dissatisfied because they brought their same problems with them to our school, and we can't fix those kinds of problems. . . . They are no longer with us.

Similarly, another teacher at this school noted that during the school's first year, parents were much more likely to send their "problem children" to the charter to get "fixed." But she noted that as time went on, parents realized that the charter school was not necessarily their solution and that the 80-hour a year parent-involvement requirement was quite onerous. "Now it is where the parents have to say, 'I am willing to come in 80 hours, I'm willing to sign that contract that says, you know, I am volunteering,' and there is not that—you know—'fix it' [attitude]."

Thus, sometimes the process of figuring out which students do not "belong" in a charter school and who are most motivated to be there takes time and evolves gradually. For instance, a teacher at one of the urban charter high schools we studied commented on the change in the student population since the school converted to charter status and thus was able to selectively recruit out-of-neighborhood students instead of taking anyone the district assigned. He explained that the students who used to be assigned to the school from poorer areas of the city did a lot of vandalizing and did not necessarily want to be there. He said that since the school became a charter school, the students and parents who were there wanted to be there.

Furthermore, although the language used to define who fits and who does not is rarely explicitly about race, in many of the contexts that we studied, these distinctions often had racial and/or social-class overtones. The degree to which race and class were conflated with who did not fit depended a great deal on local context of the charter schools and the demographics of the districts in which they were located. For example, an administrator of a neighboring school to one of the rural charters noted that part of the charter school's appeal was that there were fewer African American and Latino students there than in neighboring schools. Thus, he said that the charter school sent out messages about "safety" that were as much about race as they were about safety. He said, "After you scratch beneath all of the excuses, it's like . . . these kids are too rough and there's gangs and there's this and that."

As we discuss in more detail below, many of the parents and teachers at several of the charter schools we studied talked about valuing "diversity," "diverse cultures," the "real-worldness" of a racially and socioeconomically diverse school, and a "normal mix of cultures." However, despite this philosophy, there was a clear effort on the part of many charter school founders, educators, and parents to keep certain students of color and/or lower-income students outside of their schools and thus their cultural communities.

For instance, a school board member in an urban school district argued that one of the charter high schools in that district discriminated against Latino students by screening them out before they applied, telling parents that their children "cannot function here." She said, "To me, you violate a human law when kids are either counseled out, or excluded, or parents are not involved, and so on, and I think that Latino parents were treated shamefully in there."

Likewise, officials in another school district voiced concern that two of the charter schools in that community were created, in part, because parents did not want their children to go to school with African American students. One district administrator, in particular, argued that the segregation resulting from charter school reform was less about class and more about race and ethnicity. She noted that the charter schools in that district were more ethnically homogeneous than the school district as a whole, and demographic data substantiate this claim. A school board member remarked that she was suspicious of the motives behind the creation of one of the district's charter schools. "Their reasoning for wanting a charter schools was, in my judgment, defensive and social as opposed to [about] education, [they were about] issues of safety, many of which sort of, kind of got smoke-screened with a combination of 'we don't want to go to middle school outside of what is comfortable to us.'"

Class issues—sometimes, but not always, conflated with race—also relate in some instances to what it is people are trying to get away from in regular public schools by creating charters. For example, in one of the rural charter schools we studied, which strongly valued family "support," assumptions and perceptions about families being "supportive" were tied to socioeconomic status. That is, those with lower socioeconomic status were thought to be less supportive. The following statement, made by a board member in the district where that charter school is located, illustrates this perception about the "pockets" of students from less-supportive families:

> In one of the trailer parks over here, those are the kids we usually have the trouble with and the parents [who] are not supportive and that kind of thing. . . . I do not want to sound like a snob. I mean, they're fine people but they are just not as interested in education.

Another respondent from this community described "good" parents as those where "Mom stayed at home" and "Dad had a good job," indicating that families with working mothers and fathers with low-paying jobs were less welcome.

In this section, we demonstrated different ways in which charter school founders and operators sought to create educational communities that were free from what they perceived to be undesirable characteristics of other public schools and some public school students. In the next section, we will look more specifically at the ways in which these people formed new and distinct identities for their educational communities and how they defined who did indeed "fit."

Identity Formation: The Art of Building a Reputation

To the extent that many charter school operators define their schools as different from regular public schools, they simultaneously must put forth an image or identity of what they *are*, if they are not like other schools. Safety, academic rigor, being like a private school, popularity, parental voice, and ethnic/racial distinctions all play a role in how the charter school operators and community members defined the identity of their schools. In this section, we examine how charter school reformers craft an institutional identity and how these identity-building efforts demonstrate what they are seeking and what they are running from in the regular public schools.

Melucci (cited in Carlson, 1997) provides a starting point for thinking about the relationship between identity and the formation of charter school communities. He states that the process of establishing a social movement involves

> activating relationships among the actors, who communicate, negotiate and make decisions; and . . . making emotional investments which enable individuals to

recognize themselves in each other [and . . . participate in the process of identity building. (p. 20)

Charter schools can be thought of as localized social movements within their communities in the sense that they bring people together who share similar values and beliefs about schools. These groups then work together to create schools that reflect those values and beliefs and attract like-minded people by promoting their cultural identities and building reputations based on those identities.

For instance, charter school founders, educators, and parents often said that one of the main reasons they created charter schools was because other public schools were unsafe. At one of the rural elementary charter schools, parents and educators constantly talked about how the school provided a much *safer* environment than other nearby public schools and that it was the "safest and best spot" in the area. They expressed a lot of pride in the "country school" atmosphere of the charter. In fact, the "country" identity seemed to symbolize everything that was *not* "urban," including safe, White, and not poor. Thus, not surprisingly, the "country" identity seemed particularly attractive to White parents and students, as they chose to leave their often more racially diverse public schools to transfer to the charter school. According to a superintendent in a neighboring school district, this particular charter school sent out messages to families within his district that it was "better . . . safer . . . and smaller." Yet in reality, the charter school was not actually smaller than other nearby schools, but it was less racially and socioeconomically diverse.

Similarly, a teacher in one of the urban charter high schools we studied noted:

Students come here because their families perceive the school as being small and safe and college-preparatory. And the fact that it has [a multicultural] focus, or the fact that it's a charter school [doesn't] play as big a role as the fact that it's a small, safe, college-preparatory school.

In fact, safety was also an issue in suburban charter schools. In a suburban charter middle school that we studied, a parent explained that most of the charter school parents were "absolutely delighted" that their kids were not going to be "thrown into a situation" like the one at the nearby public middle school, especially, she said, the parents of girls. "I was just talking to my niece the other day who is in sixth grade, and it's been really tough. She doesn't feel safe in that school. And I think the kids feel pretty darn safe at [the] charter, in all ways, emotionally, physically."

Countless other counselors, teachers, administrators, and parents in most of the districts we studied also expressed an appreciation of the "safeness" of charter schools. In fact, "safety" was often a unifying theme that made the school different from other schools, or at least led parents, in particular, to believe that it was.

Another such unifying theme that helped founders, educators, and parents define the identity of their charter school was *academic rigor*. The vast majority of the schools in our study identified themselves as academically much more rigorous than nearby public schools. For instance, at one of the urban charter high schools we studied, an administrator explained, "We try to maintain a certain level of [educational] attainment. . . . Sports teams are good, but not what attracts them to this school. We have kids going to Berkeley and Harvard—we are known for that." At another charter high school, teachers noted that it was a "serious" place now that it was a charter, a "hard academic" school. Similarly, people at one of the suburban elementary schools emphasized the importance of high achievement test scores and viewed them as a marker that the charter school was better, that is, more academic, than other schools in the district.

Exactly what "academic rigor" meant or how that rigor related to certain outcome measures or instructional strategies varied somewhat from site to site. Still, with the exception of the charter schools geared toward students who dropped out or were kicked out of regular public schools, all the charter schools in our study claimed to be more rigorous than nearby public schools along one academic dimension or another.

Furthermore, in almost all of the districts we studied, people likened charter schools to private schools. It appeared that the efforts on the part of the charter schools to create an image of *being like a private school* were related to their efforts to project a sense of distinctiveness, of doing something different from other public schools in the area. One educator at a rural charter middle school explained, in the context of talking about the school's required parent involvement, "We provide a private school education in a public school." According to a former school board member in a nearby school district, the charter allows the school to be more like a private school because it can accept, deny, or disinvite students on the basis of the charter. Indeed, the principal of the charter school noted that his school was no longer limited by the rules of the state education code in terms of acceptable reasons for expelling students: "To that extent, we're like a private school. We can say, 'You are not adhering to the rules of the charter. You've contracted with us. Now either you do it or you don't go to school here. That's the rule.'"

Related to this notion of being like a private school, many people affiliated with charters cherished their schools' *popularity*—being wanted, chosen, and in demand—as an essential piece of the school's identity. The length of the waiting lists of families trying to get their children into the charter schools was an important illustration of this popularity. As a teacher at one of the suburban elementary charter schools explained, the charter school had become increasingly popular over the first 4 years of its existence. At the point at which we studied the school, it had a long waiting list and thus was able to be selective about which students would be admitted. At some charter schools, these waiting lists were used to scare students and parents into complying with charter school policies and practices. For example, at one rural charter middle school, some students and parents were warned that if they did not "shape up" they would have to leave because there was a long list of families who wanted to be there and who were willing to play by the school's rules.

Another oft-stated component of charter school identities was the supposed greater importance they placed on *parental voice*—that is, parents having much more say in their children's education and their schools' decision-making processes than they had in regular public schools. For instance, at a suburban elementary charter school, the school's philosophy strongly emphasized the value of parental "involvement," "say," "support," and "interest in their children's education." In this particular educational community, parents were expected to "buy in" and share a sense of "ownership" in the charter school.

Parents could come up with the ideas and work with a staff liaison to take care of the specifics of implementation. As one parent and governing council member explained:

> The idea, the concept . . . can either be a parent coming and saying, "Don't you think it would be fun if we did this," or, it can be an educator or the staff liaison going to a parents and saying, "We could really . . . we'd like to do something in this area." We have parents fill out background sheets, so [we] know what your hobbies are, what your interests are, what your time frame is, what your educational background and job is.

Several suburban charter school parents in our study claimed that at the regular public schools—unlike at the charter schools—meaningful parent involvement was discouraged or deterred after their children reached first or second grade. Similarly, a mother at another suburban elementary charter school explained that the teachers at the regular public schools did not know how to work with her daughter and made unwarranted judgments about her as a mother. She went on to say that the charter school teachers worked better with parents to solve problems without assigning blame.

Another aspect of institutional identity for several—but not all—charter schools was the distinct and explicit *ethnic or racial identity* of the founders, educators, students, and parents associated with these schools. This tended to be the case when charter schools were serving members of an oppressed "minority" group and thus their identity was grounded in the schools' ability to serve the unique needs of these students. A teacher in one of these so-called "ethnocentric" charter schools in our study explained that she had always wanted to teach U.S. history from her particular racial/ethnic group's perspective. In talking about the relationship between "her people" and the history she teaches, she said:

> We are U.S. history. We were U.S. history before there was the thirteen colonies, before the Declaration of Independence. We were U.S. history way before that, and we are U.S. history now . . . I wanted to teach, to teach U.S. history, our history.

An administrator at this same charter school stated that the purpose of the school was to provide young students from a particular racial/ethnic group a sense of their own identity. He talked about the school as "a way of life," and said that students identified themselves through the school.

Educators at other ethnocentric charter schools we studied noted similar issues of needing to provide their students a greater sense of ethnic pride and a stronger understanding of their own cultural identity. These are charter schools founders and educators who hoped to create "safe spaces" or "homeplaces" (Collins, 1991; hooks, 1990) for students of a particular racial or ethnic group. Many of these schools are Afro-centric, Chicano-centric, or Native American-centric in their curricular focus and orientation. But whether or not they have such a focus, they have been started by people within the local communities and thus they represent localized social movements, people of color fighting for greater independence from what they see as a hegemonic state-run system (see Wells, Lopez, Scott, & Holme, 1999).

Issues of race and class also were discussed in terms of how charter schools differed from other nearby public schools. While we heard several charter school educators and parents talk about valuing *diversity*—an issue we discuss in more detail below—what this actually meant in practice varied to some degree across sites. Still, it usually meant that diversity along racial and cultural lines was a good thing as long as it did not conflict with the core values and beliefs of the founding parents and educators who defined the school culture, as we will discuss later in the chapter. As Wells and Serna (1996) found, the "ideology of 'diversity at a distance' is often employed by white parents at strategic moments when the privileged status of their children appears to be threatened" (p. 102). Other times, for example, in racially homogeneous schools, this ideology manifests itself more along social-class lines.

Thus, these various efforts on the part of charter schools to define and affirm their distinct identities can play out differently in different contexts, with some charter schools emphasizing certain dimensions—e.g., ethnic/

racial identity—more strongly than others. But in the end, across all the sites, these identity-building efforts served a critical purpose, defining who "belongs."

Defining Who Belongs: Valued Students and Parents

Clearly, part of the process of constructing an identity for a school, is figuring out who belongs there. Thus, the flip side of charter schools' efforts to define who does *not* belong in their educational communities is their discussion and definition of who does belong there and their ability to control which students are accepted, invited, and allowed to participate in the charter. People in all of the charter schools we visited talked about wanting to serve students and parents who "care," who are "motivated" and "committed" to taking on part of the "responsibility" for learning, and willing to be held "accountable" for their actions in and out of school.

For example, at an elementary charter school in a suburban district, a parent talked about the importance of children at the school developing some sense of "personal responsibility." She explained the need for student to be "self-driven." At another charter elementary school, the staff explained that they valued students who were "doing their best" and who showed "effort." It was important to a lot of people at this school that students were "respectful" of themselves and others, that they learned "integrity," and that they were a "positive social influence in the community." As one founding parent stated:

> We are not afraid to use words like patriotism and dignity and work ethic. That's what's behind our moral code. Trying to teach them those values that we think maybe have been . . . if not lost, at least covered over a little bit in the last few years.

At a charter high school, the principal talked at length about the types of students he wanted to enroll in the school, explaining that he was hoping to recruit some children from private schools back into the public system. But he also said he was trying to attract "disadvantaged youth with potential." At one point, he summed up his efforts: "We want some private school kids, but we [also] want to go to the inner city"—as long as those inner-city students had "potential" as he defined it.

In many places, there also seems to be a shared sense of "valued" parenting practices related to concern, commitment, and accountability. For instance, parents at one of the suburban elementary charter schools talked about the importance of parents teaching children "responsibility" and "accountability" at home. We heard echoes of this at other charter schools. For instance, one respondent at a rural charter school noted, "We believe in the simple things around here like honesty and accountability. If you do something wrong, you have to pay the price."

At a suburban charter school, students and parents were given a handout on acceptable behavior and expected personal responsibility. Parents were told:

> This is our culture. This is what our staff is demanding of your child. This is what we will demand of you at every school function, every time you drop off your child at every activity, and if you can't abide by this, this is the conflict resolution procedure that we will demand of you.

As one parent explained, "And that's all [the handout, etc.] now in the parent binder. And . . . when [you] come, at the beginning of school, you're taken through and you're told this is it—this is parent behavior!"

And, at an urban high school that we studied, a teacher noted that since the school became a charter school, it has been enrolling more students who are "prepared to learn" because the school requires parents and students to complete an application process to get into the school. According to this teacher, this means her charter school is attracting parents who are more interested and students who are more willing to work.

Like at many of the charters we studied, educators at a suburban elementary school claimed to have some of the most involved parents from the local community. As one parent explained:

> I think one of the hardest things for some of the other elementary schools [in the district] was that they lost some of the parents who were the most active and who really were willing to put a lot of time into the school. They did go to [the] charter, you know. And I think that [happened] a lot. I've heard people say, "Oh, we lost [so-and-so] to the charter." They see it as losing people to the charter, and they did to a certain extent because those people are no longer there to do those kinds of things that they were doing.

Another interviewee discussed being able "to pick from people who not only just care, but also have . . . the background . . . or the knowledge . . . we just have an awful lot of people to pick their brains, to pick from . . . and for advisory [purposes]." A governance board member also talked about "valued" families in the charter.

> There is this group of homes—the first homes that provided a big jolt in our growth—were probably upper-middle-class homes, with parents

that were educated and really cared . . . and knew what they were after for their kids and knew how schools should run and knew what to expect. And they seemed happy so I think then others thought, "Oh, well, they're happy, that's where we want to be."

This same person noted, "I know what I was looking for in a private school education, and I feel that we [at the charter] come as close to it as you can in a public school situation. Not just because of the charter but because of the families involved."

A similar sentiment was expressed by those affiliated with one of the suburban elementary charter schools we studied. Several parents of students in the school are scientists. A teacher there said that it was hard to be a science teacher at the charter school because there were so many parents that knew a lot about technology and had a scientific background. These parents are valued for their skills and expertise, so much so that they are invited to teach seminars at the school.

It was clear that some parents at another suburban charter school we studied were more valued than others. One teacher there described "dynamo" parents, contrasting them to other parents in the school and the means they have—or do not have—to provide for his class. His view of "dynamo" parents shaped who within this diverse school community was most valued.

> We have some parents who go way overboard. They come to the school, and they want to do anything and everything. I have one of those in my room [this year] . . . and I love her to death! I have not had one single party where [I had to bring stuff]. . . . The first year I sent notes home, and the parents [in my bilingual class] would send like a tamale. . . . And you could tell they were pulling out of the cabinet what they could. That broke my heart. I never did that again. So I buy all the candy or all the cookies or whatever we are going to have. This year, this parent called me ahead of time and said, "Don't worry about the party." She went out and, with her own money . . . like for Valentine's day she ordered peppermint cookies from the bakery . . . beautiful cookies with boxes to put them in. A huge expense. I could never have afforded it. . . . At the end of the year, she wants to make T-shirts for all the kids, and she's buying all the stuff and having it printed.

In addition to wanting well-behaved students and parents, many of the charter school founders, educators, and parents said, as noted above, that they also wanted some degree of "diversity" at least in theory. Most frequently, they talked about diversity in terms of race/ethnicity, although some also used "diversity" to refer to socioeconomic status, English-language proficiency, or even learning ability.

For instance, a teacher at an urban charter high school described the many dimensions of diversity at his school. "I always wanted to work with a really diverse student population, so this [charter school] definitely offers that. . . . Economically, socially, racially, family order-wise, everything . . . handicaps, physical or mental, sexual orientation, the whole gamut."

At another charter in our study, a suburban elementary school, parents and educators openly discussed their interest in exposing the children in the school to a diverse educational setting. We heard comments such as:

> I went to public schools, and I feel that I got a great education, and I don't think that it should be any different. I pay my taxes. I expect my children to be schooled well. I can afford to go to a private school, it's not the real world to me—quote, unquote—real world. I want different cultures, I want different socioeconomic kids. I want . . . anything different in this school that could be there.

Another teacher expressed a similar hope for the charter school: "We want everyone to learn from each other and experience the real world of public school."

Yet while charter school founders, educators, and parents talked about valuing "diversity" in terms of their student populations, they also placed tight controls on the degree and type of diversity through the use of student and parent "requirements" or contracts. Such restrictions allowed charter schools to create so-called "diverse" communities that were homogeneous in terms of students' and parents' values and beliefs about schooling and willingness to abide by school requirements.

For instance, at one rural charter school, there was a lot of discussion about the "professional and well-educated parents" who lived in the district and sent their children to the charter school. One respondent explained:

> We have superior court judges, we have lawyers, we have, of course, school teachers, principals, superintendents. We have doctors, pilots, nurses . . . we have an awful lot of professional people living in our [school boundaries] who really care about this, and are sending their children [here] instead of private schools, which makes us feel good, of course. And they are very supportive and they have an awful lot to offer, and they were . . . many of them were on the committees when we were writing the charter.

In one of the urban school districts we studied, a school board member described one of the charter high schools as "racially integrated but not necessarily economically integrated." The board member also noted that although this particular school was "set up" to "value diversity," what that means is that diversity is valued there "as long as you're middle class in behavior and in everything else, and as long as you come with the kind of support system where you're gonna succeed regardless of where you go."

Another way of "dealing" with diversity was to keep the number and percentage of "minority" and low-income students so low that they were easily assimilated into the White and upper-middle-class culture. In other words, this was another way of saying diversity is good as long as everyone acts like "us." For instance, one teacher noted that "we still have our—you know— our migrant children and lower socioeconomic children, of course. But they're in the environment and they respond."

Holmes (1992) notes that while many parents genuinely like the idea of their children growing up with other children from varied social backgrounds, when given a choice between a "heterogeneous" school that does not conform to their educational ambitions for their children and a more "homogeneous" one that does, many will choose the latter. Thus, we saw charter school founders, educators, and parents attempting to deal with the tension between appreciating diversity and wanting to associate only with people who were like them. In other words, they strove to create "bounded diversity"—a community that could be diverse along some dimensions such as race/ethnicity, as long as everyone who attended shared similar values and beliefs about education and parent involvement. This proved to be a very difficult task and one that ultimately failed to create diverse schools.

Although the characteristics and behaviors of "valued" students and parents that charter school educators describe are also considered desirable in other schools, charter schools are able to use a wide variety of mechanisms to ensure that "valued" students and parents are attracted to, and remain, members of these educational communities. In the next section we describe these mechanisms.

THE MECHANISMS USED TO STRUCTURE
CHARTER SCHOOL COMMUNITIES

Charter school founders, educators, and parents employ certain mechanisms in their efforts to structure their educational communities to include only those who share certain values and beliefs and who appreciate the distinctive identity of the charter school. For instance, charter school educators talked about how their recruitment and enrollment processes, their student requirements and discipline/expulsion practices, and their parent-involvement requirements all shaped who became and who remained a part of these schools.

All of these mechanisms enable charter school founders and educators to create a school identity that reflects their values and beliefs about schooling. In creating such an identity, people must pay close attention to image production. Gewirtz and colleagues (1995) define this image-production process as the creation of messages about the ethos, culture, values, priorities, and "quality" of educational provision. They describe how schools convey their image to the public in a variety of ways, often through policies and practices, but also through the "glossification" of school imagery. This includes how school personnel design and present everything from the school buildings to publicity materials and promotional events, including open houses. They also can try to manipulate the press coverage of the school and the school's symbols, such as uniforms, flags, and icons. Gewirtz and colleagues (1995) explain:

> *The new symbolism is important because it carries a message about what and who is valued in schools* and because . . . it has implications for, and is rooted within, policies and processes which have practical consequences for children. Through the symbolism and associated policies and practices the market valorizes certain kinds of success, activities, behavior, *and children*, and devalorizes others. (p. 142, emphasis in original)

Charter schools use such symbols and school imagery, including icons and uniforms, as well as publicity events, brochures, open houses, tours, and so on, to help them develop and market charters' institutional identities. As Power, Halpin, and Fitz (1994) describe from their study of school choice in England:

> All state schools are now more conscious that the management of their local reputations is a central aspect of attracting parents. Certainly schools seem more concerned than ever to "market" themselves through the presentation of glossy prospectuses and open [houses]. There is also a renewed emphasis on school uniforms as an outward sign of good discipline. (p. 220)

We found evidence of such imagery and marketing in the mechanisms that charter schools used to shape their educational communities. A teacher at one of the urban charter high schools we studied described the marketing of this school.

> We are selling a product here. And we have to get that message across to parents that this is a product and, you know, this is what you will get if you come here. Nobody is going to force you to come to [this school] but [if you do] this is what you will get.

The mechanisms discussed here relate to recruitment, admissions, and enrollment; student academic requirements and discipline/expulsion practices; and parent-involvement requirements.

Recruitment, Admissions, and Enrollment Processes

Charter schools have increased control over who enrolls and participates in them, beginning with publicity, information dissemination, and recruiting strategies. In terms of *publicity and information dissemination,* some of the charter schools we studied sent out information about their schools in district-wide brochures, along with other schools in the district. Some of them posted flyers in the local community or sent out mailers to families within their attendance boundaries. Also some placed ads in the newspaper and gave tours to interested parents and students. Still others had school representatives—usually the principal and sometimes students as well—travel around, making presentations about the charter, to inform, recruit, and raise money for the school.

Yet what is most interesting about these publicity and information-dissemination tactics is that while they could be used equitably to make the charter's programs known to all students in the district, this was not always the case. Some charter schools chose to target the specific populations that were seen as "valuable" or "desirable" by the charter school community. In addition, often marketing efforts to publicize oversubscribed charter schools were curtailed altogether. As a principal at one charter high school explained:

> In the beginning, 4 or 5 years ago . . . we were marketing ourselves.
> I'm not saying we don't market now . . . but I don't have to go out
> and find more students because we have enough. We're kind of in a
> position that we don't want to over-market ourselves and disappoint a
> lot of people.

Admissions priorities and requirements exemplify another way in which charters are able to shape who is a part of them, more so than other public schools. Most of the charter schools in our study implemented some sort of admissions criteria. These criteria specified which students had priority to attend the school and which students and parents fit well into the charter school and thus would succeed in that particular educational community.

Furthermore, although many of the charter schools we studied stated that they operated on a "first come, first served basis," in reality, the process was much more complicated. For instance, the charter schools that were oversubscribed usually gave priority to certain students—for example, those who attended the school before it was a charter school, those who had siblings there, or those whose parents worked there. Beyond these priorities, the first-come, first-served policy favored parents with the most access to information about schools and choice within their districts, because of the limited recruitment strategies and the requirements associated with the admissions process.

For instance, as part of the admissions or application process, several schools required some sort of parent/student meeting with school officials. Such meetings ranged from an informal chat, where the school culture was described to families, to more of an interview, where students' abilities and interests were assessed along with parents' level of commitment to education and school service. Charter school affiliates described to us how this meeting/interview time often was used as an opportunity to make sure there was a fit between the charter identity—its mission, policies, and practices—and the family. For instance, the principal of an urban charter high school described how the meetings with students and parents provided an opportunity to gauge whether the students would be successful at his school.

> The students who don't want to be here aren't successful. Seriously. There are students whose families force them to go here, and now we've learned with our presentations and our applications processes, if you don't want to come, don't come. They'll do everything possible to flunk out or to get kicked out or just to not succeed, and who needs it? There's a couple of kids who went to a very progressive school, with no classes and independent studies. It's clear that they won't fit, so we're counseling and asking them to encourage their family [to] go someplace [else].

A teacher at another urban charter high school noted that the admissions interviews that the staff conducted with parents and students were "key" because they asked students if they knew that this was a college-prep school with a lot of requirements and no music or drama. She said, "We just want to make sure kids know what they are getting into when they come here."

In addition to admissions meetings, these two charter high schools also required students to write essays about why they wanted to attend the school. These admissions requirements allowed the charter schools' staff to filter through applicants to ensure that their shared values and beliefs were supported and upheld. The principal of one of these schools explained the importance of admissions requirements.

> What we found is . . . the applications . . . are a pretty good screening process for commitment. Lots of kids are weak. That's fine. But . . . by

getting all these things we know they want to come. The ones that aren't happy, they don't stay. We turn away hundreds and hundreds of kids, so we can fill [their slots]. It's like, "go somewhere where you're happy." And, to be honest, we're not good for everybody.

Student Academic Requirements and Discipline/Expulsion Practices

As discussed earlier, charter schools often state explicit expectations and requirements of students, in terms of academic performance, "effort," and behavior, in their charters, mission statements, and policies. Unlike other public schools, charter schools are legally able to enforce these student requirements, mainly through the use of contracts and discipline/expulsion policies and practices. Most of the charters we visited had such requirements, policies, and contracts in place. They could ask people to leave the schools if they did not "live up" to the charters or the "contract." The specific requirements within these contracts or charters varied, but they included matters related to students "making an effort" or "trying hard enough," being tardy or absent, or not abiding by the rules of the school's conduct code.

For example, a teacher at an urban charter school described how the contract was used.

I had one kid tell me—he was in the fourth grade—he told me I was full of shit, in front of the whole class, and then walked out. So what I did when class was over, I called his parents at work immediately and we had a parent conference, and what they did is put him on contract, and if anything happened for the rest of the semester he was out of here. He straightened out. They know. Just the reputation of [this school], the students want to be here, and [the school staff] are not going to let you continue to screw around and stay here.

Another parent, at a suburban elementary charter school, commented, "It is nice to have some 'teeth' when you need 'teeth' as far as discipline and having children be accountable for themselves and the work." A teacher at the same school expressed a similar sentiment about the student contract.

I just feel that it holds the students and the parents much more responsible, and it's much easier for us as teachers and [for] our principal to enforce our rules and our standards and our expectations. And I think that our school has very minimal discipline problems because of that. It's made a huge difference, huge.

Another urban charter high school in our study had an academic probation policy, which an administrator referred to as a way to get rid of students who were not trying hard enough. On the student's application to the charter school, the policy states that students with three or four failing grades are placed on academic probation, and students with five or six failing grades can be "moved out" if they do not show improvement in the next grading period. After the three or four failures, a counselor sends a letter to the student's home. If there are additional failures, the counselor refers the student to a student-success team—comprising the student, his or her parents, and educators—"to evaluate what is going on." The administrator went on to say that a lot of the failures occurred because of attendance problems, because if students missed too many classes they automatically failed the course. Furthermore, three tardies to class equals a failure. The administrator noted that students who did not improve their attendance were sent back to their "neighborhood schools." Inherent in this statement is the assumption that the students who "fail" are not the wealthy students who live near the schools and for whom the charter *is* their neighborhood high school. She also talked about enforcing a dress code at the school—no baggy pants, no hats, no dresses that look like slips—as a way to control who is in and who is out. Other charters we visited also chose to set a dress code for similar reasons. Yet, in setting such codes, the charter schools also sent messages about whose culture was valued, as some of the articles of clothing were more likely to be worn by students of certain racial/ethnic backgrounds.

In a discussion of the purpose of the student contracts at one of the rural charters we studied, a teacher noted that if families there did not fulfill the requirements of the contract, the child could be asked to go elsewhere. She remarked, "It cut through the red tape, a *lot* of red tape, other schools would have to go through. [The founder's] idea was that he didn't want people taking up space, you know, he wanted kids and families that wanted to learn."

Parent-Involvement Requirements

As with students, charter schools also specify expectations and requirements of parents in their charters, school missions, and policies; and unlike other public schools, charters are able to enforce these parents requirements, mainly through the use of contracts. Charter schools sometimes ask parents to read to their children, go over their homework, and encourage "appropriate" behaviors—those in accordance with school behavior codes, and so forth. However, the most common requirement that the charter schools we studied made was that parents volunteer at the school and participate in school activities, a certain number of either hours or events per school year. And, charters reserved the right to ask families to leave if parents did not "live up to the charter" or meet the requirements specified in the "contract."

A parent and governance council member at one of the suburban charter schools we studied talked about how her school enforces the parent contract.

> If they can't fulfill their parents' participation hours, they must request an exemption, and present their explanation and a committee will meet and determine, do we grant them an allowance, do we give them an extension, do we make it null and void?

Founders, educators, and parents at some of the charter schools we studied talked about not allowing families to re-enroll for the fall when parents had not fulfilled the required volunteer time or participated in enough school activities. Although it was not always clear how often this actually took place versus how often parents and students removed themselves from the schools, the right that charters have to remove students "scares" families into either abiding by the school "rules" or leaving on their own. For example, at an urban elementary charter school we studied, a teacher told the following anecdote: "The parents all have to [put in] 30 hours. They don't all do it, but they figure they owe us, so if you tell them their kid is screwing up, they say, 'Oh, OK, I'll get right to it, because I don't want to be [singled out] for not doing my job.'"

The superintendent of a neighboring school district to one of the rural districts we studied raised another issue about the use of contracts in charter schools. He drew attention to the relationship between the contracts and who was attracted to the school.

> I think that contract business certainly culturally fits in much more nicely with people who understand the nature of contracts and the mutual promises that, you know—you make an offer and I accept. You know that's more of a, you know, educated person shtick than it is some poor soul who's trying to slug out a living on, you know, out picking cotton, who wouldn't have a chance in a million to spend so many hours a day at the school. Most of those folks are running for their lives.

He makes the point that people who are less educated, working class, and/or have lower socioeconomic status are less likely to be familiar with contracts and therefore either feel intimidated by them or not understand the seriousness with which they are expected to take the contracts. Furthermore, they probably have less time and means to actually meet the requirements outlined in charters' parent contracts.

Returning to the very issues that frame this chapter, Holmes (1992) writes that the assumptions underlying the importance of parent-involvement requirements in schools can stand in opposition to articulated desires to serve students from diverse backgrounds. He writes that many of the assumptions behind the popularity of the liberal, common school model of parent involvement merit analysis. Such assumptions, he notes, include the beliefs that all "parents have the time and ability and the inclination to become involved" and that "parents of limited education feel confident to participate alongside more successful, more affluent parents, without humiliating their children." He notes:

> But that is precisely what is questionable. It is ironic that sharing should be so important and so practical in the very situation where there are not shared beliefs, shared philosophical and educational assumptions, shared religions and shared cultures. . . . Heterogeneity and diversity are claimed to be virtues, demands the sharing of the school's values. (p. 65)

In other words, the parent-involvement requirements and contracts of the charter schools we studied, as well as the other mechanisms described in this section, allowed charter school founders, educators, and parents to "bound" the diversity that they said they so highly valued. The mechanisms serve as symbols of charter schools' distinct identities in the landscape of public education. At the same time, they enable people in charter schools to decide which students and parents are included in these new educational communities.

CONCLUSION: CHARTER SCHOOL COMMUNITIES AND THE COMMON GOOD

Charter school reform provides a legal tool that groups of people, including founders, educators, and/or parents, can use to bound diversity within an educational community around values and beliefs about schooling. In creating charter schools, the founders and participants we studied went through a process of identity building in which they defined the distinction of their schools and understandings of who fit in and who didn't. Salient issues in this process included things like safety, academic rigor, accountability, being like a private school, popularity, parental voice, and ethnic/racial identity. As charters, they were able to use mechanisms such as targeted publicity and recruiting, admissions criteria, and parent and student contracts that let certain people in and kept others out.

Certainly, social stratification and segregation along race and class lines ran rampant in the public education system long before charter school legislation was passed, often due to housing markets, district attendance boundaries, and so forth. However, we find that charter schools emerge as sites where distinctions about who belongs and who does not tend to be more clearly articulated by educators, parents, and students than they do in regular public schools. Furthermore, charter school legislation allows members of charter school communities to act on these values and beliefs through the use of mechanisms that most other public schools cannot—or have not—implemented.

While clearly there are important perceived benefits to these community-building efforts on the part of the people who are included in them, there are obviously broader implications in terms of how these efforts affect student access to educational opportunities more generally. It is important for educational research to document this process of diversity bounding and consider what it means for the educational opportunities of all students.

Acknowledgment. We would like to thank Makeba Jones for reading a draft of this chapter and providing valuable feedback.

REFERENCES

Bourdieu, P. (1984). *Distinction: A social critique of the judgment of taste.* Cambridge, MA: Harvard University Press.

Brantlinger, E., Majd-Jabbari, M., & Guskin, S. L. (1996). Self-interest and liberal educational discourse: How ideology works for middle class mothers. *American Educational Research Journal, 33*(3), 571–597.

Carlson, D. (1997). *Making progress: Education and culture in new times.* New York: Teachers College Press.

Castells, M. (1997). *The power of identity.* Malden, MA: Blackwell.

Clark, B. (1992). *The distinctive college.* New Brunswick, NJ: Transaction Publishers.

Collins, P. H. (1991). *Black feminist thought: Knowledge, consciousness and the politics of empowerment.* NewYork: Routledge.

Cookson, P. (1994). *School choice: The struggle for the soul of American education.* New Haven, CT: Yale University Press.

Driscoll, M. E. (1993). Choice, achievement, and school community. In E. Rassell & R. Rothstein (Eds.), *School choice: Examining the evidence* (pp. 147–172). Washington, DC: Economic Policy Institute.

Ford, R. T. (1995). The boundaries of race: Political geography in legal analysis. In K. Crenshaw, N. Gotanda, G. Peller, & K. Thomas (Eds.), *Critical race theory.* New York: The New Press.

Gewirtz, S., Ball, S. J., & Bowe, R. (1995). *Markets, choice and equity in education.* Buckingham, UK: Open University Press.

Holmes, M. (1992). *Educational policy for the pluralist democracy: The common school, choice, and diversity.* Washington, DC: Falmer Press.

hooks, b. (1990). *Yearning: Race, gender, and cultural politics.* Boston: South End Press.

Lareau, A. (1989). *Home advantage: Social class and parental intervention in elementary education.* London: Falmer Press.

Power, S., Halpin, D., & Fitz, J. (1994). Parents, pupils, and grant-maintained schools. *British Educational Research Journal, 20*(2), 209–225.

Wells, A. S., Holme, J. J., Lopez, A., & Cooper, C. W. (2000). Charter schools and racial and social class segregation: Yet another sorting machine? In R. Kahlenberg (Ed.), *A notion at risk: Preserving education as an engine for social mobility* (pp. 169–222). New York: Century Foundation Press.

Wells, A. S., Lopez, A., Scott, J., & Holme, J. J. (1999). Charter schools as postmodern paradox: Rethinking social stratification in an age of deregulated school choice. *Harvard Educational Review, 69*(2), 172–204.

Wells, A. S. & Serna, I. (1996, Spring). The politics of culture: Understanding local political resistance to detracking in racially mixed schools. *Harvard Educational Review, 62*(1), 93–118.

CHAPTER 7

California's Charter School Teachers

The Embedded Context of Professionalism

Ash Vasudeva and Cynthia Grutzik

Arguably the most highly touted aspect of charter school reform is the freedom and autonomy it grants to teachers. Released from the constraints of district bureaucracies or contract-bound unions, charter school educators are supposed to create fertile sites for educational innovation (Nathan, 1996; Vanourek, Manno, & Finn, 1997). Indeed, some of the earliest supporters of this reform movement included those who saw charter schools as sites of teacher empowerment. For instance, Ray Budde (1989), a founding father of the charter school movement, saw it as a teacher-led reform that could give educators more professional autonomy. Furthermore, American Federation of Teachers' leader Albert Shanker (1994) was one of the earliest proponents of the chartering concept, noting that charter school educators had "the power to do their own thing and, presumably, to make their school what they think it ought to be—without interference from the central office or the school board" (p. 1).

Indeed, Seymour Sarason (1998), doyen of American education, writes that charter school reform has the potential to create new schools that sidestep the bureaucratized, burdensome regularities that afflict the culture of existing school systems. In this way, Sarason's hope for charter schools rests on one of the most pronounced assumptions underlying charter school reform—that these schools will be free to structure themselves in ways that work best for children and teachers rather than as regulatory or administrative bureaucracies (UCLA Charter School Study, 1998).

Adapted from Ash Vasudeva and Cynthia Grutzik, "Teachers' Perspectives on Charter School Reform," *Teaching & Change* (7/3), pp. 235-257. Copyright © 2000 by Corwin Press, Inc.
Reprinted by permission of Corwin Press, Inc.

Such optimism regarding the potential for charter school reform to provide the autonomy for teachers to better use their professional training and judgment is woven into state laws as well. For instance, educational independence and teacher professionalism were explicitly linked in the original California Charter Schools Act of 1992. The law calls for "schools that operate independently from the existing school district structure," in part, to "create new professional opportunities for teachers, including the opportunity to be responsible for the learning at the school site" (California Education Code, 1992).

Part of the purpose of our UCLA study of California charter schools was to understand what this promise of greater teacher professionalism looked like at the school level. This chapter examines charter school reform through the eyes—or, more accurately, the attitudes, thoughts, and beliefs—of teachers at the 17 charter schools in the UCLA study. We also analyzed transcripts from interviews with charter school administrators and parents, who spoke at length about what they valued in terms of teacher professionalism.

Two particularly salient themes emerged: The first was that many of the charter school teachers we interviewed expressed a great deal of pride in working in schools that were more autonomous from the public school system. The second, somewhat contradictory, theme was that their professional identity remained tied to more traditional public education-based institutions, including teachers unions and credentialing commissions, and not to their status as charter school teachers.

Thus, the first theme centered on the teachers' expression of a great deal of satisfaction in working at a charter school and their pride in being associated with a more autonomous school that was perceived to be unique compared with other schools in their local communities. For example, we learned that in California, as in many other states, charter school teachers overwhelmingly valued having greater freedom and autonomy from state and district rules and regulations (Education Commission of the States, 1995; Koppich, Holmes, & Plecki, 1998). Also, according to many of the teachers we interviewed, charter schools allowed them to create strong relationships with students and with other teachers, thereby building tighter-knit communities and often creating an esprit de corps. However, our data also suggest—as do a growing number of other studies on this issue—that this energy and enthusiasm led to few changes in terms of classroom practices and instruction (see, for instance, Arsen, Plank, & Sykes, 1999; Public Sector Consultants & Maximus, 1999; SRI International, 1997; Wood, 1999). Furthermore, our study and others have found that in addition to valuing their greater freedom, many charter school educators are also overworked and on the verge of burnout (UCLA Charter School Study, 1998; Weiss, 1997).

A second theme that emerged was that rather than being defined by the independence and autonomy they enjoyed in terms of the school organization, charter school teachers' sense of professional identity was often—although not always—intimately related to a variety of teaching contexts, including local teachers associations and state credentialing commissions. Here, we found that many charter school teachers, while appreciating the educational independence facilitated by charter school reform, also valued their membership in larger professional communities such as unions. This was much more true for teachers who previously had worked in public schools and teachers in converted charter schools and less true for teachers who were new to the profession and employed in start-up charter schools. Still, it was more pronounced than we expected to find in a reform movement partly grounded in anti-union rhetoric (see, for instance, Finn, Manno, Vanourek, & Bierlein, 1997).

Related to this theme is the finding that across almost all of the schools we studied, charter school leaders and parents valued evidence of professional training, especially a state teaching credential, for the teachers in their schools. Indeed, when charter schools had credentialed teachers, the leaders often used it as a selling point to parents interested in their schools. Thus, despite their efforts to remain distinct and different from the "regular" and bureaucratic public schools, charter school teachers and constituents often valued and relied on various aspects of that very system to accomplish their goals.

These two emerging, complex, and, in some ways, contradictory themes on working and teaching in charter schools have led us to conceptualize charter school teachers' professional lives as part of a larger educational tapestry that extends beyond the immediate domain of their schools and classrooms. In other words, the contexts that matter for charter school teachers are not limited to charter school communities. Rather, charter school teachers, like teachers in all schools, are influenced by both local and larger policy contexts. For instance, the characteristics valued by charter school teachers and facilitated by charter school reform resemble the teaching conditions advocated by educators engaged in a variety of school-based reforms—namely, smaller, more intimate settings and closer working relationships. Still, despite the fact that charter school teachers are released from the mandates, regulations, and controls of states and districts to a greater degree than their peers in traditional schools, it could well be that charter school educators, as Sarason (1998) fears, lack the time and energy to engage in the sustained pattern of reflection and revision needed for continuous improvement in education. This would explain a consistent finding in the research literature of little or no evidence of classroom-level innovation or change within charter schools (see Arsen et al., 1999; Public Sector Consultants & Maximus, 1999; SRI International, 1997; Wood, 1999). It also could explain why so many charter school teachers continue to look toward more traditional professional associations, such as unions and credentialing commissions, for validation.

With some exceptions, the charter school teachers we spoke with were attracted to, and influenced by, the same diverse mixture of local and larger teaching contexts that broadly shape teachers' work. Therefore, even while many of the specifics of their local contexts differed from those of educators in less autonomous schools nearby, their lives, like the lives of so many teachers, were influenced by a mixture of local and larger policy contexts. Their professional lives, like the lives of all teachers, were not simply circumscribed by the boundaries of their particular charter schools. Drawing from Joan Talbert and Milbrey McLaughlin's (1993) discussion of how teachers are influenced by multiple contexts, we describe the interaction between local and larger contexts for charter school teachers as the *embedded context of professionalism.*

TEACHING IN CHARTER SCHOOLS: THE EMBEDDED CONTEXT OF PROFESSIONALISM

Talbert and McLaughlin (1993) conceptualize teaching by placing teachers, students, and classrooms at the center of a set of concentric circles, with each circle representing a specific context that has the potential to influence classroom practice. Moving outward from the center, teachers' work is shaped by numerous circles, including their subject area/department, the organization of the school, the school sector (i.e., public/private/parochial) and system (e.g., district), and the social-class structure of the school's parent community. More distant, but still influential, circles include higher education institutions, local professional associations, and finally society's educational goals, particular reform initiatives, and the profession's norms of practice.

Talbert and McLaughlin (1993) emphasize that all of these multiple and embedded contexts *together* influence teaching and learning in schools. They write that the important contexts of teaching are much more "varied, embedded, and interactive in their effects on teaching practice" than assumed by relevant lines of research on the effect of context. Indeed, their schema of concentric circles summarizes "the multiple and embedded educational contexts that together shape teaching goals and practices in secondary and elementary schools" (p. 188).

Charter school reform, in theory, seemingly redesigns this schema by reducing the number of concentric circles that influence teachers' work. In other words, charter school teachers hopefully have the same initial center or focus as any non-charter teachers would have—that is, children and classrooms. But because of the autonomy that their schools are supposed to enjoy from the educational system, charter school teachers can, theoretically, be somewhat insulated from interactions beyond the school community, while traditional teachers must—also theoretically—navigate state, district, and union contexts. Yet, as noted above, our interviews with charter school teachers revealed a different picture.

Thus, similar to points made in other chapters of this book—namely, Chapters 2, 3, and 4—we learned that charter schools were not isolated islands, but rather had varying degrees of relationships with other institutions, such as unions or districts or state departments of education. At conversion schools, these relationships were much stronger than in start-up schools. However, even in start-up charter schools, these relationships existed to some extent.

Viewing charter school teachers' interactions with their multiple contexts allows us to understand the charter school movement as consistent with, rather than a departure from, broader efforts to reform schooling. In fact, our findings suggest underlying similarities between charter school teachers and teachers in other reform-minded settings with respect to the context-related effects. Thus, while we use Talbert and McLaughlin's framework for understanding teaching within context as a springboard into our discussion of the professional lives of charter school teachers, we also draw from the larger body of literature on teaching in reforming schools. This allows us to highlight the common threads connecting teachers in this particular movement with the broader teaching profession.

Also, throughout the chapter we refer to "teachers' experiences." However, it should be noted that "teachers" were defined differently across the 17 sites in our study. For example, while the majority of charter schools in our study employed teachers as they traditionally are defined, the two home study programs referred to their educators as "educational specialists" or "facilitators" rather than teachers. Although the distinctions between teachers and facilitators or educational specialists sometimes included differences in professional training and responsibilities, in this chapter they are grouped together with other charter school teachers to include the voices of all the adults in our study who shared responsibility for teaching and student learning.

LOCAL PROFESSIONAL CONTEXTS FOR CHARTER SCHOOL TEACHERS

The charter school teachers we interviewed described three critical aspects of their local teaching contexts. First, they were highly enthusiastic about charter schools that maintained personal, intimate settings, either through limited enrollment (i.e., small schools) or low teacher/pupil ratios (i.e., class-size reduction). Second, teachers commonly referred to their work as being intensely satisfying on a personal level. In start-up charters, this satisfaction typically took the form of an esprit de corps, while teachers in conversion charters often described a sense of renewal and reinvigoration. These findings are consistent with other studies of charter school teachers, in that they show how local, context-specific variables, such as a familial atmosphere and opportunities to work with dedicated colleagues, foster feelings of commitment and efficacy among teachers (Finn et al., 1997; Little Hoover Commission, 1996).

At the same time, however, we also documented a third element, the flip side to the highly motivated teaching corps often found in charter schools: physical exhaustion and fatigue, the threat of rapid turnover, and the difficulty of sustaining intense levels of commitment over time. Like the more positive contextual features of charter schools, the intense time commitment, along with the attendant possibility of burning out, also has been reported by other researchers (see Weiss, 1997). Related to this, charter school teachers often described themselves as being more committed and harder working than most other public school teachers.

Small Size and Intimacy of Schools and Classes

Many of the charter schools we studied used a variety of techniques to create an intimate, family-like atmosphere. Some schools, especially start-ups, had lower enrollments than traditional schools serving similar grade levels. Other charter schools, especially conversion schools that could not shrink their overall school size, made a concerted effort to reduce their class sizes—a reform that dovetailed with California's efforts to lower class size in all K–3 classrooms. Still others promoted stronger relationships between teachers and students by shifting the schedule to create longer classes or a longer school day. According to many of the teachers we interviewed, these efforts to reduce the "scale" of teaching and learning in charter schools humanized and enhanced their lives as professional educators.

Teachers reiterated the value of smallness at nearly all of the start-up charter schools we studied. For instance, at Foundation Elementary Charter School, a start-up school with 160 students mentioned in earlier chapters, teachers commented on the importance of keeping the school intimate. One noted:

> I just really like the small size . . . it's just a small atmosphere. We don't have 10 different lunch periods, we have two . . . so it's more intimate. I know a lot of the kids [by] name, I know what they're up to, and they come in and work with me.

Echoing the views of her colleagues, another teacher, when asked about Foundation's attributes, told us, "You don't have a mass of children. You don't have 1,200 children in a school to deal with, so . . . it's nicer that way." Similarly, at Heritage Charter School, a middle school serving an ethnically distinct student population (see Chapter 5), one teacher noted that charter schools change the nature of schooling. She said, "It becomes personal, it becomes private, it becomes special, and you can't get that at a public school . . . you cannot meet those needs in any public school system, or private school system."

While start-up charter schools focused on keeping schools small, conversion charter schools made similar efforts to create more intimacy by keeping class sizes small. In fact, educators at all four of the conversion elementary charter schools in our study—and one conversion middle school—reported class-size reduction as one of the benefits of becoming a charter school. Teachers at these charter schools clearly connected reducing class sizes with promoting a more family-like school setting. Meanwhile, two charter schools in our study offering home-based instruction—Ursa Independent Charter School and Valley Home School—took class-size reduction to its logical terminus. "We offer a class size of one!" the director of Ursa Independent Charter School told us with a proud grin.

Although these class-size-reduction strategies significantly overlapped with a statewide mandate to trim K–3 classes to 20 students each, teachers and administrators at conversion charter schools argued that they were able to implement the state initiative more quickly than traditional public schools. They also noted that in some instances they were able to affect more grade levels than K–3. For example, at Monument Charter School, a K–5 school located in a district with a rapidly growing enrollment, the need to reduce class size to no more than 28 students played a central role in the staff's decision to convert to charter status. One Monument teacher told us:

> I had 37 kids [prior to the conversion to charter status], so I was definitely in the mood for . . . a change in that situation. During that year, some parents and [the principal] had been playing around with the idea becoming a charter . . . and I think most of us felt that we needed to get control of the class size.

While charter school teachers most often cited the small size of their schools and/or classes as contributing to a sense of school community, changes in scheduling and organization also were deemed important. For example, two schools chose to extend their school days, giving teachers more time with students and with each other. One school rearranged its weekly schedule so that every Wednesday afternoon was pupil-free for teachers to spend planning and learning together. And one group of teachers pointed out that since they began working in a charter school, they were more likely to invite students into their classrooms before and after school, an arrangement they said would have been more difficult in their previous schools. It is important to note that while non-charter schools in California technically are able to make these kinds of arrangements, the teachers we interviewed felt more free to pursue them after receiving their charter.

Obviously, the appeal of more personalized working conditions—particularly small schools and classrooms—extends well beyond the boundaries of charter school reform. For example, longtime teacher, administrator, and public school reformer Deborah Meier (1995) has written at length about the virtues of small schools. She and other reformers see such small schools as the way to eliminate the impersonal, factory-like atmosphere of traditional secondary schools and facilitate more meaningful relationships between adults and students (see, for example, Sizer, 1984, 1992). In this way, Meier's suggestion that districts break up large schools and redesign them into small schools, easily accessible on the basis of choice, is philosophically in line with charter school reform. Indeed, to the extent that it allows educators to create smaller, more personal school settings, charter school reform complements the recommendations of Meier and other advocates. Thus, it represents one possible way to create the types of local educational contexts that many practitioners and policy makers find attractive and important.

Renewed Commitments and Shared Esprit de Corps

Across the schools we studied, teachers, when discussing their lives as educators in charter schools, were both challenged and invigorated by the new reform. At start-up charter schools, teachers described an esprit de corps that permeated their undertaking. Similarly, teachers at conversion charter schools took pride in their commitment and dedication to remaking public education.

Our data suggest that charter school teachers often differentiated themselves from teachers in traditional public schools. Typically, they considered themselves to be harder working, more committed, and more professional than their counterparts. For example, at Directions High School (mentioned in Chapters 4 and 5), one teacher effusively praised his colleagues.

> I love the other teachers here. I mean it's just such a great group, and I feel it's much more close-knit than almost anywhere else I could be. I like the striving for excellence. I mean the people that are here also want to be here. It's not just some school that we're assigned to. And so they all have that spirit. So you're with your fellow idealists—or fools, maybe—and that's nice to have in common with everybody else. And everybody knows everybody, and I like that. I like starting out with something, and feel like I'm helping to build it.

At almost all of the 17 schools, teachers generally spoke about—or at least alluded to—a boost in pride that accompanied their charter status. Furthermore, teachers in several charter schools said they were different from teachers in non-charter schools in several ways. For example, in three charter schools we studied, teachers described themselves as "mavericks" or "rebels," willing to push against the district bureaucracy.

While there is by no means a consensus around what it means to be a charter school teacher, our data reveal emergent attempts to define the role in opposition to conventional, and sometimes unsavory, portrayals of public school teachers. Furthermore, by distinguishing themselves from other public school teachers, a minority of charter school educators—particularly those in new, start-up charter schools—suggested that organizations such as teachers unions designed to promote teachers' interests are less necessary. Still, as we note below, this view was not at all consistent across the 17 sites.

At four charter schools, teachers expressed a greater sense of efficacy. When asked for examples of what had changed for them as a result of being in a charter school, they told us that they were able to obtain more instructional materials than they had thought would be possible. They also talked about having more freedom to design their curriculum, even though they rarely did this (see below). These findings suggest that the charter school teachers we interviewed associated greater power and control over their professional lives with their involvement in charter school reform.

Still, it was not always clear how or when their perceptions were linked to changes in their teaching practices. For example, one teacher at the home-schooling and independent study Ursa Independent Charter School described her satisfaction with leaving a traditional public school to work at a charter school. Yet, she noted that despite working in a very different organizational setting, neither the textbook-driven curriculum nor the pedagogy of teaching to the test diverged from traditional classroom practices. Even in charter schools that were not home-schooling charters, teachers could not always identify what, in terms of their own teaching, had changed as a result of being in a charter rather than a "regular" public school. Based on these findings, we suggest that charter school educators' new identities may be based on factors other than their teaching practices.

The possibility that charter school teachers derive satisfaction from factors unrelated to changes in the classroom has been noted previously in the literature. David Paris (1998) suggests that charter schools—like other types of schools—"succeed by creating a culture of belief in the moral authority of the school and the legitimacy of its aims" (p. 393). Without any other change in schooling, this culture of belief may enhance teachers' feelings of professional efficacy by diminishing tensions or conflicts (e.g., student discipline problems) over the goals, expectations, and vision for the school.

Thus, it could be that charter school teachers value working in charter schools for more organizational, as opposed to pedagogical, reasons. For example, in a separate study of charter school teachers, Grutzik (1997) noted that teachers in charter schools often considered their choice to work in a charter school to be an important part of their professional identity. Many of the teachers in Grutzik's sample identified working in a charter school as a means of favorably distinguishing themselves from colleagues in traditional schools.

Fear of Burnout/Stretched Too Thin

Despite the attractiveness of working at small charter schools, teachers were aware of the costs involved in staying small. These costs included feeling constantly pressured by time constraints, the fear of inadequate curriculum coverage, and the prospect of physical and mental fatigue. Teachers at Community Charter School (mentioned in Chapters 4 and 5) exemplified the benefits and drawbacks of working in a small, start-up charter. Sharing her enthusiasm for the school with us, one teacher remarked, "Having a small staff that has a lot to say is really wonderful, and it's overwhelming sometimes because there is so much that we all need to do above and beyond our teaching." In addition to feeling overwhelmed by non-instructional demands, this teacher wondered whether she was being stretched too thin by a commitment that offered little financial reward and would be difficult to sustain. "We have a commitment to the kids," she offered, "but I feel like in our society . . . being committed to human beings means being a martyr."

Another Community Charter School teacher feared that having too few staff members also meant taking on teaching assignments for which she did not always feel qualified. She said:

> One thing about teaching in a small school is that we have to cover everything, so I'm teaching [a course] which I don't feel particularly well prepared to teach. . . . I thought there's got to be somebody more qualified than me . . . [but] in a small school you have to be flexible, and for now, that's how we're doing it.

Even at larger charter schools in our study, teachers often battled physical exhaustion. At Imperial Way Charter School, one of the first charter schools in California, years of intense demands outside of the classroom left some teachers reeling. One teacher described having to participate in "meetings beyond belief." This teacher said that she arrived at the school in the early morning hours and rarely left before 5 o'clock in the evening at least 4 nights a week.

It was "a lot of extra time." Working 6 or 7 days a week, up to 10 or more hours a day, was not unusual among the teachers in our study, particularly those working at start-up charter schools. Another Imperial Way teacher warned teachers who were considering joining a charter school to "be in very good physical shape. Inform your family you won't be seeing them as much as you intended until it gets off on its legs."

Clearly, issues of extreme fatigue and feeling overwhelmed are not unique to charter school teachers in California (see Weiss, 1997), nor are the time pressures and fear of burnout. In fact, they fit larger patterns of the teaching profession, particularly within reforming schools. For example, Hargreaves (1994) argues that the perennial time shortages experienced by teachers reflect the intensification of teachers' work in the face of public demands for greater accountability on narrow performance measures. He writes that this "time compression" for teachers leads to feelings of guilt, inadequacy, and eventually burnout and exit from the teaching profession. Although far from conclusive, our data point toward a similar conclusion. While we did not formally track the retention rate of teachers in the 17 charter schools we studied over time, the stresses teachers shared with us and the turnover during the course of our study suggest that turnover rates were quite high, especially at the start-up charter schools. Some of these schools were losing close to half of their teaching staff each year. Furthermore, in our interviews with teachers, young teachers talked about not being able to do this job for long. They noted that as they matured and started families, they would look for less frenetic settings in which to work. On the other end of the life cycle, one teacher noted that the charter school work schedule was good for "workaholic empty-nesters" whose children were grown.

Yet, even teachers firmly committed to the dynamic, reform-minded spirit of charter schools expressed reservations about their ability to keep veteran teachers. One Imperial Way teacher confided:

> We put in the time, we put in the long hours, and now it's time that I have to look at me, where am I going to go with charter? As far as [the] charter school, I think it's great, I think the teachers that get hired, come here for interviews because they want the challenge because they want the reconstruction of education to happen, and they're open to the long hours, and the new ideas. I think it's a success but we don't have the support to support the people that stay on. And it's not going to be a success if the support does not happen. You're going to have a turnover every 5 years if that's the way it stays.

In this first section, we focused on what charter school teachers told us was important about their local professional context. As we have pointed out, their sentiments—valuing smallness, sharing an esprit de corps, and being wary of burnout—are not unique to charter school educators. Rather, they broadly overlap with the larger body of research dealing with teachers' roles in, and responses to, school-centered educational reforms. Still, it appears as though the very laissez-faire nature of charter school reform leaves teachers with less support and more stress.

LARGER PROFESSIONAL CONTEXTS
FOR CHARTER SCHOOL TEACHERS

In addition to the influence of the local context, our interviews and observations also suggested an important set of larger influences that contributed to teachers' sense of professionalism. These influences included school districts, teachers unions, and the state, as exemplified by teacher credentialing requirements. Instead of a unified movement away from traditional educational institutions or organizations, we found that charter schools and their teachers varied in the ways they chose to create, restructure, or sever relationships with districts, unions, and even the state's credentialing system. In this second section, we discuss how this broader context complicates assumptions about teacher professionalism in charter schools.

Here, we focus on three findings related to unions and state credentials that reflect the larger context of teaching for charter school teachers. First, we found that in many instances, charter schools and teachers unions were not necessarily incompatible. This finding cuts against the grain of much of the literature on charter schools, which typically portrays unions as steadfast and universal opponents of charter school reform (Finn et al., 1997; Nathan, 1998).

Second we found that even through one of the most frequently touted aspects of charter school reform is the flexibility to hire personnel without regard to state licensing requirements (Manno, Finn, Bierlein, & Vanourek, 1998), all 17 charter schools in our study either hired or preferred to hire state-credentialed teachers. Even in these highly deregulated settings, the regulatory apparatus of the state appeared to validate the quality of the teachers and the credibility of the charter schools.

Finally, we also found that charter school teachers do not necessarily equate freedom and autonomy with the termination of district relationships. While some teachers, especially at start-up charter schools, eschewed district responsibility or oversight for such items as salaries, seniority rights, and curriculum, teachers at conversion charter schools often preferred having their districts continue to provide basic services and instructional assistance. We do not describe in detail the relationship between teachers and districts in this section, in part because it is discussed in Chapters 3 and 4 of this volume. Even without an elaborated discussion of districts, however, we suggest that teachers' desire to modify, rather than terminate, traditional financial relationships with their chartering districts suggests a third area in which the larger contexts in which charter schools are situated profoundly influence their operation.

Relationships with Teachers Unions

The relationship between charter school teachers and teachers unions is mixed. For instance, rather than precipitating a general exodus away from teachers unions, charter school reform had little impact on existing union–teacher relationships. In fact, all but one of the eight unionized conversion charter schools we studied maintained their union affiliation. Meanwhile, none of the start-up charter schools became unionized during the course of this study.

The reasons why teachers at conversion charter school generally maintained their relationships with their professional associations were multiple, and these relationships affected the teachers' professional lives in many important ways. For example, the teachers at Franklin Charter Academy, a conversion charter school in the Mission Unified School District (see Chapter 3), not only stayed in the union, but also demanded that new hires be conferred the same benefits and protections as other district teachers. By taking this position, Franklin teachers opposed the district policy that allowed charter school teachers to be employees of the school rather than the district. In such instances, where teachers are employees of individual charter schools, they are more likely to be paid less and given fewer employment protections than unionized district employees. Franklin teachers' insistence that new teachers not be given short shrift reflects both strong union leadership at the school site and a belief among most of the staff that new teachers should have similar benefits to more established teachers. One teacher at Franklin Charter Academy explained that the teachers' decision to remain in the union reflected the ongoing importance of job security for teachers. Although he noted that "good teachers should be content with doing their good job and that the security comes from within yourself," he recognized the need for, and supported, contract provisions that provided specific job protections.

At a second conversion charter school in our study—Wilson Elementary (see Chapter 4)—teachers decided to retain union membership because, like Franklin teachers, they were concerned about losing seniority, fringe benefits, and retirement options if they left. This is particularly interesting at this charter school because the local teachers union fought to keep the Wilson charter proposal from being approved by the local school board. Still, many Wilson educators saw the union as an important contributor to implementing successful changes at the school. Wilson's principal exemplified the view that the union (and the sponsoring district) could help establish and sustain reform, rather than undermine it. Citing the importance of charter schools nurturing a strong relationship with both unions and districts, he said, "The really strong charter schools are the ones where the district and the union have backed up [the school] and helped them to implement changes."

Only a single conversion charter school in our study—Imperial Way Charter School—opted out of union representation. The decision was made when the union and sponsoring district required that the charter school begin paying into the teacher retirement fund, which the principal did not want to do, thereby ending the relationship. When the decision was made to abandon the bargaining unit, however, several veteran teachers chose to leave the charter school rather than lose what they had invested in the union and district over the years. Although these teaching veterans professed deep attachments to their charter school, they were not ready to abandon the rights and privileges accrued through the union. Thus, they chose to leave Imperial Way for other schools in the district.

Meanwhile, in the start-up charter schools we studied, teachers were either ambivalent about unions or strongly rejected them. For instance, teachers at Foundation Elementary Charter School expressed ambivalence about union membership, noting that it was a peripheral issue. Indeed, when asked about their relationship to the union, several Foundation teachers were uncertain about whether they were in the union.

For many teachers at other start-up charter schools, the union represented a roadblock to change. Most of the teachers at Academic Charter School, for example, felt they had no need for a teachers union, and spoke very negatively about unions and how contracts inhibited creativity. According to one of the younger teachers at this charter school, "I don't see [the union] as a need here, and if I ever got to the point where I saw it as a need, I probably wouldn't be here." In fact, Academic's founders and administrators, drawing on their experience with the union in the sponsoring district, felt that the union's rules and requirements were simply too rigid and clashed with their idea of what charter schools should be. One of these administrators noted, "I mean, in [some] districts . . . you have a union for everything. It's like, how many contracts do you have before nobody is able to operate other than like in this square box?"

Teachers at another start-up charter school, Shoreline Charter School (see Chapter 5), also rejected union representation. In part, their decision reflected the fact that unions received little political support in Shoreline's school district or the school's parent community. In fact, one of the main motivations of some of the initial founders of the charter school was to get away from the union. According to one teacher we interviewed, "The community almost unanimously was opposed to [any] union activities [in the charter school] at all." The founders of the charter school—some of whom were on the local school board—made a distinct effort to head off unionization. In part, the founders did this by making sure that the charter school offered teachers salaries equivalent to the district's salary schedule, as well as the opportunity to receive performance bonuses. As a result, teachers agreed very early on that they would not support a union. The need for a union was diminished, according to one teacher, because of the feeling that, on any number of issues, "we would work together with [the district]."

Given the emphasis on freedom, autonomy, and flexible staffing of charter school reform, it is important to understand that teachers' larger professional context—as embodied by teachers unions—was not rejected across the board by the teachers in the charter schools we studied. This finding suggests that conflicts between unions and charter school advocates, often heated at both the district and state policy-making levels, sometimes subside at the school level. While charter school teachers, like teachers in all schools, were divided in their support for teachers unions, those who had been a part of a union for many years were loathe to relinquish the benefits that unions commonly provide, such as increased job security, health insurance coverage, and pension provisions. Yet younger teachers or those who were new to the profession generally lacked a vested interest in the union and any understanding of the benefits to be derived from union membership. These teachers were much more likely to be working in start-up charter schools and to express a desire to distance themselves from the status quo. Thus, for the most part, teachers' decisions about unions followed the lines of their status as working in either start-up or conversion charter schools.

Value of Teaching Credentials

The area of teacher credentialing is a second area that continued to shape teachers' work in charter schools. Before the 1998 amendments to California's charter school legislation were passed, charter schools were allowed to employ a wide range of individuals, including non-credentialed teachers and experts from other careers. Still, we found that nearly all of the charter schools in our study preferred to hire teachers with valid state credentials for their classrooms. We learned that while charter school founders valued the concept of "at-will" employment, they also recognized the importance of having professionally trained educators on staff.

Some charter schools hired credentialed teachers because their sponsoring districts required it as part of the charter agreement. Yet charter school administrators appeared to have a variety of reasons for preferring credentialed teachers. One central theme that emerged from our data was that charter school leaders wanted credentialed teachers if for no other reason than to gain more credibility with parents. Because many parents perceived credentialed teachers to be more qualified to teach than other candidates, charter schools were forced to respond to their concerns. For example, the libertarian principal of Ursa Independent Charter School, who was skeptical that state-mandated teacher credentials were a good measure of teacher quality, still preferred to hire credentialed teachers to assure parents that Ursa was a serious school.

However, other charter school leaders who had more faith in the state credentialing process stated that hiring teachers with credentials helped to ensure a strong academic program. As one principal at a start-up charter school told us, "With charter schools you can hire teachers that may not even be certified, but . . . it is not providing the best education if you do not have professional people teach. . . . I'm going to make sure we get certified teachers that are trained as professionals."

Still, even among those charter school leaders who valued the knowledge that credentialed teachers brought to their schools, some argued that credentials were not crucial for all courses. Non-credentialed teachers sometimes were hired to teach extracurricular activities or non-core electives. For example, a consultant who was hiring teachers for a business/vocational training program offered through Mountain Peak Charter School, which was designed for students who had not succeeded in regular schools, was pleased about the opportunity to hire non-credentialed teachers, especially for courses geared toward specific vocations. He said, "It is nice because we have hired people that have certain business experience [for example, paramedics] . . . we have flexibility."

At another charter school, the principal explained that although the school encourages certification, it is not required. He stated, "If we have a Ph.D. who's an expert in biology and [that person] proves that he or she can teach young people well, we'll hire them, whether they're certified or not."

Our findings indicate that state teaching credentials remained an important element of professional identity for charter school teachers and the parents and leaders at their schools. This finding is surprising given persistent critiques by many charter school advocates of the teacher education/state credentialing process and of state regulations in general. It demonstrates that, holding other variables roughly constant, teachers who have been prepared for teaching by colleges and subsequently certified by the state are perceived by parents and many educators as being much more valuable and sometimes better qualified to teach children than other candidates. Although California amended its law in 1998 to require state certification for charter school teachers who teach core subjects, our finding suggests that even in the absence of such mandates, many charter schools preferred to fill their core teaching positions with credentialed teachers.

CONCLUSION

Through our research, we have learned that the professional lives of charter school teachers—like other teachers—are profoundly influenced by both local and larger contexts for teaching. At the local level, many charter school teachers were attracted to, and satisfied with, the opportunity to teach at small, family-like schools with dedicated, like-minded professionals. Still, they were not sure that such an opportunity had translated into profound changes in their teaching practices or that they could sustain their current workloads without burning out.

But even as teachers' local contexts were remade, their relationships to larger teaching contexts often endured. Although the touchstone of charter school reform—freedom and autonomy—suggests that teachers in these more autonomous schools are released from the bureaucratic tendrils of unions, districts, and the state licensing system, we learned that each of these contexts remained influential to varying degrees. More important, they remain valued by at least a portion of charter school teachers and administrators. Using an analytic framework based on the work of Joan Talbert and Milbrey McLaughlin (1993), we term the ongoing, nested interactions across teaching contexts as the *embedded context of professionalism*.

Through our conversations with charter school teachers and administrators, we found the idea of an embedded context of professionalism to be especially compelling. Such a perspective was helpful for understanding teaching in charter schools for at least two reasons. First, the various forces that influenced teachers were not easily disentangled from each other. Unions, districts, and state licensing requirements continually interacted with the charter school movement in California—these extended professional contexts do not simply fade away when teachers go to work in more autonomous charter schools. Second, and more important, charter schools do not change the layers of concentric circles themselves, but they do change the nature of the relationships that exist across these contexts. Although many teachers in the start-up charter schools did have looser relationships with these entities than teachers in the conversion charter schools, none of the teachers were able to simply cast off those layers of professionalism that have been deemed unimportant or cumbersome by advocates of deregulatory reforms such as charter schools.

Our evidence suggests that charter schools often provide intensely rewarding school contexts, such as the intimate personal settings of small schools and classes. Charter school teachers, for the most part, also said that they found professional pride in being among a select group of school reform pioneers. But at the same time, these contexts were constantly fluctuating, and there was little evidence of dramatic change at the classroom level, where, arguably, change matters most. Over the course of our study, teachers inundated by non-classroom responsibilities struggled with weariness and exhaustion, and openly speculated about their ability to sustain their level of commitment over the long haul.

And while we find that charter school teachers are divided in their support for teachers unions, only one conversion charter school in our study opted out of union membership. Meanwhile the start-up schools generally showed little or no inclination to move toward union affiliation. Finally, even when charter schools had the opportunity to hire non-credentialed teachers, they rarely exercised this option. This finding suggests that charter school founders valued the concept "at-will" employment, but also recognized the importance of professionally trained educators, or at least valued the credibility that credentials add to charter schools' instructional program. For these reasons, we found that charter school teachers—like teachers at traditional schools—remained, for the most part, firmly embedded within multiple professional contexts.

REFERENCES

Arsen, D., Plank, N., & Sykes, G. (1999). *School choice politics in Michigan: The rules matter.* East Lansing: Michigan State University Press.

Budde, R. (1989, March). Education by charter. *Phi Delta Kappan, 70*(7), 518–520.

California Education Code. (1992). § 47600-16, Chapter 781 (pp. 1–7).

Education Commission of the States. (1995). *Charter schools . . . What are they up to?* Denver: Author.

Finn, C., Manno, B., Vanourek, G., & Bierlein, L. (1997). *Charter schools in action: Final report.* Washington, DC: Hudson Institute.

Grutzik, C. (1997). *Teachers' work in charter schools: From policy to practice.* Unpublished doctoral dissertation, University of California at Los Angeles.

Hargreaves, A. (1994). *Changing teachers, changing times: Teachers' work and culture in the postmodern age.* New York: Teachers College Press.

Koppich, J. E., Holmes, P., & Plecki, M. (1998). *New rules, new roles: The professional work lives of charter school teachers.* Washington, DC: National Education Association.

Little Hoover Commission. (1996). *The charter movement: Education reform school by school* (Report commissioned by the California State Legislature). Sacramento, CA: Author.

Manno, B. V., Finn, C. E., Bierlein, L. A., & Vanourek, G. (1998, March). How charter schools are different: Lessons and implications from a national study. *Phi Delta Kappan, 79*(7), 489–498.

Meier, D. (1995). *The power of their ideas: Lessons for America from a small school in Harlem.* Boston: Beacon Press.

Nathan, J. (1996). *Charter schools: Creating hope and opportunity for American education*. San Francisco: Jossey-Bass.

Nathan, J. (1998, March). Heat and light in the charter school movement. *Phi Delta Kappan, 79*(7), 499–505.

Paris, D. C. (1998). Standards and charters: Horace Mann meets Tinker Bell. *Educational Policy, 12*(4), 380–396.

Public Sector Consultants & Maximus, Inc. (1999). *Michigan's charter school initiative: From theory to practice*. Lansing, MI: Author.

Sarason, S. B. (1998). *Charter schools: Another flawed educational reform?* New York: Teachers College Press.

Shanker, A. (1994, December 11). Every school a charter. *The New York Times*. Reprinted by the American Federation of Teachers, Washington, DC (pp. 1–2). [www.aft.org]

Sizer, T. R. (1984). *Horace's compromise: The dilemma of the American high school*. Boston: Houghton Mifflin.

Sizer, T. R. (1992). *Horace's school: Redesigning the American high school*. Boston: Houghton Mifflin.

SRI International. (1997). *Evaluation of charter school effectiveness*. Menlo Park, CA: Author.

Talbert, J., & McLaughlin, M. (1993). Understanding teaching in context. In D. K. Cohen, M. McLaughlin, & J. Talbert (Eds.), *Teaching for understanding: Challenges for policy and practice*. (pp. 167–206) San Francisco: Jossey-Bass.

UCLA Charter School Study. (1998). *Beyond the rhetoric of charter school reform: A study of ten California school districts*. Los Angeles: Author. [www.gseis.ucla.edu/docs/charter.pdf]

Vanourek, G., Manno, B. V., & Finn, C. E. (1997, April 30). The false friends of charter schools. *Education Week on the Web*. [www.edweek.org]

Weiss, A. R. (1997). *Going it alone*. Boston: Northeastern University, Institute for Responsive Education.

Wood, J. (1999). An early examination of the Massachusetts charter school initiative. Boston: University of Massachusetts Donahue Institute.

Conclusion
Envisioning a More Progressive Agenda

Amy Stuart Wells

What is so painfully obvious from the data and analysis presented in the preceding chapters is that charter school policies were written to serve some agendas more than others. For instance, it is clear that charter schools have gained a great deal of autonomy in terms of private fund raising, including and excluding children, and hiring and firing employees. In these ways, they look more like private than public schools, which is no doubt the intent of free-market reform advocates who see charter schools as one step down the path to full-blown voucher programs (see Wells, Grutzik, Carnochan, Slayton, & Vasudeva, 1999).

On the other hand, we see from our study and many others that charter schools are not held any more accountable than other public schools for student achievement. And, similar to the growth in income inequality in general over the past 20 years (Clines, 1999), the gap between the rich and the poor is only exacerbated under charter school reform.

In other words, despite the broad-based and bipartisan support for charter schools, the public policies under which these schools operate tend to serve a more narrow set of interests. Clearly, it is time for more liberal and progressive forces to help redefine the distinction between so-called "strong" and "weak" laws as defined by the conservative, free-market, and pro-voucher advocates of this reform.

Indeed, a whole new language for evaluating charter school laws could emerge from a coalition of more progressive and equity-minded reformers, a language that deems "strong" laws to be those that make this a more supportive and equitable reform. In other words, good charter school laws would target extra resources toward grassroots organizations trying to start charter schools in low-income communities. They also would disallow charter schools from having admissions criteria or requiring parents to sign contracts with the schools. These prerequisites are too reminiscent of private school practices, and there is no good justification for tax dollars to go to schools that exclude students because their parents work two jobs.

Furthermore, good, equitable charter schools would ensure that information on charter schools was widely distributed and that word-of-mouth recruitment was no longer the primary means by which families learned about charter school opportunities. These laws also would provide financial and other incentives for founders, educators, and parents who wanted to start racially, ethnically, and socioeconomically diverse charter schools. Yet in order for such diverse schools to survive, the states would have to pay for student transportation to and from school, especially for students who lived far from the school and those whose parents did not have the means to transport them each day.

In addition, there is a need to pick up where the systemic reformers left off by crafting good charter school laws that address the profound contradictions within the current autonomy-for-accountability trade-off. For instance, we know that under the current systemic reform paradigm, the parameters of the accountability system of state-mandated standards and tests are centralized, while access to the schools for students is decentralized. Why don't policy makers consider ways in which this formula could be turned around to some degree?

Why not use the regulatory system of the government to ensure that all students have equal access to charter schools? And at the same time, why not give charter schools (and other public schools) more space and voice to help define for what they want to be held accountable? In other words, centralize equity and decentralize to some extent the accountability mechanism that in theory drives the curriculum and pedagogy in the schools. For instance, why don't we consider a strong or a good charter school law to be one that guarantees both fiscal and academic accountability, but does so in a way that leaves charter schools more room to decide to what standards and goals they will be held accountable. In other words, policy makers could use charter schools as test sites for much-needed efforts to create more nuanced accountability systems that do not rely simply on mandated standardized tests—a system that allows educators, parents, and students to help define the very purpose of their schooling.

At the same time, tighter controls are needed on where the public funding for charter schools is going, as well as more public information about who is reaping financial rewards as a result of this reform. Financial equity across charter school sites should be a major concern, just as it should be for regular public schools.

Indeed, headlines from several states, including Texas, Pennsylvania, and California, suggest that policy makers are beginning to rethink what they consider to be "strong" characteristics of a charter school (see CANEC, 2001; Keller, 2001; Sandham, 2001). For instance, in the past couple of years, California has passed several pieces of legislation, including ones that limit the amount of public per-pupil funding that home-schooling and independent study charter schools can collect, create a lease aid funding program for charters schools in low-income areas of up to $750 per student, and require annual independent financial audit reports for charter schools each year. These are steps in the right direction.

Thus, the only remaining hope for charter school reform to have any lasting positive impact on the public educational system would be for more progressive members of this diverse and complex movement to recapture the language and symbols of what constitutes a good charter school law. Until that happens, the hopes and dreams of the thousands of social justice educators and families engaged in this reform will be marginalized and reliant on powerful and private market agents who have never served the most disadvantaged students well. It is time to leave the market metaphor to the market and to focus the educational policy lens on equal opportunities and the very hard work of teaching all students well.

REFERENCES

CANEC (California Network of Educational Charters). (2001). Legislative summary. [www.canec.org]

Clines, F. X. (1999, October 2). In "boom," more lint lines pockets of poor. *The New York Times*, p. A8.

Keller, B. (2001, June 6). Texas legislature places restrictions on charter schools. *Education Week* on the web. [www.edweek.org]

Sandham, J. L. (2001, May 2). Challenges to charter school laws mount. *Education Week* on the web. [www.edweek.org]

Wells, A. S., Grutzik, C., Carnochan, S., Slayton, J., & Vasudeva, A. (1999). Underlying policy assumptions of charter school reform: The multiple meanings of a movement. *Teachers College Record, 100*(3), 513–535.

About the Authors

Amy Stuart Wells is a Professor of Sociology of Education at Teachers College, Columbia University. Her research and writing has focused broadly on issues of race and education and more specifically on educational policies, such as school desegregation, school choice, charter schools, vouchers, and tracking and how they shape and constrain opportunities for students of color. She was the principal investigator of UCLA Charter School Study from 1996–2000. Currently, she is directing a study of adults who attended racially mixed high schools in six cities across the country. She is the author and editor of numerous books and articles, including "The 'Consequences' of School Desegregation: The Mismatch Between the Research and the Rationale," *Hastings Constitutional Law Quarterly*; co-author with Robert L. Crain of *Stepping over the Color Line: African American Students in White Suburban Schools*; and co-author with Irene Serna of "The Politics of Culture: Understanding Local Political Resistance to Detracking in Racially Mixed Schools," *Harvard Educational Review*.

Sibyll Carnochan is an education policy analyst and researcher. She most recently served as Director of Policy and Research for The Broad Foundation, a Los Angeles-based philanthropy that funds innovative efforts in governance, management, and labor relations in large urban school districts. Previously, Carnochan was a research associate for the UCLA Charter School Study. Before that, Carnochan staffed Congresswoman Nita M. Lowey on the House Subcommittee on Labor, Health and Human Services, and Education Appropriations, and served as a legislative analyst for The Council of Chief State School Officers. Carnochan has a Ph.D. in education policy from UCLA's Graduate School of Education and Information Studies, an Ed.M. from Harvard's Graduate School of Education, and a B.A. from Wesleyan University.

Camille Wilson Cooper is a Qualitative Researcher at UCLA's Institute for Democracy, Education & Access (IDEA). She is a Project Director for the Institute's Urban Teacher Education Collaborative and coordinates research that focuses on teacher preparation, urban schooling, and social justice. Cooper earned her doctorate in educational policy from UCLA. She also has an M.A. in education from the University of Michigan, and a B.A. in political science from Whittier College. Cooper's additional research interests include school choice policy, African American education, and feminist theory.

Cynthia Grutzik studied charter schools while earning her doctorate at UCLA. Her focus was on teachers' work in charter schools, and her research interests continue to center on teachers' lives in schools, and on how policies play out in those contexts. Cindy is currently the Academic Director for Teacher Education at Pacific Oaks College in Pasadena, California.

Alejandra Lopez works as a research associate at the Stanford University Center for Comparative Studies in Race and Ethnicity, where she is currently writing a report series on the changing demographics of California. She holds a B.A. in Psychology from Stanford University, and an M.A. and a Ph.D. in Social Research Methodology from the University of California, Los Angeles, Graduate School of Education and Information Studies. Her doctoral research examined race/ethnicity identification experiences of mixed heritage high school students, with the support of a dissertation fellowship from the Spencer Foundation. Other research areas include: the psychosocial impact of diverse schooling environments on students, race/ethnicity classification in American society, and demographic data collection in the U.S. Census.

Jennifer Jellison Holme is currently working as a postdoctoral researcher on the UCLA Understanding Race and Education Study, a study of graduates of racially mixed high schools. She has worked as a research associate on the UCLA Charter School Study, and the Harvard Project on School Desegregation. She received her Ph.D. in education policy at the UCLA Graduate School of Education and Information Studies, where she was a recipient of the Chancellor's dissertation year fellowship. She obtained her Ed.M. in administration, planning, and social policy at the Harvard Graduate School of Education. Her current research interests center around school choice and school integration. She has co-authored a number of articles, and her most current article, "Buying Homes, Buying Schools: School Choice and the Social Construction of School Quality," will appear in the Harvard Education Review next year.

Janelle T. Scott is the Assistant Director for Program Development at the National Center for the Study of Privatization in Education at Teachers College, Columbia University. She is a former urban elementary school teacher who specializes in race and the politics of education. Scott earned a Ph.D. in Education Policy from the University of California, Los Angeles' Graduate

School of Education and Information Studies. Her doctoral research, supported by the Spencer Foundation, examined education management organizations and charter schools.

Ash Vasudeva is an educational policy researcher based in Los Angeles, CA. He focuses on the implementation of policy in urban schools and districts. Vasudeva received a Spencer Research Training Grant to support his doctoral studies at the University of California, Los Angeles. Dr. Vasudeva's research explores the disjuncture between policy and practice by examining how accountability-based policies are shaped, filtered, and defined by the context in which they are implemented. Dr. Vasudeva has used this lense to study two national educational reforms: charter school reform and comprehensive school reform (CSR). After receiving his Ph.D. in 2000, Dr. Vasudeva served as Director of Research for the Galef Institute, developer of the *Different Ways of Knowing* CSR design. Since 2002, Dr Vasudeva has been Senior Research Associate at WestEd, where he is engaged in a national evaluation of CSR. Dr. Vasudeva has contributed to articles and book reviews for such journals as *Teachers College Record, Stanford Law and Policy Review,* and *Teaching and Change.*

Index

Abelmann, C. H., 29–31
Academic Charter School
  described, 107–108
  governing board membership, 115–116
  grant writing and fund raising, 121
  parental and in-kind support, 125
  partnership of, 117–118
  social networks and, 111–112, 115–116, 117–118, 121, 125
  state sources of funds, 90–93, 99, 100
  teachers' unions and, 172
Accountability, 3, 9, 23, 29–53
  academic, 43–47
  autonomy-for-accountability tradeoff, 44, 74–75, 179
  charter school legislation and, 37–39, 50–51
  to court orders and enrollment policies, 50–51
  fiscal, 47–48
  politics of accountability in context, 54–58
  politics of charter school, 31–33, 48–51
  role of school district and, 41–43
  to state and federal rules and regulations, 49–50
  student achievement and, 11–13
Admissions process, 151–153
African Americans
  Black Power movement, 7
  civil rights movement, 8
  racial/ethnic issues and, 139
Apple, M., 8

Arizona, charter school reform in, 10, 15
Arizona State University, 16
Arrow, K. J., 54
Arsen, D., 17, 160, 161
Ascher, C., 15
Autonomy
  over budgets, 66–67, 71–72
  over calendars, 69, 73
  over curriculum, 67–70, 72–73
  over discipline, 69–70
  over instructional materials and strategies, 67–68, 72
  over personnel, 64–66, 71
  over professional development, 68–69
  school governance structures and, 60–64, 70–71
  of teachers, 160–161
Autonomy-for-accountability, 44, 74–75, 179

Bailyn, B., 54
Ball, S. J., 13, 30, 130, 132, 150
Beck, L. G., 57, 58
Bierlein, L., 9, 56, 161, 164, 170
Bourdieu, Pierre, 105–106, 133
Bowe, R., 13, 130, 132, 150
Bowman, D. H., 1–2
Brantlinger, E., 130, 132, 133
Buckley, J., 17
Budde, Ray, 159
Budgets. *See also* Funding of charter schools
  facilities and rent, 92, 96, 97–98, 99–100, 111

185